GARDENS IN DETAIL

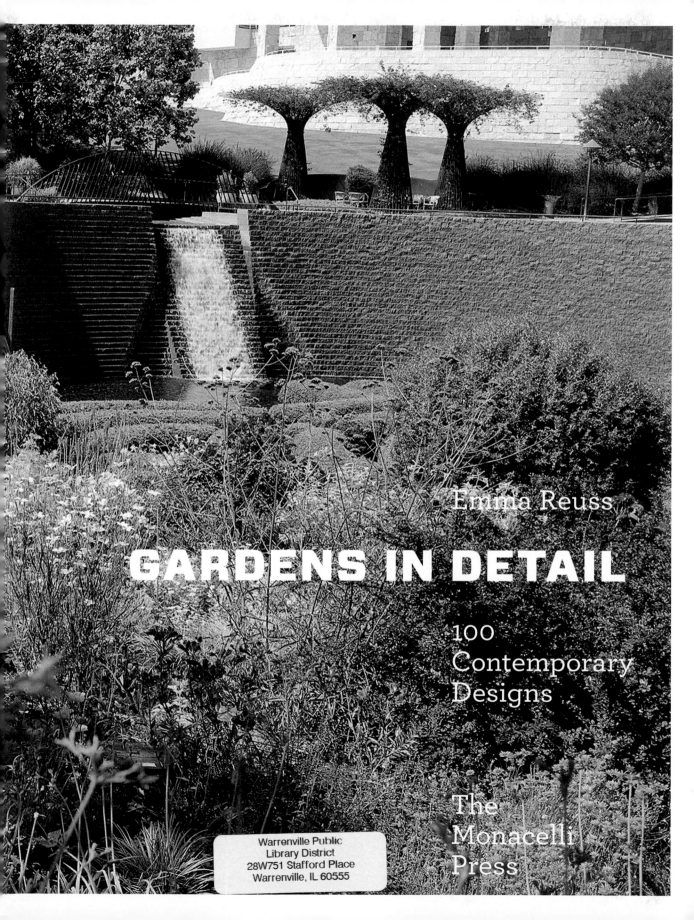

Emma Reuss

GARDENS IN DETAIL

100
Contemporary
Designs

The
Monacelli
Press

Contents

Introduction

We look at gardens. We like what we see. But why?

Good gardens deliver at a subconscious level and, more often than not, we do not register why something is 'right'. We are, however, likely to notice when something is 'wrong'. *Gardens in Detail* not only features one hundred standout gardens from across the globe for you to explore and admire, but also explains the attributes of each garden from a design perspective. The book examines the diverse components of every garden – from planting and water features to landscaping and works of art – and highlights the way each particular element contributes to the composition and how each garden design achieves its purpose.

There are many exceptional gardens around the world, and it was extremely difficult to select only one hundred examples to feature in this book. In choosing the gardens displayed I was keen to present a wide range of styles and situations and also to feature gardens that demonstrated with ease the thinking behind the design. The eclectic collection that resulted features geographically and historically diverse gardens, from 15th-century Kyoto, Japan to 21st-century São Paulo, Brazil; from grand palaces in India to tiny backyards in California; and from opulent roof gardens in Sydney to rural riversides in Maryland. Every kind of location is included, from desert to wetland, and from jungle to beach garden.

Grouped into ten thematic chapters – Art, Landscape, World, Plants, Composition, Lifestyle, Colour, Urban, Environment and Atmosphere – the gardens cover a surprising diversity of character. A range of historical styles is represented, including Islamic, Renaissance, English Landscape and Arts & Crafts, together with many contemporary gardens that have been influenced by them, such as Ossart

and Maurières's Ochre garden with its Moorish character. The influence of past design greats, such as Roberto Burle-Marx, Luis Barragán and James van Sweden, is evident in several of the gardens, while an 18th-century English landscape by Charles Bridgeman enjoys a modern artistic intervention by Kim Wilkie. There are conceptual designs by Martha Schwartz and modernist designs for two wildly contrasting locations by Christopher Bradley-Hole and Steve Martino respectively. The work of major international designers sits alongside that of gifted amateurs: what they all have in common is strong design values. This book provides insight into the intentions of the designers as well as revealing how their aims were realized.

The 'room outside' is a phrase frequently used when discussing garden design, and the principles used to design buildings and interiors – unity, balance, proportion, areas of focus – are equally relevant in the landscape. Key to successful garden design is to be true to the character of both the site and the house – the genius loci – and to take into account the views beyond the garden. Environmental conditions will also have an effect on style and planting.

Gardens in Detail will enhance your appreciation of every garden you visit, and it will provide inspiration and practical ideas that you can apply to your own garden. You can take a whole landscaping scheme or you can select individual ideas from several of the designers in the book and incorporate them all in one garden. There are a wealth of ideas you can choose from. So, whether you are looking for a water feature or a topiaried structure to add panache to your garden, let the sheer range of possibilities displayed here influence you to make some great design decisions for yourself. Above all I hope you will be inspired, as I have been, by the excitement and passion for garden design that is so evident within these pages.

KEY DESIGN PRINCIPLES

Good garden design will exhibit the majority or all of the seven design principles listed below. Combined, these tenets provide the basis for a harmonious, balanced, uncomplicated design that delivers on aesthetic and practical levels.

[1] GENIUS LOCI The character of the site, literally the spirit of the place. This abstract concept refers to the inherent ambience, mood or presence of a garden, and it is not always clear how it has been achieved by analysing each of the composite elements. Character is often driven by the location of the garden, as is evident in Steve Martino's Sonoran desert garden in Arizona (see p. 354).

[2] UNITY A central theme or idea running through the garden. There should be a relationship between the many component parts – overall style, materials used, planting or colour palette – that promotes a sense of harmony. The formal lines of Del Buono Gazerwitz's London garden and its classic theme provide unity (see p. 324).

[3] SIMPLICITY An unfussy approach to line, form, texture and colour, simplicity brings with it clarity, focus and calm. All inessentials should be eliminated or reduced. But beware! A design that is too simple can leave visitors uninspired. This is particularly important in small spaces, as demonstrated by the Hanover penthouse garden by WES & Partner in Germany (see p. 252), where the elements have been pared back to create a highly effective minimal experience.

[4] BALANCE When every element in a garden has the same or similar visual weight, perfect balance is achieved and a state of comfort created in the beholder. Qualities affecting balance are direction, size, mass and void, density and colour. If there is imbalance between any of the elements, the space will feel uncomfortable. In Hong Kong, Andy Sturgeon created a roof terrace of different levels and plenty of vertical structures to balance the large void of the adjacent swimming pool (see p. 344).

[5] PROPORTION Concerns the relationship of width, height and depth in terms of garden space and human scale. Small scale can mean intimate, comfortable and safe, but can also feel claustrophobic if the composition is not executed sympathetically. By the same token, large scale can make a grand or imposing impression, perhaps of power or even wealth, but again this approach succeeds only if the right elements of design are used and visual balance is achieved. The opulent Mughal gardens of the Indian subcontinent are obvious examples of grand scale, but look at the Getty Center garden in Los Angeles (see p. 22) for a model of perfectly balanced proportion.

[6] RHYTHM AND REPETITION If similar objects or plants are repeated at regular intervals, a natural rhythm will occur, bringing with it a sense of continuity to the area. This can be achieved by using shape, colour, texture, materials or any part of the constituent properties of the garden. One garden that demonstrates the coherence that repetition brings is the Mendocino garden by Gary Ratway in California (see p. 214), in which a line of painted wooden columns creates repeating vertical punctuation that breaks up the horizontal space.

[7] FOCAL POINTS Particular elements, or groups of elements, that draw or hold the eye for a notable length of time. Their function is to add interest, to encourage movement around the space, and to focus attention and consideration on particular areas. Jean-Charles Chiron's garden near Nantes in France (see p. 396) uses many focal points to communicate his East–West fusion and to entice visitors to explore further into the garden.

Art

Land Art

DESIGNER KIM WILKIE

COMPLETED 2009

LOCATION NORTHAMPTONSHIRE, UK

LAND ARTISTS DIFFER from landscape gardeners in that they produce artworks that are written large in the landscape. Their works may refer to, or represent, realities that have nothing to do with the landscape itself, even though they are made using the natural elements of landscape: bedrock, stones, soil and water. Often, a work of land art is only fully understood when viewed from the air.

Boughton House in Northamptonshire, UK, is no stranger to landscaping. In the 17th century, perfect rectangular canals were dug in the grounds to create a network of beautiful formal waterways. Later, a flat-topped 'Olympian mount' was raised, named after the home of the twelve gods in Greek mythology.

When restoration of the mount and surrounding canal system began in 2006, the present owner, the 10th Duke of Buccleuch, awarded designer Kim Wilkie the task of doing something with a large space in front of the mount. Wilkie proposed digging downwards to create an inverse twin of the existing mount – a hell to offset the Olympian heaven. Wilkie's work was named 'Project Orpheus' after the musician of Greek mythology who descended into the underworld and persuaded the god Hades to release his dead wife, only to lose her when he looked back to check that she was following him.

The original mount is 23 ft (7 m) high and 165 ft (50 m) square, and Wilkie's inverted pyramid was dug out to the same proportions. The stepped hole was lined with grass, and a still, black, reflective pool was created at the bottom to represent the fear-inducing entrance of the metaphorical hell.

Project Orpheus is a successful intervention in a historic English landscape. A clever inversion of a historic man-made feature, it similarly draws its meaning from outside itself. The inverted pyramid brings renewed drama and interest to a formal landscape that, due to a lack of funds, fortuitously escaped a naturalistic makeover in the 18th century.

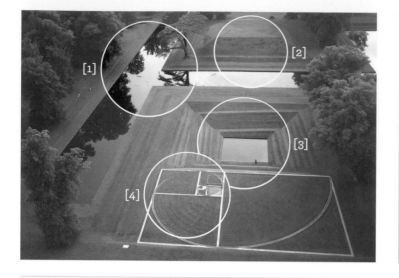

DESIGN INGREDIENTS

- Historical reinterpretation
- Symmetry
- Mass and void
- Geometry
- Allegory

[1] LAND AND WATER The 17th-century canals at Boughton House divide this part of the landscape into formal rectangles of land that look as though they are floating in a larger expanse of water. Fully filled with water, the canals act as flat, reflective expanses that seem to join the sky and the land together. The summary effect is one of simplicity, with drama and movement provided by reflections of clouds, and shadows that lengthen across the landforms, giving them a sensual and sculptural quality.

[2] OLYMPIAN MOUNT The 18th-century landscaping at Boughton is attributed to Charles Bridgeman, whose best-known work is his contribution to the park at Stowe in Buckinghamshire; the mound is believed to have been built in 1724. Mounds had been popular in landscaping since medieval times. Often circular in shape, their elevated platforms would offer views of a house, its surrounding gardens and the landscape beyond. In the 18th century, landscapers favoured classical motifs within a garden framework, hence the naming of the Olympian mount.

[3] INVERTED PYRAMID The pyramid's excavation and shaping required complicated calculations. These were made by computer and fed into laser survey equipment, which then guided the digger exactly. In order to lay the turf on the steep slopes, it was rolled down like a stair carpet and pinned at intervals using bamboo canes; these stayed in place until the turf rooted. A variety of mower types, including remote-controlled ones, are used to maintain the pristine greensward; the job takes two full days every week in summer.

[4] FIBONACCI SPIRAL Set in the ground next to Project Orpheus is a rill that delivers spring water to the pool at the bottom of the excavation. The rill's course is a Fibonacci spiral, a logarithmic spiral that gets wider (or further from its origin) by a certain factor for every quarter turn it makes. The spiral represents the geometric formula at the basis of all classical and neoclassical architecture, as well as underlying the compositional structure of many great Renaissance paintings. The formula presents the ideal aesthetic proportion and is found not only in such buildings as the Parthenon in Athens but also in nature, most famously in the distribution of features in the human face. The Great Pyramid of Giza, echoed at Boughton, conforms to the ratio represented visually by the Fibonacci spiral.

SCULPTING THE LAND

Bridgeman's sculpted landforms at Boughton are part of a long tradition in Britain that began with prehistoric burial tumuli and barrows. Geometric earth sculpting fell out of favour, but was revived in the 1930s with Art Deco. Today, organic designs, such as Alan Gardener's serpentine path at The Wrekin Garden in Shropshire, UK (above) and Charles Jencks' remarkable Garden of Cosmic Speculation in Dumfries, Scotland, testify to the continued tradition of turf-covered earthworks.

Postmodern Beach

DESIGNER DEREK JARMAN
COMPLETED 1994
LOCATION KENT, UK

CREATING A GARDEN in lush countryside where plants of many kinds can be relied upon to thrive is one thing; making one in an environment that wipes out all but the most specialized plants is quite another. Yet getting something beautiful to grow in a hostile, bleak or ugly landscape has a particular kind of poetry that can compensate for the expected setbacks and disappointments.

Such a garden was created by English artist and film director <u>Derek Jarman</u>, who completed it around Prospect Cottage, his coastal hideaway, during the last few years of his life as he faced death from the AIDS virus. The house and garden (now privately owned) lie on a flat shingle spit in Kent that juts out into the English Channel. The surroundings are bleak and, for the most part, barren: a coastal desert. Heavy on the horizon is the vast bulk of the Dungeness B nuclear power station, which adds a further degree of unearthliness to this hostile place.

Rainfall is low, and frost rare, but the site is very exposed to the wind. In summer, when the sun blazes out of a sky that seems immense above the flat, harsh landscape, the wind is drying and laden with salt spray. In winter, the wind freezes the visitor to the bone. The atmosphere of the place is uniquely, almost romantically, desolate.

The garden began one day when Jarman picked up a piece of driftwood and used it to stake a rose. Over the years he retrieved more and more pieces from the shore to protect and support his plants. It was impossible to dig holes in the shingle to add compost: the shingle simply replaced itself as it was displaced. In the end he just thrust in the plants and left them to take their chances.

In the spring and summer, colour erupts from the stones, from nothing. Poppies blaze and gorse glitters. In winter the vegetation withdraws and the structural elements remain. This is a space with no boundaries, an inspiration for art and poetry.

[1] SALT- AND WIND-TOLERANT PLANTS

Plants that thrive in extreme coastal conditions often have adapted structures to reflect strong sunlight and repel salt spray (small, thick, shiny or silver leaves); retain water (fleshy storage leaves and stems); reduce evaporation (hairy leaves); and resist the force of the wind (low-growing compact structures with strong, deep, widespread rooting systems). Jarman's garden is full of many self-seeded wildflowers, such as poppies, thrift, honesty, forget-me-not and the most common, naturally-present plant on the shingle, *Crambe maritima* (sea kale). He also planted woody, structural plants like gorse, cistus, santolina and helichrysum, the last three being Mediterranean plants but well suited to this environment. In this place, young plants usually require some sort of shelter.

[2] SALVAGED MATERIALS

Apart from the plants, everything in the garden has been found on the nearby beach or salvaged and recycled from the sea. Jarman was able to select from a wealth of random objects thrown ashore by storms, or installed on the beach some time in the past and now obsolete. Stones with holes eroded through them hang on pointed fingers of rusty steel, and metal triangles swing together as rudimentary wind chimes; garlands of cork floats adorn the driftwood, and chains lie coiled by paths like snakes of the post-industrial age. Much of the tangled wire seen in the garden was once anti-tank fencing, left over from World War II; Jarman found that, turned upside down and bunched together, it made effective frames to support plants. Everything found in the garden has a practical use or an aesthetic function.

[3] MINIATURE STONE CIRCLES

Jarman would collect stones from the seashore and bring them to the garden. Flint was his first conscious introduction, and he formed the pale grey stones into rings of standing stones that reminded him of the menhirs and monoliths of prehistoric peoples. Additionally, he used rings of stones to contain, shelter and define areas of planting, important in this boundaryless setting. Jarman would also collect stones of different colours, such as white and red, and set them in the spaces between the circles.

[4] DRIFTWOOD BEDS

Just as Jarman used collected stones to define small areas of planting, he also set out larger beds within areas demarcated by salvaged driftwood, such as the railway sleepers shown here. Jarman planted informally and relatively sparsely because dense planting would be out of keeping with the natural setting. The centrepiece of this bed is a found 'sculpture' or arrangement of jagged, rusted metal, itself a symbol of the garden's inhospitable environment. The area surrounding it is deliberately bare.

POETIC MEMORIAL

On the southern wall of Prospect Cottage a poem is set in raised wooden text across the tarred weatherboards. 'The Sun Rising' by John Donne is a jokey and joyous love poem, and it was installed to celebrate the lives of Jarman and his partner in the face of Jarman's approaching death from AIDS. The piece was made and installed for Jarman by artist and sculptor Peter Fillingham. The poetry sits very well in this landscape, with its open skies and distant horizon, and the way the verse is displayed is a work of art in itself.

Conceptual

DESIGNER MARTHA SCHWARTZ

COMPLETED 1986

LOCATION CAMBRIDGE, MASSACHUSETTS, USA

FOR CONCEPTUAL ARTISTS, the idea or concept behind their work is more important than how it is achieved or what it looks like. In garden design, the idea can be inspired by the site, or by something linked to the interests of the client or the artist. Conceptual gardens can be the antithesis of traditional 'tasteful' garden design, and are often distinguished by the use of artificial materials, surreal proportioning and humour.

The nine-storey office building of the Whitehead Institute in Cambridge, Massachusetts had a dismal tiled terrace on its roof. The 25 x 35-ft (8 x 11-m) area was surrounded by high walls and was a dreary, inhospitable space. It was overlooked by a classroom and a faculty lounge, and although there was access onto it, nobody ventured out because it was entirely uninviting. The Institute decided to call in landscape architect Martha Schwartz to transform the space into a garden that could be enjoyed by staff and which reflected the biomedical research work being undertaken there.

Schwartz is credited with designing the world's first conceptual garden, the Bagel Garden in Boston, Massachusetts, in 1979. It was the subject of some controversy when it was first unveiled, but today she is recognized as one of the most exciting Postmodernist landscape architects in the United States, and her impact is acknowledged internationally.

The Whitehead site had no water source, no maintenance provision, and a concrete decking system that would not bear the weight of compost-filled planters. With only a minimal budget, the project presented something of a challenge.

What Schwartz did was create an entirely artificial garden, a metaphor in three dimensions that referred to a technique used at the Institute: gene splicing. She 'spliced' the garden diagonally, the cut symbolizing a knife cutting through a gene to form two separate items. On one side she created a representation of a French Renaissance garden; on the other, at the opposite end of the landscaping spectrum, she created a Japanese Zen garden. The 'Splice Garden' is a graphic pun, but it is also a cautionary tale about the dangers inherent in gene splicing. A combination of two very different and arguably incompatible things, the garden is a light-hearted but still sobering reminder for the building's scientists of the risk of creating a monster.

· Artificiality

· Surrealism

· Humour

· Incongruous proportions

· Narrative concept

[1] RENAISSANCE TOPIARY One part of the garden represents the formality of French Renaissance estates, with their meticulously clipped topiary in various shapes offset by beautiful lawns. The 'grass' surfaces are merely gravel dyed green, and what appear to be examples of topiary are actually rolled steel cyclinders, cubes and asymmetrical shapes covered in AstroTurf. The 'hedges' are designed to serve as seating from which to contemplate the Japanese Zen character of the opposite side of the garden. Schwartz is denying the reality of what is normally interpreted as 'real', replacing it with the synthetic, and injecting a large dose of irony. In keeping with all conceptualist art, the work itself is simply an instrument to put forward the larger idea.

[2] JAPANESE ZEN RIPPLES Sand, carefully smoothed and then raked into neat furrows or ripples, is used in Japanese Zen gardens to foster a feeling of calm. Boulders are placed in the sand to provide focal points for contemplation. In her conceptual garden, however, Schwartz mischievously mixes up these Zen characteristics with elements from her adjoining 'Renaissance' garden. The Zen sand itself is dyed green, which makes it seem more like grass, and fake topiary globes take the place of the customary rocks. Further, what appears to be a single topiary globe fixed halfway up the green-painted back wall has a confusing effect on the senses because it suggests a bird's eye view – the observer seems to be viewing the garden from two different vantage points.

[3] TRICK OF THE EYE Viewed from the side, it becomes clear that what appears from the front to be a single topiary globe is actually a construction of three globes. Sculptural elements such as this impart energy to the space through their imaginative placement: conifers and topiary hang off the walls, seemingly defying gravity, or teeter unexpectedly on the tops of walls. The garden is full of such quirks; in the Zen garden, for example, some of the topiary globes are raised like lollipops, on trunks.

[4] SYMBOLIC DIVISION
Details of Schwartz's garden are visually amusing but they illustrate her serious point, that gene splicing carries the risk of unnatural, undesirable consequences. The low wall between the two gardens, ominously coloured black, is a bold, diagonal vector representing the power that scientists have to combine things that in nature are never combined. The two gardens appear as mutants of their respective styles, a stern warning of what can happen when nature is tampered with.

21

HUMOUR IN GARDENS

In the 'Splice Garden', Schwartz uses visual humour to make a memorable statement — the details are amusing, but they refer to dark possibilities. Using humour for a polemical purpose in this way was innovatory; previously, humour in gardens tended to be of a frivolous, slapstick kind. Water has long provided an unmissable opportunity for a joke, and Italian Renaissance gardens are full of *giochi d'acqua* or water games, where jets of water surprise unsuspecting visitors; Chatsworth House in England has a 'willow tree fountain' (see right) that showers approaching people. In the 20th century, the emergence of conceptualism created new opportunities for comedy in gardens.

Multimedia Experience

DESIGNERS ROBERT IRWIN

COMPLETED 1997

LOCATION LOS ANGELES, CALIFORNIA, USA

WHILE EVERY GARDEN offers the visitor an experience of some kind, experiential gardens are designed specifically to provide a multiple assault on the senses. Sights, sounds, still and moving water, plays of light, textures, colour and fragrance all play their part in ensuring that visitors have an unpredictable and entertaining journey as they move around the garden.

The Getty Center in Los Angeles is a campus of landmark buildings and gardens that attracts 1.3 million visitors a year. The campus is located high above the city, with lavish views of the Pacific Ocean beyond, and at its heart is the 134,000-sq-ft (12,500-sq-m) Central Garden, conceived by artist Robert Irwin in collaboration with plantsman Jim Duggan. He calls his garden 'a sculpture in the form of a garden which aims to be art'.

Here, a stream disappears below the paving and resurfaces, creating splashing sounds as it spills over boulders and stones of varying sizes. The 'spine' of the garden, it finally cascades over a carved stone waterfall into a maze pool full of azaleas below. A tree-lined path makes a series of switchback turns, traversing the stream five times. Corten steel maintains a strong presence throughout the garden, lining the paths and forming bridges over the stream. Together with the stone, it roots the garden and counterbalances the mass of the building above.

The round azalea maze pond at the bottom is enclosed by gardens containing an impressive variety of perennials, annuals, vines, roses and tropical plants. On the eastern bank the colours are cool, while the western side turns up the heat with a palette of pink, red and orange. The garden is brought to life by the interplay of colour and the reflection of light.

The garden is conceived as an arena, a theatre where a complex interaction of plants, water, stone and steel puts on an ever-changing show.

· Grand scale

· Stimulation of senses

· Feeling of journey

· Movement of light

· Colour association and contrast

[1] ALLÉE OF LONDON PLANES

Alongside the path down through the garden, an allée is populated by *Platanus* x *acerifolia* 'Yarwood'. The trees interrupt the sightline and afford 'surprises' along the way, constantly revealing and hiding. Irwin chose the tree for its sculptural silhouette in the winter months. Light is so important in the garden that when the tree canopies become dense in summer, gardeners remove one in three leaves every few weeks to reveal the movement of reflections from the stream across the garden.

[2] AZALEA MAZE
The garden's most notable feature, the azalea maze, is like nothing that has existed before. Set within a circular pond, it consists of three types of Kurume azaleas, in red, pink and white, that seem to float above the water surface. In fact, the azaleas are in specially shaped and firmly grounded containers, and the plants do not come into contact with the water. The Kurume hybrids were selected for their compact nature and small leaves; after careful clipping they resemble plump flower ropes. Their evergreen leaves add interest by changing colour through the seasons.

[3] TERRACED BEDS Examining flowerbeds and appreciating how gardeners have placed different plant shapes and colours against each other for optimal effect is a key pleasure of visiting gardens. In the Getty Center garden, some of the flowerbeds are set on slopes so that their plants can be appreciated afresh. Tall plants tend always to be set at the back, but here their height is enhanced by the terracing. Curving paths ensure that each step brings more plants into sight, with new contrasts adding to the interest.

[4] CHADAR A chadar is a carved water screen of Mughal origin (the name means 'sheet' or 'shawl'). Here, the stream that has flowed down through the garden, all the while providing a visual and auditory continuity throughout the visitor's experience, makes a final flourish with a visually dramatic fall down the surface of the long, steeply inclined screen. The sound of the stream, too, is altered by the carnelian granite screen's carved face. A second visual factor also comes into play; the screen is textured to maximize the play of sunlight on the descending water and direct it towards the azalea maze below. Thus, on sunny days, the maze is enlivened by a continual shower of twinkling light that moves across the twisting ropes of flowers.

[5] BOUGAINVILLEA BOWERS Constructed of steel, these umbrella-like structures are formed to resemble the huge swollen stems of tropical trees, such as the baobab. The constructions have various functions. Firstly, they are practical: at the very least, they are unusual-looking supports, out of which cerise-coloured bougainvillea blooms erupt and then trail downwards, rather like lava flowing from the crater of a volcano. Secondly, they are in themselves art – unique structures that add scale, height and interest in an area of the garden that is wide and relatively flat and featureless. While not being trees, they provide shade on hot days, and, like much else in the garden, they are a surprise to the visitor coming upon them.

Gallery Space

DESIGNER RENATA TILLI
COMPLETED 2007
LOCATION SAO PAULO, BRAZIL

JUST AS A PICTURE gallery provides a neutral background for the optimal display of paintings, a garden may be conceived to show off a collection of sculpture to best advantage. The clean lines and muted palette of this garden by Brazilian landscape designer <u>Renata Tilli</u> ensure that each sculpture is given the space it deserves.

In a residential neighbourhood a few blocks away from Paulista, São Paulo's financial district, Renata Tilli has conceived a garden which flows out seamlessly from the house and echoes the modernist construction of the building, designed by avant-garde architect Marcio Kogan.

The owner has a large art collection that includes many examples from important Brazilian artists and sculptors. The property was designed to accommodate the art, with sculptures scattered throughout the house and garden. The brief for the garden was unrestricted except that the design had to offer clear visual access to the pieces, and enhance rather than overwhelm them. The garden space was relatively small in size, so the challenge was to maximize the effect of the limited space.

The resulting design is minimalist and uncluttered by ornamentation, excess planting, or unnecessary structures that might divert attention from the sculptures. Everything in the garden works hard to achieve the overall goal, and each element has an intrinsic interest and purpose. Even the outdoor tables and chairs, emphatically horizontal, help to stress the long, clean lines of the design.

Contrasts are everywhere. Grass-like *Ophiopogon japonicus* is planted between the brick pavers to soften the rigid geometry of the flooring, and hewn stone and travertine marble make up the exterior walls in a juxtaposition of rough and smooth. It is these adjunct textures and forms that add appeal and flavour to the design, and light is used cleverly to create shadow play on the diverse surfaces.

DESIGN INGREDIENTS

· Flow

· Mass and void

· Equilibrium

· Minimalism

· Contrasting textures

· Limited colours

[1] MORPHING SURFACES

In one of the more eye-catching parts of the garden there is a deliberate, gradual transition from grass to brick pavers. The carefully managed merging alleviates the geometry and adds a softness to the otherwise spartan plan. The main lawn is *Zoysia japonica*, a grass that tolerates the periods of drought and high temperatures of São Paulo's subtropical climate. Between the pavers, the designer has used *Ophiopogon japonicus* 'Nana', another groundcover plant for warmer climes.

[2] TREES AS SCULPTURE

The staggered arrangement of the trees is subtly out of alignment with the garden's overall geometry. The apparently arbitrary cluster appears as a single feature – itself sculptural – whose lack of uniformity impresses informality onto the otherwise rigid space. The trees add height to the garden and break up the expanse of wall. The tree species is *Lafoensia glyptocarpa*, or mirindiba, a Brazilian tropical native, and the margin between their bases and the decking is softened by *Arachis repens*, a relative of the peanut.

[3] **SPACE AND ART** With a small sculpture low in the foreground, this corner of the garden has been made to seem very large. Everything is open to view, and the space has been kept clear of structures that might distract the viewer's attention from the work of art. Just as in an indoor gallery, the sculpture is surrounded by ample space so that it may be viewed easily from all sides against a neutral background. The modernistic backdrop was conceived to give the impression that it was built specifically to offset the sculpture.

[4] **RESTRICTED PALETTE** The decking and furniture are made from the same local Brazilian hardwood. The mixed stones of the dark wall behind harmonize with both the dark wood of the furniture and the brown, unfaded decking in the foreground, while contrasting with the lighter colour of the more distant decking that has been exposed to the sun. At the same time, the grey of the sun-faded decking chimes with the pale travertine stone of the garden's side wall, which itself extends into the house and makes a visual connection between the garden and the interior. A further visual connection is made between the decking and the wooden structural elements of the house hanging overhead. In all, the garden design exploits a deliberately limited palette of light and dark wood and stone to establish a continual visual flow and a sense of calm.

AN ELEMENT OF WATER

Behind the garden is a narrow rectangular water feature. A travertine wall of the house juts into it, serving as a dividing structure. In front of the wall, the pool becomes shallow and provides a watery setting for a dramatic piece by Surrealist sculptor Maria Martins, which shows two intertwined human forms. Here, Tilli introduces water as a fresh design element, its green colour and glassy surface contrasting with the two different stone walls, as well as the smooth, dark bronze of the sculpture. Their reflections in the water add another textural dimension.

Abstract Form

DESIGNER TOM OSLUND

COMPLETED 2001

LOCATION FRIDLEY, MINNESOTA, USA

ABSTRACT ART, whether it is a painting, sculpture or installation, depends on a visual language – form, colour and line – that can have significance without depicting reality in any literal sense. Garden designers have learned that they, like other artists, can influence the thoughts and emotions of the viewer while using their own visual vocabularies. This design approach can be equally effective for a large-scale corporate campus or a small-scale domestic garden.

With landscape design becoming increasingly dynamic, corporations have realized that staff and visitors deserve more than campuses consisting of only functional paths, benches and a collection of drab municipal plantings. Companies have been shown that the areas surrounding their offices can be inspiring and contemplative as well as functional.

It was thus that the Medtronic Corporation, a leading medical technology concern, briefed Tom Oslund to transform a potentially indifferent space within its campus into one that would positively affect the attitudes of the company's employees and provide an interesting and meaningful exterior welcome for visitors. The space would also commemorate the company's scientists and their achievements in the area of patents.

The garden space – located between a car park, a pedestrian walkway and the walls of the corporate library and research centre – was earmarked to be renovated as somewhere for the company's many employees to find respite from the rigours of their biomedical research. Oslund's design solution eschewed elaborate plantings and ornate water features, which would have been in stark contrast to the clinical scientific arena in which the garden is set. Instead, he used simple, abstract design elements and materials to create a Zen-like courtyard space full of symbolism, a garden that people would find both relaxing and uplifting.

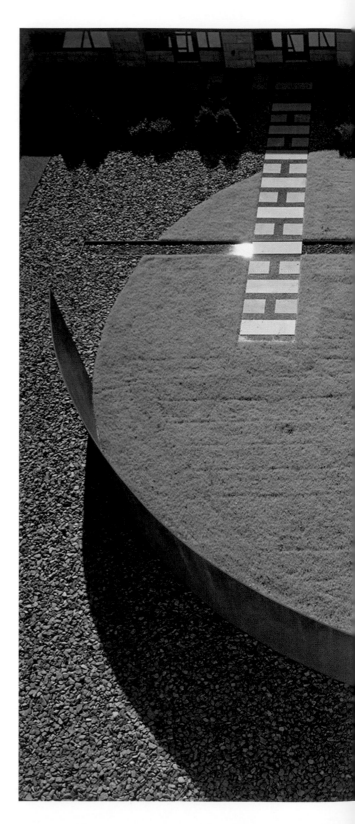

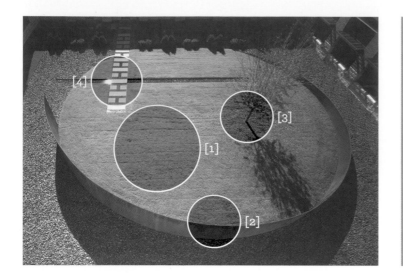

DESIGN INGREDIENTS

· Minimalist design philosophy

· Counterbalance of vertical and horizontal lines

· Allegory

· Strong geometry

[1] CIRCLE WITHIN A SQUARE

The space is a perfect square of 100 sq ft (30 sq m), incorporating a border of crushed stone. At its centre is a lawn of 70-ft (21-m) diameter, enclosed by a Corten steel wall. 'Squaring the circle' is an ancient problem of geometry that has engaged mathematicians for centuries, and the expression has come to mean trying to attempt the impossible. Perhaps for this reason, the motif of a circle within a square immediately lends interest to gardens laid out on a perfectly square plot.

[2] CORTEN STEEL SPIRAL WALL

Around the lawn a Corten steel wall spirals up from ground level to a height of 10 ft (3 m). The wall represents an ever-increasing rate of innovation, onwards and upwards. Over the past twenty years Corten has been widely used in gardens for the warm, rust-coloured appearance that it develops after only a few weeks of weathering. Usefully, the 'skin' of rust offers resistance to corrosion and makes the steel relatively long-lasting. Stainless steel studs in the wall are each etched with the number of a company patent.

[3] VERTICAL ELEMENTS

The square horizontal plane with its internal circle is counterbalanced by certain vertical elements: not only the Corten steel wall, but also a single specimen of *Acer saccharum* (sugar maple), which provides a focal point within the garden as a whole. Popular for its attractive form and foliage colour, the species is one of the most widespread in the Midwest. Its brilliant red autumn flush echoes the rusty orange of the steel wall. As the day progresses, shade patterns of the vertical elements cross the space.

[4] RILL AND PATH

Almost bisecting the circle, a narrow, reflective rill cuts its way from the stone border. Water moves over the stones of the rill and is recirculated along its course. Near its start, the rill is itself bisected by a bluestone path that, like the rill, does not arrive at the far side of the circle. The two features pose questions in the visitor's mind: 'Where do they go? Why do they stop so abruptly?' They also offer a pleasing balance with the positioning of the tree on the lawn, anchoring what looks like an unstable surface.

ABSTRACTION IN GARDENS

Allegory and abstraction have been significant qualities in gardens since the earliest Persian examples. In the 18th-century landscape garden at Stowe, England, with its Temple of British Worthies (see left), a tale of political intrigue is told by its statuary and structures. Following a long period of design in which only the aesthetic qualities of the outside space were emphasized, the garden designed around a concept or idea, and including metaphorical statements and abstraction, is making a comeback.

Sculpted Ground

DESIGNER VLADIMIR SITTA

COMPLETED 2004

LOCATION SYDNEY, AUSTRALIA

THE NOTION OF A SCULPTURE garden, perhaps designed to showcase a collection of sculpted works from various artists, is familiar. Much less common is the concept of a garden that is itself a sculpture, where it appears that the land of the garden itself has been sculpted by a giant hand to turn it into a meaningful artefact.

Sometimes, people who commission a cutting-edge architect to design a house for them end up with much more, namely a bold statement of their ambition, their wealth or their avant-garde taste. And what such a house often requires is a garden that makes an equally strong statement, created by an equally cutting-edge landscape designer.

That was how the owners of this property, perched on a ridge above Sydney, Australia, came to ask Vladimir Sitta to make them a memorable garden on the small plot of land that wrapped around their house. Sitta was given no detailed brief, bar the stipulation that the garden should accommodate a collection of succulent plants.

When someone left a red rock on the designer's desk, he realized that it would make a perfect backdrop for the succulents. Sitta traced the rock to a quarry near Alice Springs and obtained what he needed for the build. Back at the site, Sitta constructed the blocks as though they were erupting from the surrounding earth in jagged shards. It was a clever device to create three-dimensional depth in a narrow site. Beneath the artificial crevasse he placed a watering hole, actually a pond for goldfish. With the grey-blue succulents standing out against the red earth, the design embodied the harshness of the Australian outback, what Sitta called 'the burning red heart of the country'.

At first sight, the garden seems more than slightly bizarre, even challenging. But viewed in conjunction with the house, it reveals itself to be an exciting, original and daring artistic statement.

[1] HOT ROCK The soft red sandstone's vivid colour intrigued Sitta, but it was not easy to work. Diamond saws were needed to produce precisely honed outlines, and then the faces were abraded with a stonemason's tool to create a rough surface texture. The structures were built as walls, course by course, and carefully mortared into place. Surplus pieces were cut up and tumbled in a cement mixer to produce a mulch of red pebbles and gravel. The mulch was distributed among the rocks to form authentic-looking drifts.

[2] WATERING HOLE The pool, populated by goldfish (themselves highlighted by the red sandstone), is set below the massive shards of rock. It is evocative of the pockets of water that any outback traveller would be delighted to find in the otherwise parched terrain. Sitta's original plan called for water emanating from between the brick courses, but the rock was too porous for that and the resulting water loss was excessive. Instead, a single spout was drilled high in the rocks to deliver drops into the pool below, creating an echoing, cave-like dripping sound.

[3] SUCCULENTS AND GRASSES

The collection of succulent plants used in the garden includes euphorbias, echeverias, *Agave attenuata*, *Aeonium* 'Zwartkop' and the strange, bulbous-stemmed *Beaucarnea recurvata* (ponytail palm). These are planted along the boundary where they are sheltered while also providing some privacy. Their colour palette is extended with a carefully spaced grid of *Festuca glauca* (blue fescue grass), which grows in controlled drifts across the tilted surfaces of the outcrops.

[4] **EXPRESSIVE TREE** A central feature in the garden is this dead specimen of *Dracaena draco* (dragon tree, named after the red resin, or 'dragon's blood', secreted by its bark and leaves). Although a drought-tolerant subtropical species, it was clearly no match for the harsh climate of the Australian outback, where it was found. The tree emphasizes the dynamic movement of the garden by teetering at an angle, as if being pushed aside by forces emanating from underground. The tree, carefully supported with wires to prevent it from moving, provides dramatic architectural form.

[5] **VIEWING PLATFORM** This is a garden designed to be viewed from the house, and the rocks are framed by floor-to-ceiling windows. On the opposite side of the garden, a viewing platform was constructed from crisp, even, white rock to contrast with the burnished red sandstone. It runs in a straight line until it turns a corner, after which it seems to drift off like an unfinished sentence, as if inviting the visitor to venture further from the house and explore. Its pristine appearance emphasizes its status as a viewing platform, separating what is modern from what appears ancient.

Mondrian Grid

DESIGNER CTOPOS DESIGN

COMPLETED 2009

LOCATION SEOUL, KOREA

THE ART OF PIET MONDRIAN (1872–1944)
typically features an irregular grid of vertical and
horizontal black lines of varying weight on a white
background, with areas of colour infilling some of
the resulting squares and rectangles. Mondrian's
stark graphic art provided the blueprint for a
remarkable public garden in Korea, with elements
such as raised walkways and pools taking the place
of Mondrian's painted lines and colours.

West Seoul Lake Park, laid out by CTOPOS Design,
is a shining example of how to turn a neglected
open space into something usable, beautiful and
meaningful. The design for the space was
determined by what went before, specifically a water
purification plant that had long served the city but
had been decommissioned some years previously.
The City of Seoul, while in the process of deciding
to retire the facility, resolved that it should be
returned to the people in the form of an eco-friendly
park and an open cultural art space, with a view to
revitalizing a very deprived area.

In the past, whenever a site was selected for
regeneration, the automatic move was to eradicate
all signs of its previous incarnation and introduce a
completely new landscape, often something that was
infinitely less interesting than what went before. The
present need to conserve world resources demands
that such sites are regenerated sustainably, which
means retaining as much of the former construction
as possible. If executed well, the ugly can be made
beautiful, and the useless made functional.

Within the park, the Mondrian Plaza is set over
what were concrete settling tanks. The plaza is one
of the most creative areas of the park, and combines
modern art, nature and architecture. Parts of the
original concrete walls have been left standing,
separating different spaces, and high-level walkways
on a Mondrian-like plan pass over water features,
constrained block planting and wild-planted areas.
The plaza's combination of horizontal and
perpendicular lines is harmonious and pleasing.

Although eco considerations motivate designs
like West Seoul Lake Park, industrial structures that
once had a function, and which have been rendered
redundant by changing times, have a certain quality
about them that stimulates the imagination,
generating a nostalgic, almost romantic sensibility
as well as a feeling of satisfaction and pride.

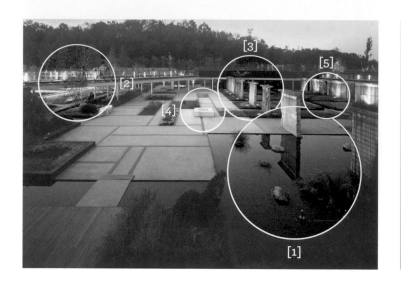

DESIGN INGREDIENTS

· Sense of place

· Evocative atmosphere

· Recycling of older structure

· Introduction of levels

[1] WATER GARDENS Shallow ponds, corresponding to Mondrian's areas of colour, contain introduced rocks that symbolize the Korean landscape. Fountains are used in the plaza to create a sense of movement, and also in the nearby lake, where water spouts send jets of water 50 ft (15 m) into the air. The jets are activated by sensors that pick up the roars of overhead aircraft, and their sound helps to neutralize the noise pollution in an ingenious and entertaining way. The planes are now welcomed for triggering the display.

[2] CHANNELS AND WALKWAYS Most of the original network of concrete water-delivery channels has been retained, and it snakes around through horizontal and vertical planes in a Mondrian-like way. The designers used some of them as the basis for a series of high-level walkways from which visitors can view the scenes below or look out into other areas of the park. Wider sections incorporate seating. The 'floating' promenade literally adds another layer to the design. It mimics and plays with the gridwork design below, adding a further dimension of interest.

[3] RECYCLED ELEMENTS The designers made no attempt to conceal or disguise the parts of the water plant that they decided to retain. Wall sections of the purification tanks were reused as structural supports, or left to stand as a robust memorial to the site's original industrial purpose. The water pipes, too, were given a new lease of life by being fashioned into signposts, bicycle racks, benches and sculptures. The overarching theme of the park is rebirth, and every retained element has been recycled and given a function in the new scheme.

[4] CONCRETE CANVAS Areas of the floor of Mondrian Plaza resemble one of the artist's canvases, but realized in rectangles of concrete with darker stone borders. In some areas, concrete is replaced by contrasting plantings, some floral and municipal in appearance, others wilder and comprising grasses and native plants. Another geometric element at this level is a single, square, white plastic bench that is illuminated from within. This feature serves as a central focus, especially at night when it offers a vivid contrast to its surroundings.

[5] DOMINANT PLANTING Variety at ground level was an important factor in the design of Mondrian Plaza. Areas dominated by water or concrete give way to sections dominated by planting, separated by wooden walkways and seating. Raised beds edged with Corten steel – which develops an attractive and protective red rust – are filled with block plantings, which contain blooms of a single colour. The Corten steel is bent into a variety of shapes to vary the feel of the borders dividing individual rectangles of planting. The overall effect is graphic and modern.

Inner-City Installation

DESIGNER HEYWOOD & CONDIE

COMPLETED 2001

LOCATION LONDON, UK

MOST GARDENS EXIST as spaces to be entered and enjoyed by the public or private individuals, but there are exceptions. Sometimes a garden is designed simply to be looked at from outside, like an installation in an art gallery. A visual refuge and a mysterious, self-contained microcosm, this kind of garden challenges passers-by to dare to look at it and work out what it means to them.

Designed by Tony Heywood of <u>Heywood & Condie</u> and installed at a busy inner-city junction – that of Edgware Road and Sussex Gardens in central London – 'Helter Skelter' is an unconventional 'garden artwork' set in a small plot of only 45 sq ft (4.2 sq m). There is no dedicated signage to it, no fanfare of any kind. It is just there, a visual haven amid the noise, speed and colour of the constantly fluctuating pageant outside its bounds.

The effect is akin to an entire landscape symbolically expressed in miniature, its elements suggesting pools, trees, hedges and rocky outcrops, with the whole revolving around itself as if in a vortex. Closer inspection reveals that the components have been carefully arranged in great detail to create a sense of energy. The dynamic is so strong that the railings and hedges surrounding the site might almost be there to protect passers-by from bits of garden that might spin out at any moment, or indeed prevent them from being sucked helplessly into the space.

For the passing Londoners and tourists, 'Helter Skelter' is a reminder that the surrounding streets are not the only reality or environment to be experienced on earth. Here is an alternative microcosm, full of vibrant colours and unfamiliar forms and textures, both organic and inorganic. Like a hallucination or a waking dream, it is an unexpected installation to find on the corner of a busy street, but one that is welcome, intellectually accessible and strangely uplifting.

DESIGN INGREDIENTS

· Movement

· Texture and form

· Three dimensions

· Multiple views

[1] SPIRAL MOVEMENT Garden designers often agonize over how to introduce a sense of movement into their designs. This garden shows how a juxtaposition of different materials and plant forms can literally put a spin on the space. The action is three-dimensional, too: elements move around the axis in a spiral but also disappear downwards into the ground and vertically, climbing up the boundaries. The planting and the hard landscaping combine into a whole that teems with energy and gives a strong sense of movement.

[2] LIVING WALL The sense that the garden is whirling out of control is heightened by elements spreading over the otherwise plain containing walls. What looks like torn, tortured metal detritus appears to have been flattened against the wall by centrifugal force, while the planting spreads vertically up the wall from the ground. The vegetation is actually rooted in a vertical framework of growing medium, but the plants seem to defy their own containment. The row of star-shaped agaves halfway up the living wall are particularly striking in the way they appear to defy gravity.

[3] SLATES AND GRANITE An important element of the revolving dynamic of 'Helter Skelter' is an area in which roughly hewn slates of various sizes jut out at sharp angles from a sparkling river of shattered blue glass. The river itself swirls around towards a central pool. The dynamic is emphasized further by curved metal railings and slates laid flat on one another, like fish scales. Beyond the slates, resembling them but much larger, leaning granite slabs increase the sense of instability and powerful centrifugal force.

[4] ROCKS AND GRASSES The garden derives much of its visual impact from pairings of contrasting materials and textures. Here, hard, latently hazardous outcrops of granite are set against gentle mounds of soft, green grass, with golden, feather-like seeding stalks behind. A further contrast of texture and colour is introduced by the adjacent area of pink-grey pebbles. The pebbles appear intermittently throughout the garden installation as a constant background that unifies the more obvious features.

HORTICULTURAL INTERVENTION ART

Tony Heywood and Alison Condie often refer to their work as 'horticultural intervention art', or visual interruptions designed to surprise and intrigue. Tony says, 'I'm particularly interested in how to emotionalize or activate an area, so I see these interventions as being things that are quite lightweight, but at the same time very sensational, high impact, advertorial.... In the eighteenth century, dioramas, panoramas, and eidophusikons were all used to present the landscape in a theatrical way and that's the path I'm interested in following.' In the work 'Split' (see right), set in Westonbirt Arboretum, Gloucestershire, UK, jagged chrome shapes bearing collections of cacti and succulents rise up from a bed of crushed anthracite.

Landscape

Coastal Hideaway

DESIGNER JO THOMPSON

COMPLETED 2011

LOCATION EAST SUSSEX, UK

A GARDEN ESTABLISHED in a seaside setting is subject to a unique set of conditions: frequent, salt-laden winds that may be very dry; prolonged periods of harsh sunlight; a lack of shade and an infertile planting environment. The secret of success is to learn what grows naturally in such environments and look for variants that will thrive while adding colour and interest to the scheme.

The owners of this house on the south coast of England had bought a plot on sand dunes directly by the beach. It contained a bungalow built in the 1920s, surrounded by a dense thicket of *Rosa rugosa* (Japanese rose, also known as beach rose). They decided to start again from scratch, and when they had approved the designs for a new house on the site they called in designer Jo Thompson to look at the garden. Being called in before the house was built gave Thompson the advantage of being able to assess the site in all seasons. She was able to design to the new house plans, and consequently the hard structures in the garden were constructed at the same time as the house.

The main challenge for the designer was to find an effective replacement for the roses, which had shielded the property not only from persistent winds (technically it prevailed from the south-west, but in reality it seemed to buffet from all directions) but also from the gaze of people on the beach, who were at liberty to walk right up to the property's boundary. At the same time, the owners had an apparently contradictory ambition to restore uninterrupted views of the sea. Thompson's answer was to create a garden that provided a seamless transition between the house and the beach. By setting the communal area low in the dunes she secured a degree of both wind protection and privacy. In its planting and its materials the space was like an extension of the beach itself, while a sheltered firepit area afforded the communal comforts of a traditional garden.

DESIGN INGREDIENTS

· Informality

· Unity of style

· Limitations of site

· Rhythm

· Relationship to the
  landscape beyond

[1] SHELTER AND PRIVACY

While the garden is set a little above the level of the public beach, there is no solid boundary to offer privacy and shelter from the wind. The seating area, created around a central firepit and rendered in white to match the house, was given a high, semi-circular back that extends at one end to the house. This creates an intimate, intriguing space, entirely hidden from the beach. Further shelter and privacy are afforded by the dunes continuing beyond the garden, their curving mounds echoing the terrain beyond.

[2] HARMONIOUS MATERIALS

As much as possible, the materials of the garden were chosen to blend in with the character of the immediate, marine environment. The fencing consists of marine rope swags suspended between simple posts. The seating structure may be viewed as an extension of the house walls. The shingle around the firepit is the same as is found on the beach. The cedar boardwalks evoke the deck of a ship. Every element reflects its setting while having an appropriate air of impermanence in a scene where features are always shifting.

[3] NATIVE GRASSES The most important plant in the palette here is *Ammophila arenaria* (marram grass). Its network of deep roots stabilizes the sand and helps maintain the dune system. The beach and dunes are protected as a Site of Special Scientific Interest (SSSI) and the garden plants were chosen with the aid of an environment agency. The marram was planted with other maritime grasses, such as leymus and fescues, in biodegradeable coir. Taller plants, including tamarisk and griselinia, are dotted along the edge.

[4] BOARDWALKS Walking on sand and pebbles can be slow and tiring, as well as exposing the feet to hidden hazards. The solution here is a network of boardwalks that traverse the property as well as give access to the beach. Made of cedar, the walkways are lightweight and do the minimum of damage to the dune ecosystem. While not indestructible, they weather the sun and salt-laden wind well, and their flexibility allows them to adapt to the changing shapes of the dunes. They can also be shifted easily to accommodate changes in the dune planting programme.

PLANTS FOR COASTAL GARDENS

Plants need to be tough to grow by the sea. Exposure to strong, salt-laden winds will scorch and stunt all but those specially adapted for such extreme conditions. However, proximity to the sea reduces the likelihood of hard frosts, so a variety of frost-tender plants may be considered for planting, and these may be helped by the higher light levels and humidity. Creating a windbreak is an important means of protecting young plants while they establish. At Little Scypen garden, in Ringmore, Devon, UK (see below), a natural barrier of shrubs and low trees filters the wind, rather than blocking it completely. Solid walls should be avoided because they create wind turbulence, which can be enough to damage and dislodge plants.

Volcanic Refuge

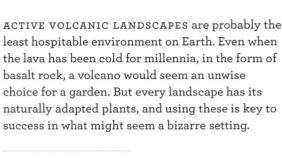

DESIGNERS	CESAR MANRIQUE AND JESUS SOTO
COMPLETED	1970s
LOCATION	LANZAROTE, SPAIN

ACTIVE VOLCANIC LANDSCAPES are probably the least hospitable environment on Earth. Even when the lava has been cold for millennia, in the form of basalt rock, a volcano would seem an unwise choice for a garden. But every landscape has its naturally adapted plants, and using these is key to success in what might seem a bizarre setting.

Tucked into the folds of a partially collapsed volcano, high above the town of Nazaret, is an extraordinary dwelling – a series of rooms and passages set in volcanaic blisters within the craggy overhang. Whitewashed walls across the cliff face offer little clue that there is a house here, but below, an extraordinary garden openly signals its existence.

The story goes that actor Omar Sharif bought the house as soon as he saw it while filming on the island. He lost the property in a game of bridge, but it retains his name: 'LagOmar', or Omar's Lake.

LagOmar was conceived by Lanzaroteño artist and architect César Manrique, and realized with the help of local artist Jesús Soto. The space is at once fantasy and folly. Like all the built components of the garden and house, the pool at its centre is whitewashed, which gives the water an opalescent luminosity. Twisting around and behind the pool are staircases and paths that lead up to and through softly curving caverns and galleries, revealing little nooks and crannies, some whitewashed and some left as natural basalt. Exploring the space feels like an adventure, or a dream. Quirky portholes or natural rock fractures offer views out across the valley towards the distant mountains and the sea.

The clean, bright and pristine construction contrasts with the murky, red-black basalt, which is softened by a variety of plants native to the Canary Islands, notably the tall, cactus-like succulent, *Euphorbia canariensis*. The property and garden exemplify a balanced synthesis between modern architecture and the natural Lanzarote environment.

DESIGN INGREDIENTS

· Environmentally sensitive

· Indigenous design and materials

· Playfulness and flamboyance

· Fusion of textures and colours

[1] PIPE CONDUIT To the side of the pool, an intriguing, round tunnel entrance beckons. Although there are other ways of moving around the garden, this definitely looks the most interesting. Inside, there are stepping stones that cross over an extension of the swimming pool, hovering just above the water line. The pipe eventually emerges at the cliff face and leads on into the rocks. The experience is a fantastical journey of discovery with no obvious end and a promise of surprises around the corner. Above all, it is fun.

[2] ARCHITECTURAL PLANTS

Fleshy-stemmed euphorbias, such as *Euphorbia canariensis*, grow everywhere on Lanzarote, and there are some fine examples here. Agaves, yuccas and palms are used architecturally for their height and form, contrasting with bougainvillea and groundcover plants such as ivy. Large areas of Lanzarote are covered in volcanic material, the climate is arid with little rainfall, and there is no local source of fresh water; coupled with the strong winds, it is interesting to see the island's wealth of flora, especially succulents.

[3] POOL ENVIRONMENT To sit in this poolside garden is a unique experience, with the black basalt cliff towering above, and the unsettling sense of a dormant volcano beneath. In this context, the spiky cacti, agaves, euphorbias and other succulents take on an alien, surreal quality – even the ivy clinging to the barren rock seems odd and unnatural. As a water jet plays over the pool, there is a sense of being in a 1970s James Bond film, or an adult jetset playground. It is an imaginary world transported from some filmic fantasy and made reality.

CESAR MANRIQUE

Artist César Manrique (1919–92) devoted his life to improving Lanzarote and campaigning against any threat to its ecological integrity. In 1993 his achievements were rewarded when UNESCO declared Lanzarote a protected biosphere. To Manrique, Lanzarote was an island-shaped canvas; he developed unique cultural attractions, and even built giant wind sculptures (as below) on roundabouts.

[4] VOLCANIC ROCK As a design element in this garden, the dramatic backdrop of bare basalt rock cannot be ignored. Its brooding bulk pushes the garden centre stage, its dark hue offsets the white buildings, lake and vegetation, and its height gives the site a sense of seclusion. Basalt is the most common type of volcanic rock. When magma (liquid rock) bursts to the Earth's surface during a volcanic eruption, it undergoes a rapid cooling process. The resulting igneous rock can vary in colour from grey to the black that is commonly found on Lanzarote. Basalt dust is used by gardeners to stimulate soil micro-organism activity, and it is known to contribute to the building up of humus in the soil.

Island Modern

DESIGNER RAYMOND JUNGLES

COMPLETED 2005

LOCATION KEY WEST, FLORIDA, USA

BUYING A PROPERTY on a small island has always had attendant risks that mainland buyers do not need to consider. Today, in the context of global warming and climate change, island properties may be subject to stricter building restrictions, and these can have a prohibitive effect on a prospective buyer's budget. Sometimes, a fresh approach is needed to achieve a great island home.

The Florida Keys, a string of islands in the southeast United States, reach westwards into the Gulf of Mexico. Key West, at the end of the string, is prone to flooding and extreme weather conditions. When a couple decided to renovate a 1940s house, they learned that they were not permitted to spend more than half of the property's value on the house itself without demolishing the structure and rebuilding in compliance with current codes. That possibility was ruled out because of the time it would take; instead, the couple called in Raymond Jungles, one of the foremost US landscape architects.

Jungles's solution was to draw attention away from the building and towards the garden, where he had a creative free hand. In the end, the interior area was slightly reduced in favour of the exterior.

Working with architect Rob DeLaune, Jungles replaced the conventional windows with floor-to-ceiling glazing, which, when open, presents no boundary between the house and garden. He also brought the garden into the house by installing glass-lined cases of plants. The shower area in the master bedroom, for example, resembles a giant terrarium, with well-placed plants offering the bather a buffer of privacy.

The garden was manipulated to maximize its space and enhance the aesthetic appeal of the house. Free-standing walls now hide the exterior of the building, and lush planting and water proliferate. The whole space has an open, dynamic feel that is simple but strong.

DESIGN INGREDIENTS

· Screening

· Tropical planting

· Geometry

· Moving water

· Flow from the house

[1] DESIGN LINES The garden is made up of a series of rectilinear lines that echo the shape of the building. Stripes of different materials – such as smooth stone paving bordering a channel filled with rounded stones of mixed sizes – have the effect of breaking up what is a small plot into separate areas, giving a sense of space, while creating repetition and cohesiveness. The strong ground plan and structural elements enforce the view outwards, diverting attention from the house and establishing a contemporary, streamlined feel. Free-standing, tall, green walls give a sense of containment.

[2] OVERHEAD STRUCTURE Aluminium has a strong presence in the garden. A trellis made of aluminium is suspended over a walkway between the carport area and the house. The trellis creates a sort of vestibule, which underscores a feeling of moving into the living space – whether the vestibule is outside or inside seems not to be an issue. The trellis provides an opportunity to introduce vines overhead, for privacy and to provide a link with the planting below. A sense of design unity is fostered by the door and its adjacent walls being made of aluminium bars, too, echoing the trellis overhead.

[3] **STEPPING STONES** In addition to a pool at the other side of the house (see below), Jungles has incorporated a rather unusual shallow pool and waterfall at the entrance, set with what at first appears to be a hopscotch arrangement of stepping stones that seem to float above the water's surface. Visitors must step across these in order to gain entry to the property. The rectangles are actually set close to each other in such a way that no hazardous hopping is required. A conformist would have placed the stones in a tidy line, but Jungles's arrangement adds an interesting dynamic.

[4] **EXOTIC PLANTS** Visible from the house, beyond the stepping stones of the entrance, is a narrow bed of exotic planting. Among the plants in the bed are a shade-loving ceratozamia cycad with fern-like leaves, and the big-leafed *Philodendron magnifica*. Above them is the grey-green foliage of *Conocarpus erectus* var. *sericeus* (silver buttonwood), with magenta bougainvillea flowers growing through it. The Florida Keys lie in a subtropical region and it is fitting that the pool planting has an exotic feel. Jungles has long been a devotee of native South American plants.

RECTILINEAR POOL

On the opposite side of the house from the entrance, Jungles has installed a large, open, rectilinear swimming pool with a deck of the same smooth stone paving. Facing the house is a raised bed, divided by a broad, oblique waterfall. Conspicuous among the plants are the orange-green leaves of *Aechmea blanchetiana*, a bromeliad from Brazil that was once rare but is now in cultivation. Jungles selected all the tropical plants surrounding the pool for their low water requirements as well as their interesting sculptural forms.

Forest Retreat

DESIGNER MARCEL WOLTERINCK

COMPLETED 2005

LOCATION UTRECHT, NETHERLANDS

[3] WATER FEATURES

At intervals along each side of the path are identical water features, each one bordered by a bracket of low-cut yew hedging. The features each consist of a minimally raised square platform of lead, with a small jet gurgling at the centre and spilling water over the edge. The 'pondless' features rely on a reservoir beneath, from which water is recirculated by a pump. Around each is a dense black carpet of *Ophiopogon planiscapus* 'Nigrescens', which contrasts satisfyingly in texture with the surface of the shiny lead platform.

[4] PERGOLA WITH WISTERIA

The garden's oak pergola is a substantial structure – two people are easily able to walk through comfortably, side by side with plenty of head clearance. Pergolas are useful devices to guide people from one space to another (in this case from the main house to the retreat) while providing a means of supporting climbing plants. The climber used here is *Wisteria sinensis*, one of the most popular climbing plants due to its fragrant, pendulous racemes of lilac flowers, which appear in May and June. Simplicity is the byword in this garden, but if winter interest were required (wisteria is deciduous), an evergreen climber could be planted alongside it, perhaps *Trachelospermum jasminoides* (star jasmine), which flowers at a different time of year to wisteria.

[5] FOREST PLANTINGS

It was important to Wolterinck's client that there should be no artificial boundary between the new garden and the natural forest. At the same time, the conjunction of the two was an opportunity for some interesting planting. Wolterinck merged the garden into the forest by using the same forest species, as well as the introduced rhododendrons that had long grown among them. It was important that the rhythm of the groups of trees that he dotted around the edge of the garden echoed those in the forest, rather than appearing like the aligned trees of a commercial plantation. In the event, the garden–forest border was one of the most aesthetically pleasing areas of the project because it drew together Wolterinck's formal elements against an informal backdrop.

Grassland Space

DESIGNER ANDREA COCHRAN
COMPLETED 2007
LOCATION SONOMA, CALIFORNIA, USA

WHETHER A REGION is predominantly grassland is determined by a number of evolutionary influences, such as wind, salt spray, fire and grazing, all of which can suppress the growth of shrubs and trees that might otherwise grow there. The open grassland of California's coastal prairies, where this garden is set, is richer in grass species than any other grassland in North America.

The owners bought the Sonoma garden site in 2001, adding it to holdings they had already developed to include a commercial vineyard, olive oil production and an organic vegetable garden that supplied local restaurants. The site contained some ancient California bay trees, oaks and buckeyes (Californian horse chestnuts), and bordered a seasonal creek that flooded periodically. Landscape architect Andrea Cochran was briefed to create a pared-back, modern area for relaxation, a garden in sharp contrast to the agricultural bustle of the rest of the property; the owners also yearned for an observatory.

Cochran's solution is one of elegantly balanced and linked elements within a serene, uncluttered landscape. The vertical structures – the observatory, a pavilion, lines of olive trees and a stone pyramid – are anchored by a rectilinear reflecting pool and a raised lap pool. The structures are clad in Corten steel, which instantly gives an aged feel, with the rusty hue sitting comfortably in the wider landscape. Meadows of drought-tolerant grasses offer a transition to the rugged landscape beyond.

Cochran believes that a garden design should respond to the surrounding landscape on an emotional level, rather than being an intellectual exercise that requires some kind of explanation. That philosophy is clear in this easily understood, understated and elegant creation.

DESIGN INGREDIENTS

· Simplicity

· Clean linear layout

· Balance of horizontal and
  vertical elements

· Ordered space

· Repetition of materials

[1] SENSE OF ORDER The flat, open, almost featureless site required strong lines dividing distinct areas, each with their own textural identity, to impose a sense of discipline and purpose on the garden, as well as to anchor the buildings in the space. Straight lines hold more authority than curves, so the plan was created on a grid, and structures were set parallel or at right angles to other features. At ground level, mown turf is contrasted with cleanly delineated areas of dark gravel and light stonework. The contrasts of colour energize the scene.

[2] CORTEN STEEL The observatory stands in a reflecting pool that is 12 in. (30 cm) deep. Attached to the structure, a mysterious staircase hangs inexplicably above the water. The observatory and other structures are constructed from Corten, a weathering steel that develops an orange–brown rust on exposure to the air. The nearer the sea or ocean, the more intense the orange colour, due to increased levels of salts in the atmosphere. Cochran saw Corten as being 'of the earth' and therefore belonging in a rural setting where rusting machinery is a common sight.

[3] OLIVE ALLEES Ancient olive trees were rescued from another grove and set in carefully positioned rows in front of the pavilion. The fact that their ancient, gnarled shapes were aligned to a grid is an example of Cochran's formal use of informal (or irregular and individual) materials. The olive allées also reinforce the overall grid plan that Cochran used to impose a sense of order and purpose on what was originally an open and largely featureless site. The trees are positioned to mirror the orientation of the pavilion and its reflective pool and walkway, and the grid plan is even confirmed by the exact siting and orientation of the table and benches. All of these elements are designed to have a calming effect on the beholder.

[4] GRASS EN MASSE Grasses planted as one mass serve to link the lawn, the pool and the olive allées. They will also improve and revive land damaged by construction. Four types of grass are layered through the planting: *Muhlenbergia capillaris* (muhly grass); *Festuca mairei* (Atlas fescue); *Pennisetum spathiolatum* (slender veldt grass); and *Schizachyrium scoparium* (little bluestem). These are all drought-tolerant plants and, seeding at different times of the summer and autumn, they bring an ever-changing variety of colours and textures to the scene. Grasses en masse create a body of fluidity, responding to every breeze, and their gauzy veil of seedheads seems quite ethereal when backlit by the sun.

ASYMMETRICAL PYRAMID

During construction, thousands of rocks were unearthed, and it was felt that these should be reclaimed and recycled in an innovative way rather than trucked off somewhere. The result is an asymmetrical pyramid (technically an irregular tetrahedron). The structure, reclining at the far end of the space beyond the shallow pool and the observatory, serves to anchor the design, not only by its weight, but also by its contrasting sculptural impact on the other elements of the garden. The pyramid's apex is positioned in such a way that the silhouette of the bay laurel stands clear.

Mountain Perch

DESIGNER DESIGN WORKSHOP

COMPLETED 2007

LOCATION ASPEN, COLORADO, USA

THE BARE SUMMIT of a mountain, subject to wild variations of temperature and exposed to wind, rain, ice and snow, might seem to be the least promising site for a garden. The truth is that few plant types will grow here, and so architectural elements must dominate. Here, an interplay of rock, water and varied heights forms a living space from which to take in the spectacular views.

This property, perched high on a steep hillside above the Roaring Fork River Valley, not far from Aspen, is backed by the dramatic mountains of the Sawatch Range of the Rockies. Thick stands of aspens embrace the house and the slopes below are thick with carpets of wildflowers.

The house and garden are stacked on top of the hillside, rather than sprawled, with the terrace acting like a green roof for the property. This reduces the impact on the surrounding landscape. The garden consists of two interlinking courtyards, with stone retaining walls defining different spaces and setting boundaries between the built and natural landscapes.

An important factor of the design was water, and this flows through the space in a variety of forms: still pools, rivulets and cascades. The terrace and landscape are visible from every part of the house. Local materials were sourced to ensure that the property blended imperceptibly into its setting.

Native plants are used throughout, which in turn provides habitat for native wildlife and further promotes the integration of the scheme into the surrounding landscape. Design Workshop conducted climate studies on the site to ascertain the pattern of rapidly changing mountain temperatures and so inform the positioning of the terraces, which are sited to provide maximum shelter from the winds while capitalizing on sunlight. The architecture complements the landscape without surrendering to it; the colours, details and stonework are all site-appropriate.

DESIGN INGREDIENTS

· Watery ambience

· Continuity with landscape

· Flow between interior
and exterior

· Response to climate

· Unity

[1] **POOL** Set before the edge of the promontory terrace is a rectilinear pool in honed black granite. Its surface is flush with the paving to provide a constant level. Shallow water is held in tension across the surface until it disappears invisibly over the infinity edge of the pool, giving almost no impression of movement. Mirroring the surroundings in its taut surface, the pool brings the natural environment into the garden, while light reflects off the water in patterns that dance across the courtyard.

[2] **ROCK WALLS** Made of rough-hewn local sandstone, the house and garden walls appear sturdy and purposeful enough to cope with the extreme climate and provide a solid foundation for the terraces. Both the sandstone itself and the way it has been roughly cut are sympathetic to the landscape. The stone shows traces of returning to its natural state; lichens are beginning to grow on its surface, and dissolved minerals are leaving tracks down the sides. The overall impression is one of a hillside fortress, or a stronghold that is literally part of the mountain.

[3] <u>DROPS AND LEVELS</u> The property follows the contours of the land, so changes of height had to be established and made traversable via terracing. The drops are steep and their precipitousness is exaggerated by the narrowness of the horizontal capping stones. The sheet of water dropping from the granite pool appears slightly dangerous, as if to emphasize the verticality of the site. The walls, heights and terraces accentuate the elevated feeling of the garden, giving it a sense of sanctuary from the inhospitable country below.

[4] <u>MOUNTAIN FIRE</u> To enable friends to enjoy social interaction away from the house, a fire pit has been tucked in by the sheltered base of the promontory wall, where the natural and built environments meet. Natural slabs of stone distributed around the fire pit serve as seating for those seeking the warmth of the fire when the temperatures dip. The fire pit is sunk into the ground, affording shelter from wind, and may be used either as a campfire or a barbecue. A wrought-iron rotisserie for spit-roasting is also available.

WATER FEATURES

Water has been used in diverse and artistic ways as a connecting element throughout the exterior parts of the residence, with the sounds of spray and cascades penetrating the silence. A short rill cuts though a gap in a wall to point out a distant peak, and a granite block overflows with mist in the entrance courtyard. Still, reflective pools dissolve into dramatic cascades that leap from the terraces in curtained planes. Rupturing and splitting when they land, they evoke the waterfalls visible on the mountainsides.

Modern Country

DESIGNER ACRES WILD
COMPLETED 2006
LOCATION HAMPSHIRE, UK

THE TERM 'English country garden' normally
conjures up generous borders brimming with
cottage garden plants and pergolas laden with
roses and honeysuckle. However, there is a way
of designing this style that manages to be at once
modern looking yet appropriate for its location.

The challenge faced by Acres Wild (the design
partnership of Debbie Roberts and Ian Smith) was
the garden's 2.5 acres (1 ha) of empty grassland. A
blank canvas is often welcomed as a starting point,
but here the sheer size of the site was daunting.

The challenge was how to 'sit' the garden
comfortably and unobtrusively in its surroundings.
Tracing the contours of the land was the solution,
marking them with broad sweeps of meadow grass
contained by curvaceous hedges and borders.

The aim was not to impose on the existing
landscape but to intervene more subtly, especially
when moving away from the house. The garden
mimics the undulations of the downland views
beyond. Hard landscaping is pared back to leave
an uncontrived and natural-looking expanse.

On plan the garden is a series of radii that ripple
outwards to provide a generous visual flow. This
graphic device made the structure easy to set out
and maintain. Indeed, the main criterion for the
spacing between the hedges and borders was the
turning circle of a ride-on mower.

It was important that the proportions were
balanced. The size of the space dictated that the
elements and their arrangement were realized on a
grand scale: large blocks of single-species planting
interspersed with generously cut turf paths. The
fairly restricted colour palette is realized in bold
swathes of ornamental grasses and tall perennials.

The exposed hilltop site meant that plants were
chosen not only for their resistance to wind damage
but also for their ability to catch every stray breeze
and produce pleasing ruffles of movement.

[1] **WATER FEATURE** Much of this Hampshire garden is designed in curves, including the pond, which imitates the natural bend of a river. Lush green planting disguises its extremities, while reeds have been incorporated to keep the water clean. A rectangular deck with loungers cantilevers over one side of the pond, its strict geometry counterpoising the soft curves of the pond's outline. On the other side, a set of elegant stepping stones traverses the water. A simple fountain adds sound and interest to the garden.

[2] **MUTED TONES** Plants are massed together as single species, striking to the eye for their sheer number and bold effect. Tones are deliberately gentle, even neutral. Bronze grasses make an impression, both floating hazily in the borders and gathered in small fields of winter barley. Set within the ripples of the design, they enhance the surrounding views. Yellow achillea and white echinacea sidle up to the grasses, while misty blocks of purple-blue caryopteris, perovskia, nepeta and lavender provide contrasting colour and maximum drama.

[3] HEDGING FOR STRUCTURE

Hedging provides the garden's backbone. Chains of planting follow the contours of the landscape and break up the garden into defined areas, while at the same time reinforcing the simplicity of the design. Here, hedging is treated informally and unusually; processions of box, each plant slightly distanced from its neighbour, are clipped to bulge agreeably. Beech hedges play a leading role in the winter months when their henna-coloured leaves offset the local evergreens.

[4] GRASSES

A natural plant scheme is achieved with the use of sweeping drifts of ornamental grasses, such as *Stipa gigantea*. Here, tall native bulrushes, *Typha latifolia,* screen the end of the pond at the path edges. The paths themselves are also turfed; bending and swelling between the hedging and borders, they disappear teasingly behind the occasional planting, enticing the visitor onwards. Gravel or other hard surfaces, even hoggin, would have been at odds with the planted areas, whereas the grass is much more companionable.

NATURALISTIC PLANTING

Rather than imitating nature, the design makes reference to it with planting that is natural looking, uncontrived and informal. Grasses and perennial plants are combined or interspersed in a meadow style. Natural schemes require plants that thrive in the same conditions, otherwise they will not co-exist as a community. A mix of contrasting forms (spikes, umbels, feathery plumes, strappy leaves) is desirable, with varying heights. Plants with attractive seedheads provide sustained interest through the winter months.

Woodland Terrace

DESIGNER DESIGN WORKSHOP
COMPLETED 2003
LOCATION JACKSON HOLE, WYOMING, USA

COMPARED TO CONIFEROUS forest, deciduous woodland can have a light and open feel. The tree canopies are less dense, with pale green leaves turning dark, then red and gold, in contrast with the uniform dark green of conifer needles. A woodland garden can take its cue from this natural openness, and trees chosen for the colour of their leaves and bark can make a statement against a background of natural woodland.

The location of this former cattle ranch in Jackson Hole, Wyoming is stunning. Set in wooded plains, it is surrounded by mountains with dramatic views of the Grand Teton and its neighbouring peaks. The design of the property's elegant, streamlined garden was deeply influenced by the owners' respect for the vegetation that grows naturally along the region's many watercourses. In the hard landscaping, too, their appreciation of the natural environment was the driving force behind the use of local materials. The striking modernist design ensures that the garden sits comfortably in the rock-strewn environment of the Wyoming plains.

Building a garden here, 6,100 ft (1,860 m) above sea level, was a challenge because the climate in Teton County is thoroughly unforgiving. The winters are virtually arctic, the summers are warm, windy and humid, and temperatures can fluctuate dramatically between night and day. All of this meant that the plant choice was extremely limited.

Design Workshop's brief was to create a variety of outdoor spaces among the contemporary single-story stone and stucco buildings, while encouraging the establishment of microclimates to shelter planting. Another important request was that the banks along the property's spring creek, which had become degraded during the site's former use as a cattle ranch, be renovated ecologically.

It was realized that the cattle had compacted the rocky soil so much that plant growth would be seriously hindered. But after studying the terrain, the team was able to plant layers of wetland trees, shrubs, grasses, forb plants and rushes.

Design Workshop's garden makes a bold statement. It complements the house's modern architecture while mixing open and enclosed spaces, movement and calm, texture and detail. It connects the buildings to the mountain, woodland, plain and river landscapes that characterize Jackson Hole.

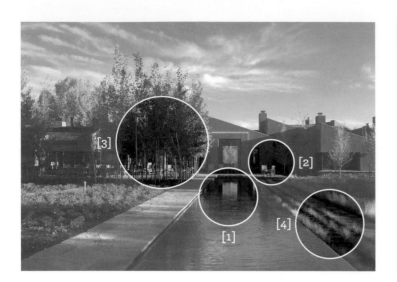

DESIGN INGREDIENTS

· Pattern

· Repetition

· Contrasting textures

· Sympathetic materials
  and planting

· Regulated informality

[1] REFLECTIVE WATER

A reflecting pool extends for more than 100 ft (30 m) from the great room terrace. It is a confident statement feature that extends the terrace out into the wilder areas of the garden. Shallow and still, the water integrates the trees and sky in its glassy surface, and viewed from inside it presents a constantly changing scene. The terrace extends along one side of the pool, but on the other side there is no edging, so the water appears to drop magically off the edge into infinity. The effect is clean and minimal.

[2] STONE TERRACE On the

south side of the building there is a terrace for outdoor entertaining. It is a broad expanse that enables guests to take full advantage of the sun when it is out. Built a little below the level of the internal ground floor and accessed by broad steps, the terrace seems to recede into a meadow of native lupins. The main area of flooring is inlaid with bands of small river cobbles, and a boundary of low walls may be used as seating. Building the terrace out of the local stone and river pebbles tied it in with the landscape, making it a part of the whole.

[3] STAND OF ASPENS A formal grid arrangement of *Populus tremuloides* (quaking aspen) has a number of roles, both practical and aesthetic. The trees are organized in a shelterbelt pattern that screens the property from the prevailing westerly winds, and also lends dappled shade to the terrace. The tight, columnar effect parallels the lines of the pool and complements those of the house, as well as linking the informal personality of the wider landscape with the more structured geometry of the architecture.

[4] RANKS OF GRASS Three parallel lines of *Helictotrichon sempervirens* (blue oat grass) separate the native meadow from the pool's edge, running along its entire length and providing a soft border. The effect of the three lines is geometric and yet is achieved using grasses, which are not the most obvious material for a task requiring a precise delineation. The grass lines effect a clever transition from the hardscape of the pool edge to the softscape of the meadow beyond, which is populated by *Schizachyrium scoparium* (little bluestem) and other grasses. The infinity edge of the raised pool is especially striking against the soft grasses because it is more usual to set an infinity edge against a correspondingly 'clean' edge such as that of a stone wall, or against an uninterrupted horizon.

WHITE ACCENTS

Pool reflections introduce the light of the sky into the garden, but on dark days the garden might tend towards the gloomy. Design Workshop's solution has been to introduce bold white elements that lift the mood whatever the weather. A large, white granite sculpture by Richard Deutsch puts a vertical visual stop to the pool, extended by its reflection in the water, and a granite table to the left of it provides a horizontal balance. Also important in the scheme are the white trunks of the quaking aspens on the right.

Riverside Meadow

DESIGNER ERIC D. GROFT, OEHME VAN SWEDEN

COMPLETED 2005

LOCATION MARYLAND, USA

WHEN DESIGNING a garden on the side of a river, the waterfront has to be acknowledged and celebrated, never ignored. At the same time, the garden space potentially displaces the natural vegetation of the shoreline, and this may deserve conservation, partly to preserve the view from the river. The trick is to secure all the amenities of a garden within the parameters of the natural asset.

This property lies to the side of a tributary of the Choptank River, which flows into Chesapeake Bay. The owners were sensitive to the beauty of the river and the natural setting of their house, but there was nowhere for them to settle and enjoy them, and they had other requirements of their garden too.

The couple chose to call on the landscape architecture practice Oehme van Sweden for advice. Oehme van Sweden is widely recognized as having pioneered the New American Garden style, which favours broad sweeps of flowering perennials and ornamental grasses to create a naturalistic look that takes inspiration from the North American prairies.

Eric D. Groft, principal at the landscape company, took up the challenge. The couple liked the idea of a prairie-style meadow, agreeing that it would be a sympathetic addition to the native landscape, but they also wanted a lawn for their grandchildren's play, and border flowers like roses. It was decided that the latter elements were best suited to being adjacent to the house, while the meadow would be designed to merge them gently with the natural surroundings of the river.

A swimming pool was built at the back of the house, with a dramatic cascade at one end and a low wall affording privacy from the riverside. The lawned area was set to the side, hidden discreetly behind tall perennials.

The result is a relaxed, intimate and private space that does not compromise the views while fusing seamlessly with its natural surroundings.

DESIGN INGREDIENTS

· Sympathy to genius loci

· Naturalistic planting

· Privacy

· Framing views

· Wildlife-friendly planting

[1] RIVERSIDE PLANTING

A key presence in Oehme van Sweden's New American Garden style is *Rudbeckia maxima* (Black-eyed Susan), and here it is used to dramatic effect in a drift through the meadow, its black cones skirted by golden, recurved petals. Other plants ensuring that the garden will be a prime destination for bees and butterflies include *Buddleja davidii* 'Black Knight', a butterfly bush cultivar with sumptuous purple cones, and *Pycnanthemum muticum* (mountain mint), which has velvety grey foliage.

[2] MEADOW GRASSES

Panicum virgatum 'Northwind' (a switchgrass cultivar, growing in the foreground) weaves in front of another native prairie grass, *Schizachyrium scoparium* (little blue stem). No meadow is complete without grasses, and on this property they blend with perennial plants to form a tapestry of moving textures and colours. The grasses provide a continuity through the space and melt into the surrounding landscape. They offer a sense of privacy without impeding views through to the water and the opposing shoreline.

[3] MEADOW WALKWAYS

Paths are carved through the drifts of perennials in natural meanders, following the contours of the land. Tamped gravel, covered with bark chips, provides a rustic surface that is suited to the natural setting, and the chips help to suppress weeds, at least for a while. As elsewhere in the garden, there is a satisfying contrast between the horizontal plane, established by the distant water and the low-lying meadow planting, and the architectural pines, whose bare trunks do not impede the sightline.

[4] DRIFTWOOD FEATURE

A sculpture-like installation of vertical bundles of weathered, grey driftwood, set in a circle by artist Ben Forgey, bursts up from among the meadow perennials and beckons visitors to an intimate, concrete-floored seating area. The installation is robust enough to support a hammock slung between its spars, offering a perfect retreat on a warm summer's day. The ubiquitous *Rudbeckia maxima* makes another appearance here, its golden petals harmonizing with the sunlit trees across the water.

PRIVATE POOL

Tucked away behind the house is an attractive swimming pool, screened from the river by a low wall. Purple-flowering *Buddleja davidii* 'Black Knight' and *Perovskia atriplicifolia* wrap around the space, spilling over the edges of the decking and softening its hard edges. Soft grasses contrast with mown lawn in the distance. The overall effect is one of cool, shaded seclusion.

World

Japanese Traditional

DESIGNER UNKNOWN
COMPLETED 15TH CENTURY
LOCATION KYOTO, JAPAN

A JAPANESE ROCK GARDEN or Zen garden (*karesansui*) is a miniature dry landscape with carefully arranged rocks, moss, trees and bushes, surrounded by raked sand or gravel and enclosed by a wall. The creator usually designates a vantage point from which to meditate on the scene. Many such gardens are found by Buddhist temples in Japan, including the famous Ryōan-ji, which translates as 'The Temple of the Dragon at Peace'.

The Ryōan-ji temple in Kyoto, which for more than a thousand years was the imperial capital of Japan, is thought to have been erected in its first incarnation around 938 CE, after which it was rebuilt many times. The garden is believed to have been part of a reconstruction that took place around five hundred years ago. Measuring 82 x 33 ft (25 x 10 m), it contains fifteen rocks, some of which are underlaid by patches of moss, all arranged in an expanse of raked gravel. The garden is enclosed on two sides by a wall. Apart from some judicious raking to remove leaves and reshape the gravel, the garden requires very little maintenance.

There are many theories about what the garden represents. Most see islands in water, but other interpretations include mountain peaks rising above clouds, swimming tiger cubs and mathematical notions related to geometrical equilibrium. Recent analysis revealed that the design is precisely arranged to align with the architecture of the temple. The placement of the stones is said to be related to an axis following a sightline from the main hall, thus creating a branched tree shape on the ground. But author Günter Nitschke resists such speculation, claiming rather that the garden is an 'abstract composition of "natural" objects in space', one that is intended to prompt meditation.

Underlying these opinions is a common theme: that the enigmatic appeal of the garden lies in our unconscious perceptions of its arrangement.

DESIGN INGREDIENTS

· Mass and void

· Rhythm

· Simplicity

· Tranquillity

· Atmosphere

[1] RAKED GRAVEL The central tenet of Zen Buddhism is emptiness, and that is something the garden evokes very well. The gravel suggests water, raked into waves. Achieving perfection of line is not an easy task, and Zen priests rake the gravel to sharpen their concentration in readiness for meditation. The patterns may change, and developing pattern variations is regarded as a creative challenge. The raking immediately around the rocks suggests ripples caused by their falling into calm water. Gravel is preferred to sand for its resistance to rain and wind.

[2] OILED WALL The two-sided boundary wall is called an *aburadobei*, or 'oil-earth wall'. It is made of loam that has been boiled in rapeseed oil, a process that creates a very durable surface capable of withstanding years of exposure and changes of temperature. A deeply pitched, overhanging roof of bark tiles caps the wall and protects it from erosion by rain. Over the years, oil has seeped out and stained the wall in tones of brown and orange. The wall completes the still mood of the garden by sheltering it from onlookers beyond.

[3] ISLANDS OF MOSS At Ryōan-ji, moss encircles the rocks to signify land surrounded by a gravel sea. As ground cover, mosses strongly express the presence of land, but at the same time they are too fragile to step on. This coexistence of apparent strength and physical fragility is what makes mosses so compelling in Zen gardens. Moss is a very popular plant material in Japanese gardening for its behaviour, texture and colour. Its shade of green changes through the seasons, being brightest in early summer and fading in autumn.

[4] STONE PLACEMENT The most significant part of making a *karesansui* is the selection and placing of its rocks. Very specific rules exist, and misfortune is said to befall the owner who pays insufficient attention to them. Rocks are classified as tall vertical, low vertical, arching, reclining or flat. Individual stones rarely play a leading role because the emphasis is more on the harmony of the composition. At Ryōan-ji, fifteen stones of different sizes are assembled in five groups; one of five, two groups of three, and two of two stones. The stones are placed so that they cannot all be seen at one time; from any angle, only fourteen are simultaneously visible. Traditionally, it was only through attaining enlightenment that a person could also perceive the fifteenth stone.

QUIET CONTEMPLATION

The purpose of the Zen garden is to encourage onlookers to meditate on the space, especially the 'void' created by its emptiness, and to fill that void using their imaginative powers, with the hope of achieving *satori* (enlightenment). Doubtless, many of the international visitors of today do not subscribe to Buddhist philosophy, but few spectators are unaffected by the quiet and reverent atmosphere of the garden. There is a dignified stillness that irresistibly inspires contemplative thought.

Indian Formal

DESIGNER SIR EDWIN LUTYENS

COMPLETED 1918

LOCATION NEW DELHI, INDIA

THE MUGHAL DYNASTY, which ruled most of India and Pakistan in the 16th and 17th centuries, produced architecture and gardens that were Islamic and geometric in character. When the British seized power in the mid-19th century, their buildings and gardens in both dominions drew on Islamic tradition but with the introduction of style elements that reminded them of home.

Formerly the palace of the British viceroy, Rashtrapati Bhavan is now the official residence of the Indian president. Built of rose-coloured sandstone, the palace and garden was the culmination of the work in New Delhi of <u>Sir Edwin Lutyens</u> (1869–1944), who had been appointed as part of the planning committee for the new city of Delhi some years earlier. Inspired by gardens he had visited in other parts of India, Lutyens created next to the palace what is one of the best 20th-century versions of a traditional Mughal garden.

The main part of the 13-acre (5.3-ha) garden features four crossing channels of water that divide the garden into a grid of nine squares. Where the channels intersect, there are elaborate, flower-shaped fountains. Bridges cross the channels at geometrically spaced intervals. Height is provided by lines of trees clipped into perfect domes. Yet parterres of box hedge, expanses of immaculate lawn for entertaining and colourful planting echo the English garden style. The amalgamation of the two traditions seems harmonious and apt.

The garden boasts a collection of more than 250 varieties of roses. These flower most of the year, although the main season comes just after they are pruned, in October. The roses give the planting a feeling of permanence. There are numerous cultivars named after famous people, such as 'John F. Kennedy', 'Mr Lincoln', 'Christian Dior' and 'Queen Elizabeth'; naturally, Indians are represented too, in roses such as 'Mother Teresa', 'Bhim' and 'Dr B. P. Pal'.

DESIGN INGREDIENTS

- Balance
- Symmetry
- Strong geometry
- Rhythm
- Symbolism

[1] WATER FEATURES A fountain theatrically propels a jet of water into the air from a decorative stone base carved to look like an arrangement of eighteen circular lotus leaves. Water is used throughout the garden in cascades and fountains that fill the space with cool air and soothing sounds. The use of running water has its origins in the *chahar bagh* garden style of ancient Persia, such as the palace garden of Cyrus the Great (*c.* 530 BCE) at Pasargadae, where a symmetrical layout was divided into four by water channels.

[2] VIBRANT PLANTING Borders are laid out in blocks and swathes of herbaceous annuals and perennials, which add to the formality of the space. Typical British choices more usually associated with cottage gardens include violas, stocks, wallflowers, alyssum, phlox and petunias, and these associate with Asian species like cannas and strelitzias to produce a lavish, vibrant display. Some of the beds bristle with a kaleidoscope of different dahlia varieties. The planting is seasonal and renewed twice yearly in preparation for a series of garden openings.

[3] HEAT-RESISTANT GRASS

The large expanses of lawn must be able to survive the demanding Indian climate, so *Cynodon dactylon*, or dhoob grass, is the turf of choice. Called 'Bermuda grass' in other parts of the world, it remains green through the hot Delhi summers, although it turns brown in winter if the temperature falls below 50°F (10°C). Grass that has turned brown is removed every year before the monsoons, and seed is sown into new topsoil. The grass takes three weeks to regrow into verdant lawn.

[4] TAILORED TREES

Avenues of fragrant, evergreen *Mimusops elengi* (Spanish cherry, or moulsari in Hindi) are pruned into mushroom shapes. Curves and circles are recurring motifs in Mughal gardens, and these clipped domes contrast with the rectilinear structure of the garden layout. Other evergreen trees add structure to the space, notably specimens of *Cupressus sempervirens* (Italian cypress). The sculptural cypresses punctuate the axes vertically at regular intervals to provide formality and height.

ROUND GARDEN

Travelling away from the palace in a westward direction, the geometric garden's central axis extends outwards into new territory. At first it passes through a narrow, walled garden, planted with roses and bougainvillea and featuring a rose-covered pergola; it then culminates in a round pool garden (see right) of descending tiered beds abundantly planted with blocks of colour-themed annuals.

Chinese Classical

DESIGNER SHEN BINGCHENG

COMPLETED 1874

LOCATION SUZHOU, CHINA

NOWHERE IS the classical Chinese approach to garden design illustrated more completely than in the nine gardens of Suzhou, which are generally accepted as masterpieces of the genre. Built by retired bureaucrats and politicians between the 11th and 19th centuries, during the Ming and Qing dynasties, the gardens displayed the cultivation and aesthetic taste of the owners, while at the same time transmitting a philosophical message.

Marco Polo, when he visited this area of China in the 13th century, called Suzhou 'the Venice in the Orient'. He was referring to the network of numerous rivers and canals, crossed by many small bridges, that now combine with the gardens to make Suzhou one of south-east China's most visited cities.

The Couple's Garden Retreat dates back to the early 18th century. It is surrounded on three sides by a canal, and the pool around which it is located is accessible directly from the canal by boat. The original garden was built by Lu Jin, prefect of Baoning district, and it was later purchased by Shen Bingcheng, magistrate of Susong County, who rebuilt it in its current form.

The name 'Couple's Garden Retreat' is a reference to the garden's two parts – the East Garden (see left) and the West Garden – and alludes to a couple who retire there. A couplet by Shen Bingcheng's wife is displayed by a window overlooking the garden. It reads: 'A loving couple lives in the couple's garden retreat. A poetic city was built at a corner of the ancient city.'

Several Ming-style buildings flank a stretch of water of the East Garden, but the major feature is a dramatic wall of yellow rock that rises from the pool. Covered walkways circle the water, and a zigzag bridge connects the two sides. A platform with a pavilion hovers over the centre of the pool. The West Garden is more subdued, with limestone hills pierced by interlinking caves and tunnels.

DESIGN INGREDIENTS

· Symbolism

· Balance

· Scale

· Detail

· Constructed views

[1] ZIGZAG BRIDGE Bridges over water are a common feature of the classical Chinese garden. They rarely follow a straight, level course, either zigzagging (see right) or arching. Their purpose is to lead visitors by a predetermined course from one carefully staged garden 'event' or focus point to the next. The zigzag course has the Zen philosophical purpose of focusing visitors' attention on the present moment and current locality. The zigzag bridge also illustrates a Chinese proverb: 'access to secrets is gained by detours'.

[2] SYMBOLIC WATER Viewing places are strategically placed around the pond to create different vantages. According to Taoist philosophy, water and rocks are opposites that must exist together and complement each other: water's yin to rock's yang. Like rock, water is a central component of the classical Chinese garden. This garden connects to an open canal, but enclosed pools often contain goldfish or carp, as well as lilies or lotus, to add another viewing dimension. Water represents lightness and communication, and the carrying of life on a journey through valleys.

[3] STACKED ROCK The rock in the centre of the pool represents a mountain, one of Confucius's Isles of the Immortals, with the peak symbolizing stability, endurance and virtue. The stacked rock construction is an essential feature of classical Chinese gardens. This example, made of yellow stone and bound together with iron bands and sticky rice paste, was built by Zhang Nanyang, a rockery master of the late Ming period. It presents an almost sheer face to the garden and is especially precipitous on one side; on other sides it steps down gradually to an area filled with planting.

[4] PLANTING The early-flowering *Prunus mume* (Chinese plum) represents nature reawakening in spring. Here, it has been artfully arranged to grow almost horizontally, so that it is reflected to best effect by the surface of the pool. Many of the plants used in classical Chinese gardens have specific meanings that could be 'read' by the well-informed Taoist scholars originally invited to view the gardens. Here, the trees and shrubs contrast with the straight lines of the surrounding buildings. Changing through the seasons, they offer sensory experiences through smell, touch and sound.

NEW YORK CHINESE

Constructed by a team of forty artists and artisans from Suzhou, the New York Chinese Scholar's Garden (see right) is a part of Staten Island Botanical Garden. Its materials were landed on the island in 1998 and the garden opened in 1999. Typically, the garden is enclosed by walls and includes ponds, rock, trees and flowers. In their composition and man-made elements, classical Chinese gardens were regarded as a manifestation of nature as constructed by man, or even of man's artistic ability to improve upon nature.

Middle East Contemporary

DESIGNER KAMELIA ZAAL, SECOND NATURE
COMPLETED 2011
LOCATION DUBAI, UNITED ARAB EMIRATES

THE DESIGN of any garden in the Middle East must take two factors especially into account: high temperatures and lack of water. When the design is on a large scale, as it is in this complex of communal gardens attached to an enormous, prestigious residential development on the outskirts of Dubai, design decisions can have a significant positive impact on the ecology of the area and the conservation of its natural resources.

Meaning 'wilderness' in Arabic, Al Barari is the name of a large group of luxury villas that are surrounded by gardens for the residents' use. Landscaping is key to this development: more than 80 per cent of the site is given over to green space.

The work of landscape designer Kamelia Zaal for her firm Second Nature, the garden space is subdivided into six main themes: Contemporary (see left), Mediterranean, Water, Woodland, Balinese and Renaissance. A man-made watercourse links all parts of the site, seen in different guises according to the theme of the garden through which it flows: it appears as a rocky stream, formal canals, reflective ponds, cascades, rills and naturalistic pools. In each case, the garden design complements the character of its waterway. The water system, relying on the contours for its movement around the site, performs in different ways to create varied images and sounds.

Inspiration for the Contemporary Garden came from the plan of central Paris, in which axes cross the city at different angles. Here, the axes are represented by subsidiary streams flowing out of and into the main pool. Their courses are highlighted by lines of silver-leaved *Conocarpus erectus* and clerodendrum hedging.

The tenet of the design is 'less is more', with the simple structure placing emphasis on the planting. The garden, designed to be used, helps entice the residents outside, and its abundant shade is welcome in the blistering heat of Dubai.

DESIGN INGREDIENTS

· Contrasting textures

· Cool palette

· Flow and continuity

· Simplicity

[1] DRYLAND TEXTURES The uncomplicated design of the garden is set off by simple planting. The plants are arranged in blocks of colour and texture that work well with the hard edges and sharp angles of the design. Their palette is restricted – purple, white and silver with different tones of green — and for that reason texture was important in setting up contrasts. Stiffly erect, blue-grey stems of *Juncus inflexus* guard the waterway; purple and grey *Tradescantia spathacea* stretches between defined sections, and variegated *Agave americana* continues the spiky theme. In contrast to the sharp-leaved plants, velvety zoysia grass provides a dense emerald background.

[2] LINEAR WATERCOURSE Wide, precision-cut stone terraces guide the water down into a large, reflective pool, creating sound and a sense of movement. Large rocks interrupt the flow of water suggesting that a natural, less built, landscape once existed here. Another cascade drops down into a *falaj*, or water channel, altering the direction of the water and leading the visitor on through the garden. The waterway, 10 miles (16.4 km) long in total, creates different moods as it progresses through the gardens. It has a narrative: gushing in parts, slow in others, still elsewhere. Natural-style streams, weaving around the site, eventually feed into this different, contemporary, linear waterway.

[3] HARD SURFACES Horizontal paving structures 'float' above the pool, creating the impression of oversized stepping stones across a much larger expanse of water. Subtle changes in colour on the sides and tops of the cantilevered platforms highlight the changes of level and assist safe passage over them. Most of the hard landscaping is constructed from concrete in a palette of white, grey and black. Crystal Inlay, a sort of 'jewelled' render, is incorporated into the surfaces of certain areas to accentuate them and add sparkle.

ECOLOGICAL FOCUS

Al Barari is one of the UAE's first sustainable residential projects. The gardens are wildlife-friendly and are home to many species of birds. Water in the channels (see below) is recycled for irrigation, the shade reduces evaporation, and plants are selected for their low water needs. An in-house site composts all green waste material from the development, and LED lighting, which requires less power, is used.

[4] ISLAND PALM The expansive central reflective pool features a sculptural centrepiece in the form of an island bed, designed to look as though it is floating. It contains a fine specimen of *Bismarckia nobilis* (Bismarck palm), named after the first chancellor of the German Empire, Otto von Bismarck (1815–98). Endemic to western and northern Madagascar, the palm is the only species of its genus. The fanned grey-blue fronds capture the breezes and recirculate them, while their reflections make an attractive display in the water. The palm, which in the wild can grow to 80 ft (25 m) in height, looks monumental in its prominent setting in this low-lying part of the garden.

PARADISE ON EARTH

The word 'paradise' has its roots in many ancient words meaning garden. Some of the first structured 'pardesu' or 'pairi daeza' gardens existed in the Persian Achaemenid Empire in the 6th century BCE. In the 4th century BCE, the word 'paradeisos' was adopted in Greece to mean pleasure park, and later brought to Rome as 'paradisus'. 'Pardes' describes ancient pleasure gardens of Jerusalem.

The spread of Islam and Arab culture transported this garden concept to the Mediterranean, a surviving example of which is seen in the 14th-century Generalife Gardens in Granada, Spain (see above). 'Moorish' gardens integrated the Persian model into what would become established as the medieval European garden style of 'hortus conclusus', or enclosed garden. The Persian garden is the prototype for all geometrically designed gardens across the world.

[3] LUSH PLANTING Blocks of bright orange *Tagetes patula* (French marigold) contrast with banks of verdant foliage and ornamental plants such as *Santolina chamaecyparissus* (lavender cotton), with its grey-green foliage and yellow, button-like flowerheads, and ostcospermum. Just as the garden's freely flowing water would have seemed almost unbelievably luxurious to the inhabitants of the surrounding parched landscape in the 19th century, its lush planting and brilliant colours would have astounded them.

[4] FRAGRANT ROSES Even the earliest of the Islamic *chahar bagh* geometric gardens contained flowerbeds of fragrant plants, such as roses, jasmine, narcissi, violets and lilies. The scent of those flowers, like the sight and sound of water and the cool refreshment it offered, was a reminder that the garden was a representation of heaven on earth. Roses had a spiritual significance in Sufism too, and the *Gulistan-i Raz* (The Rose Garden of Mystery) by the 13th-century poet Mahmud Shabistari is considered to be one of the greatest works of Persian Sufism.

English Arts & Crafts

DESIGNERS GERTRUDE JEKYLL, THEN
ROSAMUND WALLINGER
COMPLETED 1908, RESTORED IN 1988
LOCATION HAMPSHIRE, UK

GARDENS ARE CREATIONS with a place not only in space but also in time. Nature soon reclaims them if they are not maintained, and they may end as no more than a memory. Sometimes, however, a distinguished but neglected garden finds a saviour who is prepared to invest time and money in restoring it to its original glory.

When John and <u>Rosamund Wallinger</u> bought Upton Grey Manor House in 1984, they had no inkling that the overgrown garden that encircled the manor was a 'lost' garden by <u>Gertrude Jekyll</u>. The 4½-acre (1.8 ha) garden was designed in 1908 for Charles Holme, founder of an influential arts magazine and devotee of the Arts & Crafts movement. Researching the history of the house, the couple were eventually able to find copies of Miss Jekyll's plans.

The acreage is roughly split between the Wild Garden, with its winding grass paths, a copse and drifts of bulbs, and the Formal Garden, which is set out geometrically (see right), with additional double borders, roses, and bowling and tennis lawns. The geometrical garden is typical of the Arts & Crafts style that prevailed at the time, with lichen-covered dry-stone walls, clipped yew hedges and abundant herbaceous planting that spills out of borders and softens the appearance.

In the geometrical garden, beds surround two square and raised stone planters containing *Canna indica* and *Lilium regale*. In the borders, as well as roses (not shown here) are peonies, lilies and *Stachys byzantina* (lambs' ears). In the side borders are narrow drifts of delphinium, phlox, poppies, hollyhocks, campanulas and daylilies, arranged according to colour, from cool tones to hot ones.

The planting schedule was designed by Miss Jekyll to provide successive colour from spring through to autumn. Today, Upton Grey Manor House is acknowledged as one of the most accurate reinstatements of a Jekyll garden in existence.

DESIGN INGREDIENTS

· Romance

· Informality

· Structure softened by planting

· Sensual pleasure: scent, colour, texture

· Framing views

[1] COTTAGE GARDEN PLANTING The turn of the twentieth century saw an enormous rise in the middle classes in Britain. Occupying smaller houses than their Victorian forebears, the new professional classes – doctors, lawyers and businessmen – found the strict formality of Victorian estate gardens unsuited to their available space. The Arts & Crafts garden retained some formal structure, but instead of Victorian bedding and shrubberies it featured beds filled with romantic cottage garden planting. There was no uniform style; the approach relied more on creating a particular atmosphere, with natural materials enclosing small planted courtyards, uncontrived topiary, clipped hedges, pleached trees, orchards, lilies, old roses and scent.

[2] WALKWAY OF FLOWERS The pergola at the top of the geometric garden consists of ten hefty oak support posts that are connected by rope swags, rather than the more conventional wooden beams. The climber-covered pergola forms a connection between the house and garden and frames a view of the garden from the vantage point of the house. In a departure from the norm, the planting allowed to climb the structure is not restricted to one species, or even one genus of plant; as well as roses, Miss Jeckyll planted aristolochia, jasmine and Virginia creeper. The different species extend the flowering season for an unusually long period, as well as introducing an unexpected variety to the pergola in terms of flower colour and leaf shape.

GERTRUDE JEKYLL

Gertrude Jekyll was born in 1843 into an affluent and artistic family. Having studied art, at first she made her career in writing and art, but later concentrated on gardening. She designed about 400 gardens, of which, regrettably, only a handful still exist (including that at Hestercombe House in Somerset, right). She wrote books and articles, in which she described the importance of structure, proportion, colour, scent and texture in gardens. In her forties, she met the young architect, Edwin Lutyens, who at that time was in his early twenties; their friendship was one of the most influential partnerships of the Arts & Crafts movement.

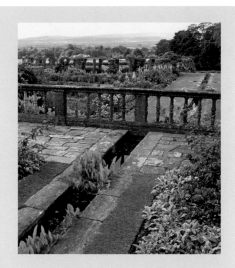

[3] **VARIED TOPIARY** The Upton Grey garden makes subtle use of simple topiary. Here, an area of the garden is partitioned by one of several straight, formal box hedges; a path passing through the hedge is signalled from afar by box 'pillars' – cuboids with raised tops sculpted from the ends of the divided hedge. Topiaried yew appears in the garden as simple shapes, mostly balls (see centre), which punctuate the space, offer formal contrast to the exuberant planting, and emphasize turning points of the bedding.

[4] **DRY-STONE BORDERS** Made of Purbeck stone, the dry-stone walls frame the garden steps and provide edging for the upper beds. Miss Jekyll crammed the beds with plants that would fill the area with colour from late February onwards. Toning in with the grey-coloured stone, blue-grey plants – such as iris, lavender, cerastium, acanthus and santolina – prevail. In Britain, dry-stone walling is still a popular choice for informal gardens. Environmentally friendly, it provides a habitat for wildlife while its crevices can usefully accommodate rock plants.

French New Baroque

DESIGNER PATRICK AND SYLVIE QUIBEL

COMPLETED 2002

LOCATION NORMANDY, FRANCE

THE GARDEN STYLE known as 'French baroque' is most strongly associated with the reign of Louis XIV (1638–1715). The key aspect of the style was its imposition of a mathematical formality on the natural world, one that was symbolic of humankind's domination of nature. In a baroque garden, nature's informality was replaced by geometrical beds and pools, clipped hedges and straight lines stretching to the horizon.

In a flat, windy field in northern France, designers and owners Patrick and Sylvie Quibel created Le Jardin Plume, a garden so remarkable that thousands of people have visited it since it opened in 2002. Its status as one of Europe's most significant new gardens was confirmed in 2003 when it won Best Modern Garden in France, and in 2008 when it was made *Gardens Illustrated* garden of the year.

A reinterpretation of the French baroque garden style, the new garden's layout integrates the original's underlying formality with a modern lack of restraint, especially in its planting. For example, a parterre with neat box hedges crammed with orange and red herbaceous perennials provides an exuberant invitation out of the house. Beyond this, an orchard of apple trees, each tree standing beside its own large square of unmown meadow grass, bridges the gap between the formal planting near the house and the wild fields beyond, softening the transition between the two.

To one side of the orchard is a potager (kitchen garden), again arranged in a grid and evocative of an earlier time, but here the formal lavender and box hedges are filled with the poppies, verbascum, nigella, campanulas and lupins of a cottage garden.

A 'plume garden' occupies an area on the other side of the parterre, crammed with tall, prairie-style planting that towers above head height, producing movement, texture, sound and visual excitement. The wind agitates a surging sea of veronicastrum, sanguisorbas, thalictrums and grasses. *Stipa barbata*, *S. calamagrostis* and *Calamagrostis* x *acutiflora* 'Karl Foerster' toss up foaming clusters of flowerheads in a welter of sounds.

The Quibels created the garden to promote their nursery, which specializes in tall perennials and grasses. The garden's success lies in their deep understanding of plants and garden history, which they have combined in a thrillingly lavish display.

DESIGN INGREDIENTS

· Rhythm

· Classical geometric structure

· Contrasting structure
  and planting styles

· Transition through to wider
  landscape

· Grand scale

[1] STORM-TOSSED HEDGES

Echoing the surging Atlantic to the west, hedges are tightly clipped in the shape of waves that 'run' past the planting, adding further movement to the scene. The hedges divide the mass of plants, breaking it up, while also serving to soften the boundaries between the different planted areas. In the spring the hedges help to protect new growth from winds that race across the flat plains of Normandy. Their precise outlines contrast dramatically with the mayhem of the adjacent planting.

[2] WINDOW OF WATER

A square reflecting pool, sharply drawn into the ground to match exactly the patchwork of squares that make up the grid of meadow planting behind, lies at the entrance to the orchard. The reflective plane of black water bounces light off its surface and changes colour along with the changing sky. The pool's simple definition, without a border or ornamentation, makes a powerful statement. This part of the garden has a peaceful atmosphere, one that is largely engendered by the symmetry of the pool and the areas of planting.

[3] <u>GRID PLANTING</u> The flatness of the landscape lends itself to the 'new baroque' geometric grid that informs the ground plan of the garden. Generous walkways, or 'allées', a nod to classical baroque, are mown between rigidly controlled 'parterres', or squares of grasses and perennials. The long paths, disappearing into the landscape beyond, open up the garden and create a sense of space. The French formality contrasts cleverly with the wanton behaviour of the grasses. A large area is given over to this, and the effect is dramatic.

[4] <u>SOFTSCAPE</u> In terms of the planting, rather than the layout, the designers admit to being influenced by the Dutch perennial or prairie style. Herbaceous perennials are non-woody plants with an indeterminate lifespan, but usually surviving beyond two years in favourable circumstances. They grow to maturity every year, then die back in the winter. They are valuable to gardeners because they flower in the year of planting – there is no requirement of years of growth before a flower is seen. Planted en masse, perennials support each other, there is no need for staking, and the density of planting leaves little room for weeds. The main maintenance task they require is to be chopped back in early spring, after which they quickly produce new shoots. These factors have made them a popular choice in planting schemes in the last few decades.

[5] <u>GEOMETRIC HEDGING</u> Aside from its overall geometric grid, the main feature that aligns the garden with baroque antecedents is its formally shaped and meticulously maintained hedging. Neat, low hedges of *Buxus sempervirens* (box) have defined areas of planting in vegetable and herb gardens since the Renaissance, when they made up the compartmentalized framework of knot gardens; often, each compartment would contain a different planting. Box hedges were widely used for edging in French baroque gardens, too, partly because the small-leaved plants were easily trained into the neat circles, geometric shapes and arabesques that appealed so much to the baroque taste. The hedges here are maintained just as carefully, but their precision is offset by wild, loose planting, rather than mirrored by equally precise planting.

Italian Romantic

DESIGNER ARABELLA LENNOX-BOYD
COMPLETED 2004 TO PRESENT
LOCATION LAZIO, ITALY

WHILE AESTHETICS underlies the thinking of garden designers, there is another important, practical consideration – maintenance. A high-maintenance garden uses up time, manpower and money, but there are ways of minimizing the costs. If the site already has natural assets, working with these is often the best design solution.

Dominating a hilltop overlooking the small village of Oliveto, an hour north-east of Rome, is Palazzo Parisi, an ochre-coloured medieval fortified house and the childhood home of garden designer Arabella Lennox-Boyd. When her father died in 2003, she decided to refurbish the interior of the castle and open it for rental to summer visitors.

The palazzo had never had a proper garden before, just fields for arable crops. Lennox-Boyd added avenues of cypresses and olive trees planted in a grid design. She also introduced shady terraces to take advantage of the beautiful views across the Sabine Hills and a swimming pool surrounded by Mediterranean plants and local grasses. The designer wanted to create a romantic setting for the house, one that reflected its character as well as that of the surrounding Italian countryside.

The plan had to be simple, though, to keep maintenance to a minimum – she did not want an army of gardeners disturbing her guests. More importantly, she wanted to use horticulturally undemanding shrubs and other plants that would enhance the pleasures of the surroundings: the warmth, breezes, scents and the buzzing of insects.

The garden is most structured near the house, where the terraces are garnished with clipped box, pale blue plumbago and white hydrangeas. Beyond, the cypresses and olives are underplanted with fragrant shrubs; progressing further, the structured planting gives way to a meadow full of colourful annuals, which itself merges gently into the surrounding natural flora.

DESIGN INGREDIENTS

· Vertical accents

· Relaxed planting

· Structural geometry

· Sensual experiences

· Capturing light

[1] EVERGREEN ACCENTS *Cupressus sempervirens* (Italian cypress) is one of the trees most associated with the traditional styling of the Italian countryside. As well as establishing a cypress avenue to link the palazzo with its adjacent chapel, Lennox-Boyd planted cypresses throughout the garden. At first glance the trees might seem randomly placed, but their positioning is actually carefully devised to provide vertical balance through the space. They also frame the house, as well as – seen from the opposite direction – the views.

[2] IRIS WALK When Lennox-Boyd inherited the palazzo, the track leading from the main building to the family chapel was just a barren stretch of land. The designer introduced cypresses and olive trees to frame the path, which is now lined by beds filled with lilac-blue *Iris pallida* and pale pink *Rosa* 'Felicia', creating a fragrant and atmospheric approach to the chapel entrance. The climber *R*. 'Iceberg' threads its way through the branches of the cypresses, its white blooms peeping out invitingly through the foliage.

HILLSIDE POOL

Walking down between terraces that follow the contours of the hillside, the visitor follows a rustic, pebbled path to arrive at a simple, rectangular infinity pool, carefully designed to blend with the surrounding landscape. Fringed by olive trees and a pink *Nerium oleander* bush, the pool looks out over a splendid Italian vista of hilltop villages and olive groves.

[3] INFORMAL PLANTING The beds running from the house down to the swimming pool, terraced with wattle hurdles, spill over with Mediterranean flowering plants and native grasses in an exuberant mass of colours, textures and forms. The long, arching stems of *Ampelodesmos mauritanicus* (Mauritian grass), with their plume-like panicles, tower over perennials such as perovskia, lavender and santolina, which have been chosen for their ability to withstand periods of drought during the long, hot Italian summers.

[4] FLOWERING MEADOW

Looking out towards the landscape from the house, the eye is drawn to the wildflower meadows that flow around the garden. The planting includes early-season flowering natives such as *Leucanthemum vulgare* (ox-eye daisies) and *Centaurea cyanus* (cornflower, or bachelor's buttons), followed by the shell-pink and white shades of *Cosmos bipinnatus* (see right). Paths are mown through the 'meadows', subdividing the space and leading visitors around the garden; following the paths, they discover new features and vantage points.

Swedish Country

DESIGNER ULF NORDFJELL
COMPLETED 2004
LOCATION OCKELBO, SWEDEN

IN THE PAST, it was not unusual for garden designers to regard a fresh plot and its natural environment as a blank canvas, to be filled with whatever plantings they desired. Today it is more common to take cues from aspects of nature, such as the local stone and native plants. What is far rarer, though, is a garden that is wholly concerned with celebrating all aspects of a region's natural environment, both as it is and how it used to be.

In 2000, Swedish gardener Lars Krantz set about resuscitating Wij, a forgotten country estate 130 miles (210 km) north of Stockholm, near the little village where his father was born. The results have transformed the property, and it now draws 50,000 visitors a year.

Krantz was interested in the views of the local villagers because he wanted a plan for the park that would help to revive the community. Something new and different was called for that would result in investment in its future. The estate was located deep within a pine forest and hitherto had been mostly used for mixed agriculture. No garden existed to suggest a foundation for future plans.

Krantz consulted landscape designers Simon Irvine and Ulf Nordfjell about creating gardens on the estate. Their joint plan constituted a series of seven areas of distinct hard landscaping and planting: rose and forest gardens, herb and kitchen gardens, a students' garden, a shadow garden and a landscape park. In each, the aim was to actualize a space that transgressed the boundaries conventionally seen to exist between the nature of a site, garden horticulture and local building traditions. The arts of the landscape gardener were not rejected but the work was to adhere to classical principles of garden design.

Irvine undertook the Rose Garden, and Nordfjell was commissioned to design the Forest Garden, a space that celebrates the history and landscape of the area, and in particular the strong relationship that the Swedish people have with their forest regions. The garden would take up a long strip, 360 x 40 ft (110 x 12 m), set in cornfields in an open agricultural landscape. The strip was divided into a series of rooms, and only one is examined here. Entitled 'With the Sky for a Roof', this part of the Forest Garden is a deconstructed room without a ceiling, with the garden on the inside.

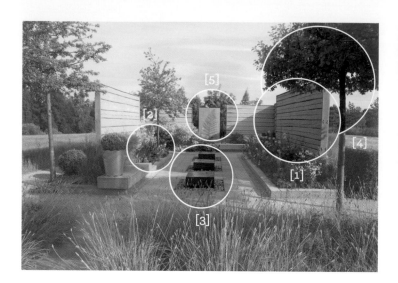

DESIGN INGREDIENTS

· Architectural vernacular

· Modern reinterpretation

· Muted colour palette

· Strong vertical presence

· Interaction between interior and exterior

[1] STAGGERED WALLS Walls of rough-hewn wooden panels, set in a staggered rectangle, reflect local building practices. The panels have steel supports and are kept in place by traditional wooden wedges and dowels. Their granite foundations raise the wood out of the wet and provide a contemporary elegance. The staggered panels offer glimpses in and out, creating a dialogue between the internal and external. They are a reminder of the staggered hedges in the Italian Renaissance garden at Villa Gamberaia, Tuscany.

[2] PERENNIALS The perennial plants selected by Nordfjell for the panel-sheltered flowerbeds were either native species of meadow plants or cultivated plants derived from those. They include maroon-flowered *Knautia macedonica* (red scabious), a white-flowered gypsophila and the slim, black-stemmed, purple flower spikes of *Salvia nemorosa* 'Caradonna'; a white-flowered phlox stands to the rear. Dense plantings of perennials are self-sustaining once established, and weeds are suppressed by the density of the planting.

[3] WATER STONES Three granite blocks advance in single file. The three squares appear identical but their top surfaces each have a different subtle grade, making water issuing forth from a central spout run off in a particular direction. Each block appears to float slightly above a bed of cobbles that conceals a reservoir beneath. The gentle sounds the water makes on the stones, along with its mesmerizing movement, help to create a space in which to relax while sitting on one of the granite benches set around the edge.

[4] CRAB APPLE TREES In the foreground is a grove of four *Malus* 'Evereste' crab apples with canopies pleached to form a continuous square 'umbrella'. The trees produce a mass of white blossom in spring, and generous clusters of yellow-orange fruits through the winter. The shape of the pleaching provides a 'roof' to counterbalance the vertical structures of the garden. Beneath the trees are perennial plants and grasses that soften the edges of the beds. The plants have been selected for their ability to thrive in poor, sandy soil, as well as for making the most of the short summers.

[5] SCREEN SCULPTURE A rolled-steel screen 'sculpture' forms a backdrop to the garden and continues the formal central axis created through the space by the three granite blocks or water stones (see above). The sculpture is actually a digitized image by Norwegian sculptor Anne-Karin Furunes of a frond of *Matteuccia struthiopteris* (ostrich or shuttlecock fern), a forest-dwelling species. The shape of the leaf is formed by manipulation of perforations in the steel. The sculpture is a reminder that true nature does not exist in this garden; it is all reinterpreted.

Dutch Spectacle

DESIGNER JAN DAVID ZOCHER
COMPLETED 1850s
LOCATION LISSE, NETHERLANDS

ALTHOUGH IT IS dependent on the weather, the flowering season of the Dutch flower industry is typically from the end of March until the second week of May. Every year, people travel from all over the world to see the flower fields in their spectacular abundance. Bulbs are the jewel in the Dutch plant-growing industry crown, and the tulip is considered the national flower of the Netherlands.

While the bulb fields of the Netherlands are extraordinary, more than 700,000 people a year make a pilgrimage to the industry's showpiece garden of Keukenhof in the town of Lisse. They are drawn by the incredible displays of tulips, hyacinths and daffodils. Every year sees a new display established in the almost 80 acres (32 ha) of garden.

Keukenhof translates as 'kitchen garden', and in the 15th century the park was exactly that, a garden used to grow food for nearby Teylingen Castle. Centuries passed and the estate underwent various changes until it was remodelled in the mid-1850s by Jan David Zocher, assisted by his son, Louis Paul Zocher. Landscape architect to William I of Holland, Zocher senior was a great admirer of the work of English landscape designer Humphry Repton.

A hundred years later, the Keukenhof Foundation acquired the property for development as a display garden for the Dutch bulb growers. In 1949, the gardens were opened to the public for the first time as an open-air flower exhibition; highly popular, this became an annually recurring event, and the exhibition continues with great success today.

More than seven million bulbs fill the gardens with their flashes of bright colour, including over a hundred different varieties of tulip. Thirty gardeners hand-plant the bulbs every autumn; in early summer, when the plants have flowered and the foliage has started to die back, they are lifted from the ground. With the arrival of autumn, new bulbs are planted according to a new design of the next year's display.

DESIGN INGREDIENTS

· Framed views

· Unity

· Repetition

· Contrasting colours

· Drama

[1] RIVERS OF COLOUR *Muscari armeniacum* (grape hyacinth) flowers make a river of blue as they pass through the throngs of tulips, crocuses and daffodils that adorn the undulating landscape, hugging its contours. Bulbs are planted in blocks and bands of single colours, so that visitors can best appreciate individual varieties. Flamboyant drifts of vivid yellow, red and orange tulips at first hold sway, eventually giving ground to more subdued colour combinations of white, pale and dark pink, violet and purple-black.

[2] ENGLISH STYLING The land is sculpted and contoured, and slopes gracefully down towards a lake. The groundwork, completed by Jan David Zocher and his son in the mid-19th century, is in the English landscape style, which had been fashionable since the previous century. A reaction to the orderliness of formal gardens (they had come to be seen as sterile), the English style shunned straight lines and geometrical regularity. Weaving among the trees, almost 10 miles (16 km) of winding paths provide the visitor with a succession of surprising vistas.

[3] TOWERING TREES The *Fagus sylvatica* (common beech) trees of the park were probably part of Zocher's 19th-century plan. Their height balances the ground-hugging bulbs, and the dark trunks calm the bright colours while framing views through to other parts of the garden. Their late-showing citrus-green foliage admits plenty of light through to the bulbs, and complements their vivid colours. It is the trees that distinguish Keukenhof from the industry's open bulb fields.

[4] SINUOUS WATERWAYS In these extensive gardens, flowing water is arranged as lakes, canals and winding rivers. Like the tulips, the waterways are synonymous with Holland, and these gardens have plenty of them. Here, the path of the water is mimicked on the bank by a serpentine path of hyacinths. The pale and bright yellows of crowded drifts of daffodils are reflected in the water, while a few red tulips are allowed to interrupt the colour scheme and form an unexpected highlight.

TULIPS AND THE DUTCH

Originally from the Middle East, tulips were brought to Holland in the 16th century. They were an instant hit, and, at the height of tulipomania in the 1630s, the price of bulbs skyrocketed, boosted by speculation in tulip futures by people who never saw the bulbs. In 1637 the bubble burst and fortunes were lost overnight. Tulipomania was a disaster for those investors, but the Dutch love affair with bulbs persisted. Today, the Dutch produce more than nine billion bulbs annually; of these, the tulip fields (see left) produce three billion bulbs.

Brazilian Innovation

DESIGNER ROBERTO BURLE MARX
COMPLETED 1948, RESTORED IN 1980s
LOCATION PETROPOLIS, RIO DE JANEIRO, BRAZIL

MANY GARDEN DESIGNERS, even when they are highly aware of the landscape in which they are working, deliberately create a contrast between the man-made garden and the natural landscape, as if the garden is defined by its introduced, exotic elements. The Brazilian landscape gardener Roberto Burle Marx, however, preferred to play with this contrast in his work, at once drawing on the existing landscape and bringing in artificial, constructed elements.

One of Burle Marx's earliest and most famous gardens was created for the residence of a friend, Odette Monteiro. The house is situated in a wide valley encircled by a dramatic mountain range. The temperature is about 15°F (10°C) lower than nearby Rio due to its being 2,600 ft (800 m) above sea level. Clouds scud across the sky at speed, altering the patterns of light falling on the garden.

The landscape forms an integral part of the design. Burle Marx preserved the topography, only

altering the course of a stream to make a lake in front of the brightly decorated house. Plants near the house echo its colours. Clumps of spear-like *Alcantarea imperialis* litter the sweeping lawns and painterly, curving carpets of flamboyant rock plants hug the contours of the garden. A waterfall tumbles down towards the lake, and this in turn mirrors the rocks, the plants and the continually changing sky. Crossing the lake, a sinuous path leads from the house, only to disappear into the distance.

All of Burle Marx's gardens boast a wealth of indigenous plants. He was an accomplished botanist, and his philosophy was to celebrate the local flora rather than use imported species. He went on trips into the Brazilian interior to collect plants, which he propagated in his home nursery for use in planting schemes. His garden designs were inspired almost entirely by the colours and forms of his beloved native plants, and the exuberance and vitality of his work owes much to their qualities.

DESIGN INGREDIENTS

- Asymmetry
- Block planting for bold effect
- Inclusion of artworks
- Sympathy to genius loci

[1] DYNAMIC INTERVENTION

A powerful and deliberately artificial-looking waterfall interrupts the garden's natural curves with solid, geometrical blocks. It also creates a link with the architecture of the house nearby. Constructed in concrete, the waterfall introduces a man-made statement to the scene. The blocks divide the descending water into sections, so it falls in sheets on several levels, creating movement and interest. Waterfalls feature in many of Burle Marx's gardens, where mountain gradients provide perfect sites.

[2] ORGANIC LINES

Burle Marx's work is characterized by curvaceous, flowing contours. Flowerbeds and ponds are laid out in amoebic forms, the former filled with blocks of flowering plants in primary colours. The visitor moves between the spaces, encountering new vistas at every turn. The layout of the Odette Monteiro garden was planned on the ground, rather than on paper. Burle Marx called this design method 'painting on site'. His lines follow and imitate the silhouettes of the mountains beyond and the undulations of the less extreme terrain below them.

[3] TILED MURAL Although known primarily for his plants and landscapes, Burle Marx was also an artist. His paintings and sculptures feature in many of his landscapes, and he also made jewellery and textiles. He used walls as decorative features, often covering them with colourful tiles (this panel was designed by Haruykoshi Ono, his partner). Although Burle Marx's use of tile panels made reference to the traditional decoration of Portuguese architecture, his own tiles were modern and abstract in character.

THE INFLUENCE OF ROBERTO BURLE MARX

No other landscape designer has had such an impact on the identity and appearance of a country as Burle Marx on Brazil. Appreciation of his work has spread worldwide; the American Institute of Architects named him 'the real creator of the modern garden'. During his lifetime, he created almost 3,000 landscapes and gardens, including one (see below) at his home, Sítio Roberto Burle Marx in Rio de Janeiro. Using same-species block planting in primary colours, he created fluid shapes that defined space in unexpected ways. Shunning foreign imports, he sought out and grew native plants for his projects, as well as foraging materials from demolition sites to recycle in his gardens. His work inspires landscape designers to be sympathetic to nature, and also to preserve the ecology and history of their countries.

[4] ROCK PLANTS As an advocate of natural-looking planting, Burle Marx took a special interest in rock plants, partly because they would grow in urban, concrete-dominated gardens and required very little soil. He favoured wide swathes of same-coloured plants (as above) because that is how they occur in nature. He was an avid collector of rock plants, too, always taking the ecological advice of botanist companions and claiming knowledge only of 'botany applied to gardens'. Even so, he discovered about 100 plants then unknown to science.

Mexican Colonial

DESIGNER DESIGN WORKSHOP
COMPLETED 2005
LOCATION TUCSON, ARIZONA, USA

THE COLONIAL MISSIONS and plazas established by the Spanish in Mexico from the 16th century onwards have a strong cultural and aesthetic identity. Pumpkin-coloured walls of rammed earth and adobe; shadowy alcoves and shaded verandas; social areas clustered against a background of splashing water, and vibrant planting can contribute to a desirable, family-friendly space that is modernist and yet traditional.

This 3-acre (1.2 ha) property, surrounded by the Sonoran Desert, is located to the north of Tucson in the foothills of the Catalina Mountains in Arizona. The owners wanted to create a unique retreat for family and friends that took its design cues from the colours, textures and outdoor living environment of the surrounding desert landscape.

The upper terrace has as its focal point a *placita* (small courtyard), whose angles and vivid walls contrast with the softer, more organic colours, shapes and textures of the lower terrace garden, which incorporates a deep swimming pool surrounded by walls and desert-style planting. Throughout the garden, native plants help to blend the architecture into the desert beyond. A raised fountain, typical of those found in traditional Mexican courtyards, tinkles quietly, as if aware that water is precious in this dry landscape.

The owners collaborated with Design Workshop, not only to capture the unique qualities of the desert environment but also to develop and install an ecological system for recycling water from the home to enable a diverse range of plants to be grown. They succeeded in bringing a barren space to life with a variety of plants, insects and birds.

Rustic materials and native planting are used in a contemporary way, along with expressive colour and subtle use of detail. What has resulted is an extraordinary outdoor living space that fully reflects the history and ecology of its location.

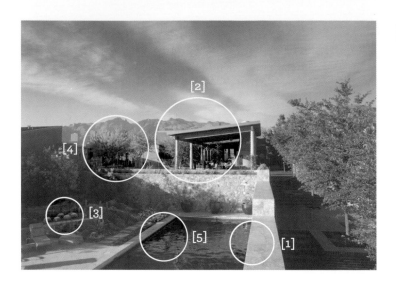

[1] MORE THAN WALLS Every wall in the space seems to do double duty as a colourful backdrop. Alongside the swimming pool, a mosaic-tiled mural by Santa Fe artist Sam Leyba draws the eye; its design is reflected in the still pool. The mural, depicting the Aztec god Quetzalcoatl, the feathered serpent, comes alive at night with embedded tiny lights that represent the constellations. The walls also serve to discourage unwelcome visitors; along their tops are narrow beds containing agaves and other plants selected to deter intruders.

[2] RAMADA Next to the house, at the back of the *placita*, the *ramada* (open-sided porch) is arranged to accommodate the outdoor living habits of the residents. Groups of tables and chairs, an outdoor kitchen and an open fireplace are set beneath distinctive, star-shaped Mexican lanterns that hang from the rafters. The cobalt and ochre of the walls and pillars are picked up in the porphyry pavers that cover the ground. A central fountain, sculpted to evoke ancient stone artefacts of Mexico's Aztec past, provides a focal point with a strong cultural identity.

[3] DROUGHT TOLERANCE

Following a study of the site's potential wind patterns, it was possible to place the native plants in groups according to their degree of drought tolerance. Relatively lush and thirsty plants were placed in the shelter of the house, while tougher, less demanding species were sited towards the more exposed boundaries. The complex palette at the owners' disposal included nearly thirty species of cacti and succulents, twenty species of native shrubs and forty species of drought-tolerant ground cover.

[4] **IRONWOOD TREES** The *placita* is framed by three specimens of *Olneya tesota* (desert ironwood), whose pale trunks and branches stand out against the brightly coloured walls. *O. tesota* is found only in the Sonoran Desert, where it can attain a height of 33 ft (10 m), despite the dry conditions. A member of the pea family, *O. tesota* produces clusters of white to pale pink flowers in early summer. The common name 'ironwood' is not to be taken lightly – the wood actually sinks when immersed in water. The soil in which the trees are growing is covered by pink and grey river stones that tone in with the flagstones.

[5] **RECYCLED WATER** Fresh water is in short supply in the Tucson area, where a paltry 12 in. (30 cm) of annual rainfall is not enough to fulfil the needs of one of the largest cities in the country. Drawing off precious mains water for garden irrigation is clearly unethical, but using 'grey' recycled water is a positive solution. The system draws on all the household plumbing fixtures except sewage, with water from the pool filtration purge line and downpipes from the roof reducing the property's mains water consumption by 40 per cent. The garden is a good model for the future.

New Zealand Haven

DESIGNER ANTHONY PAUL

COMPLETED 2005

LOCATION KERIKERI, NEW ZEALAND

THE ISLANDS OF NEW ZEALAND, lying between the Pacific Ocean and the Tasman Sea, experience hot and dry summers while bearing the brunt of blustery, salt-laden winds. European immigrants arriving by sea would long for their first sight of the coast, and this garden, perched on a hill above Te Puna inlet on the North Island's north-east coast, represents the havens that they built far from their original homes.

The landscape in this region was known to the Māori as *kerikeri*. While there is some doubt surrounding the definition of the word, it is believed to mean 'dig dig' in reference to the widely distributed gardens that the Māori cultivated in the area before the arrival of the European settlers. Today the fertile land is used for the commercial growing of oranges and kiwifruit (also known as the Chinese gooseberry).

The garden, designed by Anthony Paul, was created with a bold sense of colour and geometry, with the patterns formed by the structure and planting producing a clean, minimal feel. In the dry, windy conditions, the planting is necessarily understated. The simple geometrical structure lends a polished sophistication to the space. Water plays a leading role and appears in many different forms, while the colour palette takes elements from the surroundings and the sky. The open site takes full advantage of wide-ranging views across the inlet.

Anthony Paul's interest in Māori culture provided much of the inspiration for the design. *Koru* is the Māori word for the coiled form of a new fern frond, and in Māori culture this symbolizes growth, strength, knowledge and peace. The koru is used widely in such Māori art forms as woodcarving and tattooing, and is a recurring theme throughout the garden. Although modern in style, both the house and garden take cues from ancient culture and demonstrate a strong sense of time and place.

· A space to display art

· Continuity with wider landscape

· Geometry

· Simplicity

· Sympathetic colour palette

[1] SPIRAL WATER FEATURE

A representation of the koru, or coiled fern frond, this eye-catching concrete feature has black slate pebbles set into its surface; these provide texture while exaggerating the movement of water whirling around and down into its centre. This is the final journey for a flow of water that starts in a large header pool and spills into a long, narrow rill that runs the length of the garden. The rill then morphs into a moat that flanks the house and reflects light back into the exterior and interior living spaces.

[2] GRID PATTERN

The long, low terrace, providing views of the sea, is laid out to a geometrical grid using soft beige sandstone. Micro-hummocks of *Scleranthus biflorus* (Canberra grass), a native, sun-loving, moss-like perennial, spread randomly across the squares, and black slate pebbles fill the spaces in between. The acid-green 'lime lava' provides a strong contrast, both with its colour, which zings against the dark stones, and its velvety texture, which softens the hard edges of the built elements. Grids work well with vistas because the lines continue outwards to infinity.

[3] GENTLE COLOURS

The colours of the garden work in harmony with the architecture. The designer painted the house and surrounding structures duck-egg blue, and introduced silver and cream into both the hard surfaces and the planting. This background palette is very relaxing and natural, reflecting the gentle colours of the sky and the adjacent landscape. The inclusion of bold, lime-green groundcover plants, however, lifts and brightens the scheme, just as the introduction of dark slate ties the garden together.

[4] SCULPTURE

The owners are enthusiastic collectors of art, with a passion for modern sculpture. The uncluttered space of the garden acts as an outdoor gallery, with carefully selected pieces placed where they can be best appreciated. Here, a spiral cone in terracotta by Felicity Aylieff is offset by a cobalt wall, as is the sculptural form of the tree alongside it. The art was chosen for the clients by the designer, who sourced various sculptures from his wife's gallery: the Hannah Peschar Sculpture Garden, in England.

[5] RURAL CONTEXT

Anthony Paul thought it important to establish a connection between the garden and the landscape beyond. He achieved this by using location-appropriate, wind-tolerant grasses around the terrace to blur the boundaries. Planted en masse, *Anemanthele lessoniana*, (pheasant's tail grass) behaves as a single entity when the wind catches it; the stems move in waves and reflect the light. This grass is also known as 'New Zealand wind grass', for good reason. The views and the 'borrowed' setting play a spectacular part in the overall drama of the garden.

Plants

Lavender Masses

DESIGNER ANDREA COCHRAN

COMPLETED 2008

LOCATION ATHERTON, CALIFORNIA, USA

WHEN A GARDEN designer decides to make a single genus or species the highlight of a project, it does not follow that the presence of that plant or family must be ubiquitous or overwhelming. Used sparingly, perhaps in a single line, as an artist might make a single, bold brushstroke, the mass of a single colour can define the style of a garden.

Builder Stephen Ackley and his wife Maryan, finally deciding that it was time to turn their attention to the exterior of their property, began to think hard about what they needed – certainly more than the existing basic combination of a patio and lawn, which had been underused. What they required was somewhere private that catered for the needs of the whole family: a kids' play area, a pool and a space for entertaining. Ackley had seen the work of landscape architect Andrea Cochran, and he liked the pared-back, contemporary restraint of her modernist style. He commissioned her to introduce some order into his awkwardly shaped plot, but with a fairly strict brief that allied with his desire for moderation. He was looking for an understated design that flowed naturally from the character of the house and the surrounding area.

Cochran's response was a landscape of classical lines that followed those of the house: a formal design with spatial architectural aesthetics. The planting is understated, in keeping with the structure, but at the same time its presence plays a palpable role. The underlying scheme consists of shades of green and white, galvanized in late spring by the dramatic appearance of lilac-blue, in the form of extensive sweeps of lavender. The wide bands of a single lavender species give the garden an elegant composure. The other materials are limited, too, and the finish is clean and crisp. Every different area of the garden makes an impression of space, and this is achieved by discipline and balance in the selection and arrangement of the components.

DESIGN INGREDIENTS

· Unity

· Repetition

· Restraint

· Framing

· Limited colour palette

[1] LILAC HAZE Mass planting of *Lavandula* x *intermedia* 'Provence' has resulted in rivers of subtly different lilacs and mauves weaving through the design, separated by bands of box. Although the cool, predominantly green and white palette offers a surprising variety of colour in itself, through its diverse range of hues and shades, the colour marriage of lavender and lime is especially lovely. The effect is fresh, with the most distant swathe of lavender appearing like a bank of lilac mist drifting down the hillside.

[2] CONSISTENT STONE
The wall is constructed from split-faced tiles of Wisconsin pewter limestone, with the face of each tile left with a rustic edge for a natural effect. The light grey limestone wall separates the upper and lower slopes of the garden, contrasting with the cool colours of the planting. Cochran used pewter limestone consistently throughout the garden and its constant presence is a unifying factor, tying the different areas of the space together. For the paving, the stone was sawn to achieve precise edges, then honed for a smooth, matt appearance.

WELCOMING SIGHT

A water wall constructed of stacked quartz stands at the end of the entrance terrace, screening the front door from public view and creating a sense of mystery. In front of it, a graceful avenue of *Tilia cordata* 'Greenspire' (a lime cultivar) greets visitors. The gentle sound of water trickling down the stone combines with the dappled shade of the trees to provide a refreshing welcome and a calm place to pause and unwind. A box hedge behind the wall extends to the edges of the terrace.

[3] RIBBONS OF COLOUR

Beyond the wall, wide rows of single species stretch across the slope and lift the eyes. Behind the first and second box hedges are the compact bumps of *Pittosporum tobira* 'Wheeler's Dwarf'. Standard bay trees (*Laurus nobilis* 'Saratoga') measure the width at regular intervals. The green bands appear as a decorative edging to the expanse of lavender above them. The repetition of the cool shades is soothing, and grey-blue gravel between the hedges picks up the colour of the lavender above.

[4] CONTRASTING ACCENT

Restricted to specific beds in the garden, masses of *Hydrangea paniculata* 'Limelight' add some exuberant, frothy relief from the garden's formality and straight lines. The white hydrangea flowers have a green tinge, which tones in well with the garden's fresh greens and blues, but the pale blooms still shine out. The plants are kept in check by low enclosures of cloud-clipped box. Further up the hillside, the hawthorn *Crataegus viridis* 'Winter King' interrupts the blue lavender expanse with its graceful, silver-barked stems.

Herb Parterre

DESIGNER DARINA ALLEN

COMPLETED 1980s

LOCATION COUNTY CORK, IRELAND

HERB GARDENS differ from most other garden types in that the owners are constantly in attendance, snipping off leaves and flowers for their cooking (or their remedies). This need for ready access is perfectly served by the parterre, where gravel paths lead to contained parcels of specific plants. A herb parterre is practical, and it is also a great opportunity to create a formal visual treat, to be enjoyed amid incomparable scents.

When the Ballymaloe Cookery School was established by Darina Allen at Shanagarry in County Cork in 1983, the gardens of the property had been left to their own devices for around thirty years. Penetrating the wilderness presented a sizeable challenge to the owners, but what began as tidying became a passion. Gradually the family began to uncover and identify old plants and trees that had survived the long years of neglect.

The Gulf Stream moderates the temperature in this part of Ireland, creating the conditions that give the countryside its quintessential 'Emerald Isle' appearance, and in turn ensuring near-enough perfect agricultural conditions. It is small surprise therefore, that the world-famous cookery school would grow local foodstuffs in its own gardens.

The herb garden is sheltered by deep hedges and laid out as an elaborate, formal, box-edged parterre. Over seventy different herbs are grown here, including lemon balm, bronze fennel, purple sage, lovage, summer savoury, sweet cicely and angelica. Clipped standard bay trees give height to the garden, and its herbaceous borders are punctuated by dark Italian cypresses.

In 1988, a sundial, carved from Kilkenny marble by Tanya Moss, was added to the northern part of the garden. It is calibrated exactly for its location: the latitude and longitude are inscribed on its plinth. It is correct for Greenwich Mean Time; all that is needed is some sun to cast the necessary shadow.

DESIGN INGREDIENTS

· Formality

· Vertical accents

· Symmetry

· Shelter

· Functionality

[1] FORMAL DESIGN Arranging herb crops in small beds contained by box hedges leads almost inevitably to a geometric overall design because the interlocking beds optimize the use of space. Densely planted within the beds, the sometimes fragile plants support each other and are sheltered at low level. A herbal parterre also offers a good means of organizing a large number of different plants in a logical manner. The use of small beds is helpful in containing invasive plants, too – plants like thyme or oregano cannot be expected to coexist happily with rampant mint or nettle, for example.

[2] PLANT SUPPORTS Providing vertical punctuation in the centre of the garden, as well as supporting sweet peas and runner beans, decorative steel obelisks take the place of the humble tied canes that more usually serve the purpose. They are fully incorporated into the parterre design by being enclosed individually by circles of box, made large enough to accommodate the planting. Set out in a precise line, the obelisks bring height and structure to the essentially baroque design of the garden. The wrought-iron scrolls at their tops echo the formal details of baroque gardens.

[3] <u>BEECH HEDGES</u> The beech hedges that form the backbone of the gardens date from the late 19th century. By the 1980s, however, they were fast becoming trees. Radical chainsaw work was necessary to convert them back to hedging, and, thanks to careful pruning, their bases have bulked out once more. Their presence creates a sheltered microclimate for the herbs, some of which could not thrive otherwise. In the winter, the bronze beech leaves do not fall, and so the hedge remains an effective windbreak for the parterre.

[4] <u>PLANT ARRANGEMENT</u>
The organization of herbs into different box 'compartments' means that tall plants – such as *Foeniculum vulgare* (fennel) and *Cynara cardunculus* (cardoon) to the rear of this view – do not crowd out smaller plants. In visual terms, the compartments favour uninterrupted drifts of foliage colours (here, grey and green) and flower colours (here, yellow and purple). Just as in any other type of garden, the plants may be juxtaposed to achieve attractive contrasts of colour, texture and height.

147

CHATEAU DE VILLANDRY

The inspiration for Ballymaloe's herb garden came when Darina Allen visited the kitchen gardens at the Château de Villandry (see right) in the Loire Valley, France. Villandry's gardens, although modelled on Renaissance examples, were created in the early 20th century by a Spanish-born doctor, Joachim Carvallo. Four levels of garden are connected by long avenues of lime trees. Immaculately maintained box parterres extend for an almost unimaginable distance, filled with herbs, vegetables, flowers and topiary.

Contemporary Roses

DESIGNER ANDREW WILSON

COMPLETED 2010

LOCATION SURREY, UK

FEW GARDEN DESIGNERS think first of roses when it comes to planning a contemporary garden. While rose gardens have a long history, dating back to China 1,000 years ago, and preconceptions rule that roses are traditional and lovely, using the plants en masse tends not to be an avant-garde priority. There are ways, however, of crafting a fresh and modern space that fully exploits the beauty and scent of roses.

The Savill Garden, part of the Royal Landscape of Windsor Great Park, is a series of interconnecting themed areas that was laid out over 35 acres (14 ha) by Sir Eric Savill in the 1930s. Since the 1950s its Summer Garden has included a conventional rose garden, but this was in need of a facelift. The Crown Estate, which manages the park, brought in Andrew Wilson to come up with a modern scheme that would showcase the roses, especially their fragrance. The management wanted visitors to have a strong reaction to the space and to fully engage with it – something which Wilson has achieved.

Wilson freed up space by removing existing hedges and then planted 3,000 roses, most of which are perfumed and repeat-flowering. He added a sleek and modernist raised pier that slices into the heart of the space like the prow of a ship, taking visitors over the roses and right into the garden's centre. The garden is sunk into the landscape and remains quite secret until the visitor chances upon it.

Twenty-eight varieties of modern roses were chosen for the scheme, in shades pale to dark, from the white *Rosa* 'Glamis Castle' and *R.* 'Princess of Wales', the pale pink of *R.* 'Queen Mother' (all roses with royal connections), the mid-pink of *R.* 'Gertrude Jekyll', and on to the darker *R.* 'Burgundy Ice'.

At the Savill Garden, Wilson has succeeded in reinterpreting one of the most sacred English garden features in a fresh way that is guaranteed to excite the 21st-century visitor.

DESIGN INGREDIENTS

· Movement and organic lines

· Use of different levels

· Contrasting textures

· Colour journey

· Unity of plant species

[1] ROSE-LIKE STRUCTURE

Swirling pathways converge onto the nucleus of the space, where they centre beneath the tip of the viewing promontory. Experimenting with the plan on paper, Andrew Wilson drew arcs curving inwards and realized that the resulting structure was an abstract representation of an open rose flower. This unintentionally but neatly provided another resonance to the design. The shape of each of the curved beds is emphasized by planting roses in blocks of colour; mixing the colours would dilute the effect.

[2] VIEWING PROMONTORY

Curving, 20 ft (6 m) long, and built of oak, pine and steel, this construction brings the space firmly into the present. Wilson made clever use of levels to construct a soaring observation stage that offered an opportunity to view the roses from a different perspective, as well as enjoy the scents carried up by warm air. At the tip of the 'prow' an open steel grille replaces the timber floor, revealing the roses beneath. Here, few visitors will fail to relive the irresistible 'I'm the King of the World' scene from the film *Titanic*.

[3] PROGRESSIVE SPIRAL

The shades of the rose varieties
develop and deepen as visitors move
towards the centre. Roses in the outer
beds are in shades of white and cream,
and their colours graduate towards
darker, crimson shades in the middle.
The visitors' experience of the roses
intensifies during the journey inwards
along the spiral, not just through colour
but through richer concentrations of
scent. The slightly depressed and thus
sheltered site of the garden helps to
prevent the scent from being dispersed
by the wind.

[4] **GRASS BREAKS** Hazy, golden-
headed brackets of *Molinia caerulea*
'Heidebraut', a cultivated variety of
purple moor grass, curve outwards
into the outlying areas of the scheme
and effectively extend the design.
Closer to the roses, textural blocks
and wedges of *Miscanthus sinensis*
'Ferner Osten' contrast with the rigid
framework of the rose bushes, as well
as providing structure in the beds.
The grasses have a practical function
as well an aesthetic presence: they
inhibit the movement of the incoming
wind, which helps to retain the scent
of roses in the garden.

TRADITIONAL ROSE GARDEN

The new Savill rose garden is unusual in containing only
showcased roses at its swirling core. More traditional is a
mixed planting of roses and perennial plants, as seen at
Old Westbury Gardens on the North Shore of Long Island
in the United States (see below). At Old Westbury, climbing
roses clamber over supports, with the resulting tall blocks
of colour providing a backdrop for the perennials' varied
foliage and flowers. At Old Westbury, roses are just one,
albeit dominant, element of the planting, while roses are the
sole focus of the Savill garden.

Structured Grasses

DESIGNER CHRISTOPHER BRADLEY-HOLE
COMPLETED 2003
LOCATION HAMPSHIRE, UK

DECADES AGO, a garden covered almost completely by grasses would have been ridiculed in the United Kingdom as being of little more interest than a field waiting to be ploughed. Today, it is a mark of many contemporary gardens that the planting acknowledges the natural environs. Close and distant relatives of the native flora now vie with exotic species as the focus of interest.

On the border of Hampshire and Surrey in England, Bury Court has the distinction of having different gardens designed by two eminent international landscape designers. The rear garden was designed by Dutch master-plantsman Piet Oudolf; the front, west-facing space is the work of garden designer Christopher Bradley-Hole.

A modern take on a grassy meadow, the garden forms a connection between the old brick-and-stone farmhouse and the surrounding countryside. The underlying hardscape is formal, but this is almost concealed by naturalistic planting that blurs the boundary edges and invites in the landscape.

One of Bradley-Hole's hallmark ideas is to plant new areas to a rectilinear grid layout. As here, he offsets rectangles within rectangles; twenty square beds are set in an arrangement within larger rectangles of shingle, forming a slight trench around each bed. Corten steel edging defines the different areas and raises the beds themselves from the surface plane. The shingle borders contrast with the compacted fine-gravel paths that weave in between the beds. The execution of the hard landscaping is precise, and this close attention to detail narrows the focus and draws the eye.

Just off-centre within the space is a green-oak 'pavilion' consisting of two interlocking cubes, one at ground level, the other just above it. The pavilion's staggered outline is reflected in the inky black surface of the pond, where it looks elongated as though the structure were set on stilts. The pond lies almost flush with the ground and occupies one of the grid squares, as does the pavilion.

The geometry of the space is confused by the towering height of the planting – mostly grasses but also perennials – which pulls the grid out of the ground plane. The experience of being within the planting is rather like being in a maze. The impact of the display is just as strong in February (before it is given its annual cut) as it is in the summer.

153

· Proportion

· Geometry

· Contrasting texture

· Sense of place

· Rhythm

· Repetition

[1] PERENNIALS Bradley-Hole's selection of plants was guided by their relationship to meadow species, although he favoured plants that require no staking. The colour scheme is hot: fiery shades of red and orange from *Sanguisorba officinalis, Eremurus x isabellinus* 'Cleopatra' and *Macleaya microcarpa* 'Spetchley Ruby', shot through with eruptions of yellow kniphofia (see above). It was important that, at the end of the season, when their colours had faded, the dead plant structures would provide winter interest, their attractive, blackened forms standing out from the bronzing grasses.

[2] MISCANTHUS Seven different species and cultivars of miscanthus are used in the planting plan. They vary in size from the towering *Miscanthus floridulus* 'Giganteus' to the compact *M. sinensis* 'Little Kitten'. A favourite is *M. sinensis* 'Gracillimus' (maiden grass), for its structure, movement and grace. The grass forms vary from plumply arching to more upright and structural. The strappy leaves develop quickly, and summer brings elegant flourishes of silky, plumed flower panicles, flushed through with colours from deep purple to bronze and silver, which persist through the winter.

[3] MOOR AND SWITCHGRASS

Molinia caerulea (purple moor grass) and *Panicum virgatum* (switchgrass) create a layer that fills the breaks between the other plants. When the flowerheads are open and less individually distinct they create a hazy effect; especially when planted en masse, and with the benefit of a low afternoon sun, they are transformed into a shimmering mirage of translucent movement. Significant cultivars in the garden include *M. caerulea* subsp. *arundinacea* 'Skyracer' and *P. virgatum* 'Strictum'

[4] GOLDEN OATS

One of the most magnificent of the ornamental grasses, *Stipa gigantea* (giant feather grass, or golden oats) does not register as especially noteworthy until it throws its tall, arching stems of golden panicles up to 8 ft (2.4 m) skywards, to wave around above the clumps of arched leaves below. *S. gigantea* cuts a very distinct form in the border for the length of clear stem beneath each flowerhead. Growing naturally, the stems look as though they have been arranged artfully in their own green, leafy vase.

GRASS SCREENING

Grasses can be difficult to tell apart, but this one is instantly recognizable for its forceful, erect habit. *Calamagrostis* x *acutiflora* 'Karl Foerster' is often used for its architectural qualities, either juxtaposed with plants that are more horizontally inclined, or, as here, planted en masse. Used next to a building, it provides a screen that is at the same time dynamic and mobile. The massed stems form an almost solid entity, but one that responds in different ways to the seasons, the light and the wind. Here the grass has the task of anchoring the garden to adjacent buildings.

Contrasting Perennials

DESIGNER PIET OUDOLF
COMPLETED 1982
LOCATION HUMMELO, NETHERLANDS

GARDENS OF PERENNIAL PLANTS are not only aesthetically fulfilling, they are also a busy gardener's dream. They are quick to establish, in that the plants will provide a full 'show' the same summer they are planted, and can be gratifyingly easy to maintain compared with the traditional mixed border. A garden of perennials assures maximum effect for minimum maintenance.

Dutch designer and nurseryman Piet Oudolf has had more impact on planting design in the last couple of decades than almost anyone. Hailed as the king of the New Perennial movement, Oudolf has spent years experimenting with the structure and form of perennials and grasses at Hummelo, his garden near Arnhem. Oudolf's naturalistic planting style has had a palpable influence and may be accountable for the increased presence of ornamental grasses in many domestic gardens.

The perennial aesthetic is driven strongly by mood; there is a romance in the use of light, movement, texture and harmony in the planting combinations. There is potential for repetition and rhythm in the plant choices, and for a changing show throughout the year. Growers of perennials have a strong urge to get in among the plants, rather than stand back and admire the whole tableau.

In Oudolf's garden, most plants are at their best in September, when the blooms of eupatorium, persicaria and helenium are burning through the tawny-russet autumn show. And at this time, above all the colour and drama, the grasses are beginning to turn gold, producing billowing gossamer clouds of flowerheads on delicate stems.

In general, perennials do not need staking or feeding to perform well, and they can be tidied up by a comprehensive chopping back in late winter. Certain perennials are somewhat shortlived, but plants like asters, veronicastrums and persicarias will flourish for years with virtually no attention.

DESIGN INGREDIENTS

· Repetition

· Informality

· Contrasting form and texture

· Evergreen structure

· Multiple perspectives

[1] SCULPTURAL FORMS When Oudolf told plantsman and writer Noel Kingsbury that 'a plant is not worth growing unless it looks good when it is dead', he was only half joking. In winter, plants that have finished flowering can have interesting forms and textures. One example, shown here, is *Angelica gigas*, whose drying dark umbels provide height and drama throughout the cold season. Oudolf does not believe in cutting back plants at the end of the summer, because they are still beautiful; and he enjoys their varying shades of brown.

[2] COLOUR COMBINATIONS Oudolf pays little heed to colour considerations when planning his planting combinations. He 'thoroughly dislikes "suitable" colour schemes', believing that colour can 'look after itself'. Here, pinky-red *Persicaria amplexicaulis* is combined with burnt-orange helenium, violet *Lythrum virgatum* and even some yellow achillea. Grasses and foliage between the plants serve to neutralize the colour, and because the effect is naturalistic the colours do not appear to jar. To some beholders, any 'clashes' simply heighten the interest.

[3] PERENNIAL PLAN Plants for perennial gardens should be able to look after themselves reliably without becoming invasive. Perennials, grasses, ferns and bulbs are united in a natural way – in swathes or clumps, or mingled in contrasting heights, textures and forms – to create a balanced, naturalistic whole. Here, the upright form of the grass *Calamagrostis* x *acutiflora* 'Karl Foerster' contrasts with the felted silver 'lamb's ears' of *Stachys byzantina*, and is mimicked by the red flower spikes of persicaria.

[4] YEW COLUMNS The merry, colourful mayhem of the beds of perennial plants is offset by the solid backdrop of shaped yew hedges. Reinforcing this contrast of solid and ethereal, broad cylindrical columns of yew grow in the beds, their course zigzagging slightly drunkenly up towards the rear of the space. They provide height and seem to order or punctuate the garden. Like policemen, the yew columns seem to have an authoritative presence, as though their solid bulk is calming the unruly milling about of the perennials.

FRAMED BY HEDGING

At Hummelo, yew hedges are clipped into organic undulations, staggered a few feet apart with overlapping gaps that create a sense of anticipation, especially from the far side of this area, where they partly block sightlines back into the garden, the gaps allowing teasing glimpses of the garden. The flowing profiles of the tops of the hedges encourage the visitor to become involved with the space, rather than just walking through without paying it attention. Viewed from a distance, the tiered waves promote a sense of perspective. The formal sculpting of the yew contrasts with, and anchors, the looseness of the naturalistic planting, offsetting its buoyancy and animation.

Exotic Surprise

DESIGNER WILL GILES

COMPLETED 1980S

LOCATION NORWICH, UK

GLOBAL WARMING brings with it all kinds of changes, some of them alarming, but for one kind of gardener it can bring opportunity. Warmer winter conditions in the last few decades, when coupled with a favourable, sheltered site, have made it possible to grow more tender plants in temperate areas than previously thought possible.

Before plant collector and author <u>Will Giles</u> created his garden in Norwich, the county town of Norfolk in eastern England, many of its plants were considered viable only in the warmer climate of south-west England. Giles bought the run-down garden in 1982, and began the slow task of clearing it. A series of trips to far-flung lands persuaded him to start experimenting with tropical species.

Thirty years later, his Exotic Garden is a miniature jungle of exciting plants. Everywhere there is something unfamiliar. Hotly coloured bromeliads, spiky orange *Strelitzia reginae* (bird-of-paradise plant) and bright scarlet *Erythrina crista-galli* (coral tree) mix in with more familiar dahlias and *Magnolia grandiflora*. Palms, trachycarpus, bamboos and phormiums create the backbone of the garden and provide its structure in winter. Softer textures – such as colocasia, ginger and brugmansia – bulk out the show during the summer months. *Musa basjoo* (Japanese banana) is the ultimate exotic plant, yet its roots can survive temperatures as low as 5°F (–15°C) if well insulated.

Clearly, not all the plants must be exotic to be included; bamboo, euphorbias and daylilies are all well known to English gardeners. But they must make a statement, with their leaves, flowers or form.

Most of the plants here – like cannas, colocasias, bananas and paulownias – grow quickly, knitting together in a fusion of different forms. In high summer, when the garden is at its best, they are a riot of colour, while the scent of jasmine, ginger and brugmansia flowers hangs heavy in the air.

161

DESIGN INGREDIENTS

· Contrasting texture and form

· Bright colours

· Big leaves

· Informal assortment of planting

· Sheltering trees

[1] POTTED PLANTS Some of the more tender plants are grown in pots, which enables them to be brought indoors to overwinter without disturbing the garden. Frost is, of course, the greatest threat to tender plants, but Norwich's proximity to the coast reduces the risk of frost in the garden. The pots themselves are simple terracotta so that they do not compete with the drama of their carefully arranged contents. Pots also provide the flexibility to fill gaps in the planting that occur at different times of the year.

[2] SHELTERED BY TREES

Trees around the garden site create a relatively mild microclimate within the space and shelter plants from direct wind, rain and snow. Transplanted exotic plants will only thrive in the right conditions. The garden is on a south-facing hillside, which maximizes the available sunshine. The soil is free-draining, so plants do not sit with their roots in water (which kills drought-tolerant species). A few plants, like the strelitzias, are dug up and brought in to overwinter, but here that is the exception rather than the rule.

[3] TROPICAL COLOURS

Tropical plants produce a riot of bright colours in their native habitats. Some of them are available as houseplants in cool-climate countries, although they do not necessarily flower. One of Giles's ambitions with his garden was to 'liberate' species that he had collected as houseplants by planting them outdoors. Plants such as *Chlorophytum comosum* (spider plant), *Impatiens walleriana* (busy lizzie) and tradescantias (spiderworts) all proved hardy enough to thrive in his mild-climate garden.

[4] CONTRASTING TEXTURES

No plant family speaks more loudly of the tropics than the palm, and here a fine specimen is backed up by hardy cordylines that echo its spiky fans. At ground level, a phormium's leaves support the theme. In the foreground a large hosta – not a tropical plant – offers contrasting heart-shaped leaves. Foliage of varied greens, red and black is cleverly juxtaposed. While this garden's exotic atmosphere owes much to flower colour, it is in the varied textures of the foliage that it really comes into its own.

XEROPHYTIC LANDSCAPE

In 1997, Will Giles added a xerophytic landscape to the garden. Xerophytes are plants that have evolved to survive in an environment with little water – not only hot, dry deserts but also regions covered by unmelted ice or snow. Giles's collection is mainly of drought-tolerant desert plants, such as cacti, agaves and other succulents. British native succulents also get a showing here, with sempervivums and sedums spreading around. The landscape makes much use of local flint; the fragments buried in the planted areas help to keep the soil adequately drained.

Succulent Levels

DESIGNER ISABELLE GREENE

COMPLETED 1984

LOCATION SANTA BARBARA, CALIFORNIA, USA

NATIVE PLANTS of dry, arid landscapes, succulents have evolved fleshy, thickened leaves and stems for the purpose of storing water. Most Western gardens are likely to contain a few succulent species (sedums are particularly popular), even more so if there is a featured rock garden, but it has taken drought and global warming to lift succulents to greater prominence.

Lying at the foot of California's Santa Ynez Mountains, on a steep and stony site of a few acres, this was one of the first gardens of landscape architect Isabelle Greene to be widely publicized. The unorthodox design attracted much attention because it overturned traditional design principles. Decades later, it can be seen as pointing the way towards a modern, more water-aware approach to gardening. It was built during a period of extreme water shortage in the area, and Greene took every precaution to minimize the need for irrigation. Her planting included many succulents, and she optimized the drainage and water recycling.

The garden, inspired by views of cultivated land, especially Indonesian rice paddies, was designed to be viewed from above as well as from ground level. The layout consists of a series of curving terraces that follow the contours of the natural topography, each retained by a low, rose-coloured, concrete wall. The terraces resemble field patterns in miniature, and are filled with swathes of mat-forming succulents in a variety of different colours. The adjoining pueblo-style house, with its sharp angles and large expanse of blank white wall, seems to float above the many-coloured strata. The sense of foreshortened distance was deliberately fostered by Greene.

Taller plants rise up out of the low-growing ribbons of succulent planting. Including grape vines, fruit trees and huge agaves, they are sometimes arranged in twos – flouting the rule that favours groupings of plants in threes or fives.

DESIGN INGREDIENTS

· Unity

· Drought tolerance

· Symbolism

· Colour

· Texture

[1] CONCRETE RETAINERS Each level of terrace is retained by a rose-coloured, poured concrete wall, originally cast in cedarwood formwork and still bearing the imprint of the woodwork. The earth in each of the terraces is slightly angled down towards the back, which helps to slow the passage of water down to the lowest level. The tiers, following the site's natural contours, spill down the slope from the house, making naturally flowing shapes that contrast with the rigidly geometrical architecture of the building. The concrete used for the terraces is roughly textured, contrasting with the house's smooth concrete finish.

[2] ARCHITECTURAL SPIKES *Dasylirion quadrangulatum* (Mexican grass tree) erupts out of the carpeting layer of succulent plants. This large relative of the yucca and agave family, which has a lifespan of about thirty years, eventually grows a thick, attractively scuffed trunk. The leaves appear as long, thin spikes and their dramatic display is made even more spectacular by being paired with specimens of the statuesque *Agave americana* (century plant or maguey). The agave produces a sweet liquid called *aguamiel* (honey water) from the cut flower stalk which is fermented to produce a drink called *pulque*.

[3] STREAM OF SLATE Broken slate and grey granite chips cover the soil in the stepped terraces, appearing like a continuous stream of water. The garden was designed during an excessively dry period and water is represented visually throughout the garden by slate. The dry stream unites the garden and takes the place of some plants, reducing the garden's irrigation needs. The stone provides a permeable surface through which rain can flow freely into the soil below. Blue-grey succulents in the beds suggest additional flows of water.

[4] SUCCULENT CARPETING

The terraces contain coloured 'carpets' or 'lakes' of low-growing succulents like *Senecio serpens* (blue chalksticks, see right), grey *Echeveria elegans* (Mexican snowball) and the pink and orange *Sedum rubrotinctum*, (pork and beans, or jellybean plant). It is the thickened leaves and stems of these succulents that give the carpets their substance, solidity and texture. The tall, spiky leaves of *Dasylirion quadrangulatum* stand in architectural contrast to the smaller, ground-hugging plants.

WHITE TREE TRUNKS

At the perimeter of the succulent planting are small fruit trees that have been painted white (see left). The effect is dramatic, especially at dusk, and was done partly for aesthetic reasons as the white echoes that of the pueblo-style house. However, in this hot environment the trees are also painted white to protect them against winter sun scald, which can cause bark to split, leaving trees vulnerable to infection.

Cactus Terraces

DESIGNER CESAR MANRIQUE

COMPLETED 1990

LOCATION LANZAROTE, SPAIN

THERE IS A beautiful simplicity about a garden arranged around a collection of plants of related families. The purpose of such gardens is to highlight the plants' similarities and differences – to create a theatre in which the plants will be properly appreciated. In a dramatic representation of the plants' natural habitat – be it desert or jungle – each plant has an opportunity to shine.

El Jardín de Cactus was the final contribution to the island of Lanzarote from <u>César Manrique</u> (1919–92), celebrated abstract artist, sculptor and architect. His work was always interwoven with the character of the Lanzarote landscape, and here he showed how, even in the harshest of environments, it is possible to create a verdant oasis. As with his other projects, the garden is itself a work of art and a place of great beauty, not simply a place with a cactus theme.

Lanzarote owes its existence to volcanic activity, with giant, puckered lava flows opening in jagged blades across its plains. The wind is relentless and annual average rainfall is a meagre 5½ in. (14 cm), making the landscape savage and hostile. Even so, vineyards pockmark the lower slopes of the volcanoes, each individual vine sheltered by a semi-circular stone windbreak, and there are cereal crops and sweet potatoes in the central plains. .

Manrique created his 'amphitheatre of plants springing out of the rock' in an abandoned quarry. Its location is heralded from miles away by a green metal cactus, 26 ft (8 m) tall, rising out of fields of prickly pear. Inside the garden, immense numbers of cactus are arranged in every conceivable shape and form. An ancient windmill, retained by Manrique, stands sentinel at the far end, and interlinking pools of water assuage the parched scene.

The garden is an artistic statement about the relationship of humans with the land. It represents a union of art and nature, where the aesthetic directly responds to the natural environment.

DESIGN INGREDIENTS

· Environmental awareness

· Humour

· Architecture of scale

· Juxtaposition of form
  and texture

[1] TOPOGRAPHY Around the sides of the former quarry, terraces of wide retaining walls double as paths. A network of stone walkways allows visitors to get close up to the plants. The oval contour of the quarry's artificial crater is hunkered down in volcanic rock. Varied seams of rock were exposed by the original excavation, and the well-arranged walkways criss-cross the site, highlighting the different levels. The walkways define a series of plots and terraces, not unlike those used by farmers in Lanzarote's mountains.

[2] CACTUS REEF The experience of descending into the garden is like diving down to a coral reef. The shapes and forms are astonishing. Succulent plants in the forms of shells, snakes, paddles, sponges, antlers, pillars, pebbles, fans, eggs, worms, rugs and corkscrews are all arranged as if in a crazy botanical drama. Most of the plants are from the cactus family, but there are also aloes, agaves and around fifty types of euphorbia. The garden contains more than 7,000 plants from the Americas, Africa and the Canary Islands, including some 1,100 distinct species.

[3] MONUMENTAL SCULPTURES

During the original excavation of the quarry, strangely shaped vertical monoliths of compacted volcanic ash were revealed; they tower out of the ground like natural abstract artworks. Manrique described them as 'monumental sculptures, fantastic obelisks that stand out from the cactus as if they were petrified cactus themselves'. These bizarre, encrusted, iron-oxide coloured columns merge with and mimic the cactus, adding an otherworldly element to the scene. The extrusions bear testament to the volcanic activity that shaped the region.

[4] DRAMATIC DISPLAY

Fat pincushions of *Echinocactus grusonii* squat in groups; muscular, furry echinopsis reach skywards; extraterrestrial worms of *Mammillaria spinosissima*, straight from the set of a sci-fi horror film, writhe across the black volcanic sand. As the shadows lengthen, the light provides a final fibre-optic show, enhancing the plants' colours and illuminating the halos of hairs and bristles around the plant silhouettes. Rather than being organized as a scientific botanical collection, the plants were deliberately and imaginatively arranged as a dramatic show.

TROPICAL STYLING

At El Jardín de Cactus in Lanzarote, succulents are displayed in a harsh setting that evokes their natural habitat. In recent years, however, gardeners have felt free to set the awe-inspiring forms of succulents in contexts that owe little to the desert landscape. One example of this practice, staged for the RHS Chelsea Flower Show in London in 1997, was the Yves Saint Laurent Garden (see left), designed by Madison Cox. This garden pays tribute to the Jardin Majorelle (owned by Saint Laurent, see p. 286) in Marrakesh, Morocco. In both gardens, succulents are displayed against a backdrop of lush tropical plants typical of rainforest, an entirely different habitat. In both gardens, too, the plants are offset by blue stonework.

Tree Fern Grove

IT IS REMARKABLE how the atmosphere of a garden may be influenced by repeated use of almost any key species, and how that feel can be changed by replacing the dominant species with another. Thus, a grassland feel may be replaced by a woodland one, or desert by lush water meadow. Even more extraordinary, the introduction of an ancient species can have the effect of making a garden seem to travel back through time.

Landscape designer Tom Stuart-Smith has secured prestigious commissions and gold medals at the Royal Horticultural Society Chelsea Flower Show in London. Yet, less than a decade ago, between designing grand-scale historic landscapes and country estates, he created a London back garden measuring just 66 x 28 ft (20 x 8.5 m).

Where nondescript planting grew before, suddenly there existed a garden like a living snapshot of the Jurassic landscape. Now the visitor seemed more likely to see a pterodactyl or a stegosaurus than a humble sparrow or squirrel. The explanation of this transformation was that Stuart-Smith had planted a grove of *Dicksonia antarctica* (tree fern), which is among the oldest plants in the world. No wonder the garden is immediately redolent of the dinosaur age.

The clients had just transformed the rear of their house with a two-storey wall of glass, and they wanted a garden that suggested escape – something simple but wild that required little maintenance. With high boundaries giving a feeling of enclosure, the planting was simple and evergreen to maintain a sense of theatre all year round. A crushed granite path winds upwards between the trunks of the ferns to a secret children's area at the top of the garden. The tree ferns themselves lean randomly, their fronds joining overhead to form a lacework canopy. All these factors combine to give a sense of peace and seclusion that lures the visitor further in.

DESIGN INGREDIENTS

· Simple

· Low-maintenance

· Bold planting

· Limited planting palette

· Texture and form

[1] TREE FERNS Tree ferns have been used in this garden for their architectural form and exotic foliage, especially in shady parts of the garden. The plants were mature when bought. Native to Australia, *Dicksonia antarctica* is frost-hardy to 14°F (−10°C), although the foliage is likely to die back at 28°F (−2°C). Protecting them in winter is done by stuffing the crown with fallen leaves or straw and wrapping it in frost fleece. The woody stem tissue does not form as the plant grows; rather, the thick mass of roots that makes up the trunk expands somewhat slowly, at the rate of 1 in. (2.5 cm) a year. Nutrients are absorbed through the trunk, so the plants need feeding and watering by spraying the crown and stem. Tree ferns will grow in most soils but should not be allowed to dry out.

[2] POLISHED CONCRETE While the path in this garden consists of crushed granite, the single step halfway along the path, separating its gradient into two levels, is made of polished concrete. The terrace that links the house to the garden (see foreground, above) is made of the same material. Polished concrete has many advantages as a surface type, and it especially suits contemporary designs. The concrete is poured into a frame and allowed to set (colour pigments can be added to the mix if required). The concrete is then polished with grinders before finishing with a non-slip sealer. The beautifully smooth, hard-wearing surface that results is versatile enough to be used both internally and externally to achieve a seamless continuation from an interior into a garden space, as was done here.

[3] WALL CLADDING Pre-existing boundary walls were clad with hardwood slats, which are used further in the children's play area. The wooden cladding provides a frame for climbing plants, which are beginning to scramble up it. When the slats become covered by plants, the space will seem even more verdant. For the moment, the light-coloured cladding provides a benign backdrop for the lush planting, as well as a 'canvas' for the play of shadows across its surface. The cladding has a modern feel that contrasts with the ancient tree ferns.

[4] PLANTING PALETTE The secret to planting in small spaces is to limit the number of species used. Here, box (*Buxus sempervirens*), a grass (*Hakonechloa macra*), and three climbers, *Pileostegia viburnoides*, *Trachelospermum jasminoides* and *Hydrangea anomala* subsp. *petiolaris* (climbing hydrangea), are used in addition to the tree ferns. Most are evergreen, and what the planting lacks in variety of colour is more than made up for by texture and form. Fern fronds splay above dark trunks, while balls of box litter the ground below.

KEEPER'S COURTYARD GARDEN

The year 2013 saw the completion of another design by Tom Stuart-Smith, again with *D. antarctica* as its dominant species (see right). The site, a cramped, dark, ugly basement housing an electricity sub-station, is next to London's Royal Academy of Arts. Stuart-Smith kept the grey patina of the walls and used it to offset the lush planting. Matching narrow Flemish bricks were used for the floor; furniture of grey metal completed the look. Additional plants included the compact evergreen shrub *Pittosporum tobira* 'Nanum' and, again, the grass *Hakonechloa macra*.

Architectural Statement

DESIGNER DECLAN BUCKLEY

COMPLETED 2003

LOCATION LONDON, UK

ARCHITECTURAL PLANTS are those with strong outlines and conspicuous habits. Some are architectural because they have big, exotic-looking leaves, like *Fatsia japonica,* or spiky leaves, such as irises and phormiums. Or it may be their form that makes them architectural, just as the vertical forms of Italian cypresses (*Cupressus sempervirens*) lift the eyeline as they break out of stone pines on a Mediterranean hillside.

Architectural plants are not shy. They grab the eye, adding visual punctuation as they contrast with less noticeable plants. En masse, architectural plants have presence, as they certainly do in this garden, but they can be used equally successfully as individuals, providing single, dramatic features.

The owner of this small garden – it measures 18 x 60 ft (5.5 x 18 m) – wanted a constant reminder of his beloved Morocco. The garden is open to view from the house through glass walls and doors, so it had to be attractive all year round. It needed to be inviting and provide a lush green backdrop to the contemporary, open-plan interior. It was also desirable to disguise the narrowness of the garden.

Designer Declan Buckley knew that using non-deciduous architectural plants with dramatic forms would make the garden look good all year while giving it an 'exotic' feel. The plants he used are hardy in the UK if adequately sheltered, and consist of evergreen trees, shrubs, palms, climbers, bamboos and grasses. The plants, selected for their varied foliage, produce a richness of sizes and shapes, so the interest of the garden is not reliant on colour or flowers. Ferns and a few bright-flowered perennials act as visual highlights through the year.

As Buckley commented, 'Tiny urban gardens need hard-working plants that offer more than a fleeting moment of interest'.

DESIGN INGREDIENTS

· Lush planting

· Contrasting textures

· Geometry

· Proportion

· Repetition

[1] CONCRETE PLANTERS
Oversized planters frame the edge of the deck outside the rear of the house, sending a signal to the visitor that they are entering a new space. Because the planters achieve the same height as the kitchen countertops, there is a visual dialogue between the interior and exterior. The render used on the planters has a slight tint of ochre, and the effect is warmer and sunnier than that of plain concrete. The minimalist treatment of the planters lends a simple, functional edginess to the garden.

[2] WATER FEATURE Continuing an oversized theme established by the large planters, a centred wall at the end of the garden is designed to be strongly dominating; there is no attempt to play down its powerful presence. In the middle is a perforated steel panel that allows light to flicker through at night; the effect is that of a giant lamp from a North African souk. The pale, ochre-rendered walls on either side act as blank canvases, picking up shadows as well as dots of light reflected by the water. The shadows and light create a hypnotic play over the blank surfaces.

[3] VARIETY OF FORMS A plant's form is commonly referred to as its habit, which accounts for its recognizable outline. There are endless plant habits that may be contrasted to good effect: tall, straight, narrow, cascading, mounding, prostrate, spiky. Also, of course, the gardener can play with the habit of many plants by clipping. Balanced garden designs include plants with a combination of forms. Juxtaposed forms – spikes against rounded leaves, for example – create contrasts and make the garden more appealing.

[4] RED HIGHLIGHTS The dominant design principle in this garden is the juxtaposition of the leaf shapes of architectural plants; the colour palette has been kept almost exclusively green so as not to distract attention from the foliage shapes. A few colour highlights have been allowed into the garden, however. Here, crocosmia has been chosen both for its bright red-orange flowers on tall stalks and its narrow leaves. Elsewhere, the tall dusky-white flower spikes and etched leaves of acanthus provide both contrast and interest.

CONTINUED LINES

The grooves of the decking flow straight out from the kitchen. The boards, cut to the same width as the interior boards, are aligned with them to provide continuity with the inside. The beds to either side of the lawn extend the lines further until everything is brought to a halt by the intersecting water feature with its stepping stone and high wall. The tall architectural plants in the borders pull the eye upwards. These elements combine to shorten and widen what is actually a long, narrow space.

Bamboo Minimalism

DESIGNER VLADIMIR SITTA

COMPLETED 1992

LOCATION SYDNEY, AUSTRALIA

A SPACE BURSTING with flowers is no longer everyone's idea of a perfect garden. The minimalist style in architecture and the arts is based on an understanding that 'less is more' – that there is beauty in a scene stripped of superfluous ornament. A minimalist garden features pared back, restricted planting that complements the clean lines of modern hard landscaping.

Landscape architect <u>Vladimir Sitta</u> drew on the related principles of modernism and minimalism to create this seminal garden in a Sydney courtyard. What it lacks in variety of planting, the garden makes up for in strength of character, while the building materials and bamboo immediately call to mind the formality of Japanese styling.

The ground plan is graphic – a linear arrangement that delivers formal structure. The vertical lines, produced by black bamboo culms alone, are extremely dramatic. Unusually, the bamboos are arranged as single stems, enabling them to be viewed individually and in isolation. The spaced planting draws attention to the beauty of the stems and their varnished-looking surfaces. The gloss of the stems is echoed by a black marble water feature; this acts as a mirror, bringing light into what is a relatively sombre space.

A raised pathway of pale marble contributes a light-reflecting surface to the space, becoming luminescent when hit by direct sunlight in the middle of the day. Light and shade are important in this garden, with the different elements arranged to behave in certain ways as the light passes through.

The plants are used for their architectural forms rather than other aesthetic qualities. The bamboo forms a series of easily penetrable barriers, with *Soleirolia soleirolii* (mind-your-own-business) making bands of green carpet to accentuate its upwards journey. Here, soft elements mimic the hard ones; the effect is stark, uncluttered and calm.

DESIGN INGREDIENTS

· Unity

· Mass and void

· Capturing light

· Contrasting textures

[1] REFLECTIVE SURFACE

What appears to be a rectangular pool is actually a slab of polished black marble with a slightly indented top surface. Water, contained by the indentation, moves imperceptibly across the surface of the stone; the result is a mirrored surface that reflects both the black stems of bamboo and the colours of the changing sky. Set on both sides of the path, the paired marble water features are generously proportioned, running to the same length as the beds of bamboo.

[2] BLACK BAMBOO

In horticultural terms, the garden is very much a showcase of the virtues of *Phyllostachys nigra* (black bamboo), whose jet-black culms make it highly useful as an ornamental. Very few plants are truly black, and for that reason the bamboo is valuable as a dramatic element. Being a 'clumper' rather than a 'spreader', the species tends not to be invasive. Normally, the culms grow together in groups, but here they have been divided into single stems for greater drama. Stripping the culms of new growth achieves a better outline.

[3] **BANDS OF GRAVEL** Wide paths of gravel in what seems to be a natural brown colour are part of a repeating pattern, alternating with strips of marble and narrow beds containing bamboo. Water features interrupt and punctuate the pattern. Examined closely, the gravel has elements of green, grey, black and brown stone. The effect of the gravel is to soften the look of the parallel hard edges made by the other combinations, as well as add another colour to the scheme. The gravel provides non-slip access to the bamboos, needed for tasks such as stripping the stems and sweeping up fallen leaves.

[4] **MIND-YOUR-OWN-BUSINESS** The black bamboo stems erupt through bands of *Soleirolia soleirolii*, a creeping perennial that forms dense mats of tiny rounded leaves. The plant's common name of 'mind-your-own-business' refers to the way it densely covers the ground, hiding everything beneath. It is a plant that easily gets out of control, especially if it establishes in a lawn, but here it is held in check by a narrow edging of marble. Growing the bamboo through the green ground cover makes the black stems stand out more and confers an interesting sense of artificiality.

[5] **MARBLE PATH** The veined, grey-hued marble of the path has been installed in its unpolished form to provide a slip-proof surface. The main pathway through the garden, it continues with steps up to the door. The path is given a dominant role in the garden; it occupies the central axis and is raised above the level of the beds. In that way it feels like a grand entrance route, from where the visitor is invited to survey the garden. The use of the same marble elsewhere in the garden, as strips around the planting and as square stepping stones, ties those elements together.

Composition

Enclosed Water

DESIGNER ANNE CHAMBERS

COMPLETED 2000

LOCATION GLOUCESTERSHIRE, UK

AN UNDERUSED tennis court takes up a lot of room in a garden, and its empty, static space can impose a forlorn atmosphere. A tennis court requires maintenance, too, and always poses the question of whether money allocated to it is well spent. Alternatively, if there really is little demand for tennis, the enclosed rectangle offers many possibilities for imaginative renovation.

Set on a steep ridge on the edge of the Cotswold hills and, usefully for visitors, just five minutes' walk from Hidcote Manor and its famous garden, is another splendid landscape, Kiftsgate Court. Like Hidcote, Kiftsgate tends to fall under the Arts & Crafts umbrella, having been originally laid out in the 1920s, but ever since the year 2000, visitors have enjoyed something completely different here; a secret space that is unexpected and breathtaking.

This is a family affair: three generations of women, each of whom made their mark on the garden. In the 1920s, Heather Muir made paths, planted colourful hedges of copper and green beech, cut terraces into the steep slopes, established brimming borders and discovered a famous rose: *Rosa filipes* 'Kiftsgate', a vigorous scented climber.

When Heather and her husband retired to the lodge, their daughter, Diany Binny, took up the challenge and continued to develop the landscape, adding a semi-circular pool in the lower garden and redesigning the white garden.

Diany's daughter, Anne Chambers, came to live at the property in the early 1980s. Her best-known accomplishment has been the transformation of a tennis court into what is now the Water Garden, an emphatically restrained space in comparison to earlier parts of the garden. Its emptiness has a profound impact, inspiring deferential admiration and hushed tones. Its purpose is to provide a place of contemplation, as well as respite from the abundance and colour elsewhere in the garden.

[1] GOLDEN LEAVES Twenty-four gilded cast-bronze philodendron leaves sway on fragile stems. Sculpted by Simon Alison, they are set in two parallel rows at the back of the pool. Despite being slender, they add up to a substantial water feature, their ample height being balanced perfectly by the many horizontal planes in the garden. Against the backdrop of the dark green yew, the gold leaves jump out and immediately draw the eye. Dripping water, the leaves animate in a timed sequence – refreshing the senses both aurally and visually.

[2] REFLECTIVE WATER The limited colour palette in the garden – green, black, white and gold – creates an impact precisely through its deliberate limitation. The water of the pool itself is completely opaque in its blackness, probably achieved by using a dark pool liner and some black dye. The result is an almost solid-looking reflective mirror in which to see the clouds and surrounding trees. When the philodendron-leaf fountain springs into life, ripples run across the surface, turning the still reflections into abstract squiggles.

[3] STEPPING STONES

A pathway of slender, white, beautifully aligned stepping stones offers the visitor a route to the central island. The material of the stones matches that of the pool surround. Their slimness gives the impression that they are floating above the water, an impression that is reinforced by their reflection in the black waters below. The pristine whiteness of the stone acts as a brilliant foil to the black pool as well as the rich emerald turf. The visitor is drawn to look for symbolic meaning in the scene.

[4] TURF PLATFORM

Turf is an important component in the garden, both surrounding the pool and covering the pontoon in its centre. Visitors' footsteps are rendered silent by the grassy surface, which adds to the calm, restful atmosphere. There is something singular about the central island; it is a geometrically perfect square set in the rectangle of the pool and garden, and the white pathway suggests that it might represent an attainable ideal. In its moated isolation it provides an inner sanctuary for contemplation.

[5] YEW SURROUND

The yew hedges were long established by the time the new Water Garden was built, having originally enclosed the tennis court. Now they provide a sense of enclosure for what is essentially a refuge of tranquillity. Square windows have been cut into the yew, providing visitors outside with tantalizing glimpses of the space. When the Water Garden was revealed to the world in 2000 it excited a certain amount of controversy in gardening circles for being unlike the rest of the garden, but the hedges permit it to be distinct with impunity.

Walled Prairie

DESIGNER TOM STUART-SMITH

COMPLETED 2011

LOCATION CHESHIRE, UK

IN THE CENTURIES before supermarkets made food relatively cheap and available, and before garden labour became largely impossible to afford, larger properties would often raise their own food supply in walled gardens that sheltered the crops from inclement weather. Many walled kitchen gardens, unused since the early 20th century, have never been put to another use, and yet their walls survive as a potentially valuable garden asset.

About halfway between Manchester and Chester in England, and set in its own 100 acres (40 ha) of rolling countryside, stands a classically proportioned late Georgian brick mansion with an Ionic portico. In 2004, when the current owners moved in, the garden was a neglected wreck.

They had a big decision: should they recreate a classic garden to go with their house, with formal topiary, shrubberies and a landscaped park, or put a modern but sympathetic stamp on the landscape? Deciding on the latter, they called on landscape designer Tom Stuart-Smith. Together with Dutch planting pioneer Piet Oudolf, he had restored the nearby historic Trentham Gardens to huge public and media acclaim. Dramatic use of drifts of perennials was a key part of their design approach.

Close to the house, the temptation to replace the formal topiary was quashed. Instead, informal box hedges were clipped into caterpillars that wind around unstructured plantings in blue, white and mauve: nepeta, thyme, blue and white agapanthus, *Euphorbia seguieriana* and *Sedum telephium* 'Matrona'. The effect is rather gorgeous, but without doubt the crowning glory is the restored walled garden. It had once been a dynamic hub for fruit, vegetables and cut flowers for the house, but by 2004 all that productivity was long in the past.

Stuart-Smith created a series of separate areas in the space, linked by an overall geometry and an informal planting style. There are no open spaces, apart from a terrace and a long, still, rectangular pool strewn with waterlilies. Around the pool, the planting is arranged to a rectilinear design. Stuart-Smith aimed for a different mood on either side of the pool: one side has grasses and cloud-pruned trees, and is contemplative and calm; the other is a rush of colour and energy. The walled garden, juxtaposed against the openness of the rolling landscape beyond, is now a secluded retreat.

DESIGN INGREDIENTS

· Energy

· Sculptural structure

· Geometry

· Flow

· Form and texture

[1] SCULPTURAL PAVILIONS

Against the walls of the garden are permanent pavilions made of bronze sheeting, their golden-brown tones picking up umber tints from the planting and harmonizing with the warm brick. Their sculptural presence contrasts with the relaxed naturalism around them, providing strong fixed points in the otherwise fluid environment. The bronze structures were designed by Jamie Fobert Architects; a variant had already appeared at Stuart-Smith's exhibit at London's Chelsea Flower Show in 2010.

[2] CLOUD-PRUNED HORNBEAMS

Entering the garden, the visitor at first notices an avenue of eleven hornbeams with their foliage pruned into cloud forms. The trees are set in square plots planted out with shade-loving plants chosen for their attractive foliage, such as *Rodgersia podophylla*, *Hosta* 'Devon Green' and the frothy flowered *Selinum wallichianum*. The square beds at the foot of the trees begin to put a geometric stamp on the garden, while the pruned shapes of the trees are truly eyecatching and contribute to the garden in a sculptural way.

REFLECTED HEAT

The main advantage of a walled space is that plants are protected from extreme weather, but there are other advantages, too. Walls often create a plant-friendly microclimate by reflecting heat they absorb from the sun back into the ground. This can mean that plants normally too tender for the area may be grown. The walls are also useful as support for shrubs, such as the *Photinia* x *fraseri* 'Red Robin' (see right). Fruit trees may also be trained to grow flat against walls (espaliered); their radiated warmth helps to ripen the fruit.

[3] ORNAMENTAL GRASS From a distance it seems that a rectangle is simply set with *Molinia caerulea* subsp. *caerulea* 'Poul Petersen' (purple moor grass). This bold statement captures the changing beauty of the grass through the seasons. In late summer, the purple flowerheads rise hazily above the rectangle and breezes ripple through them. Closer to, however, lines of low box hedging are revealed through the grasses, and a pattern is seen from certain angles. The box gives structure in winter when the grasses are cut.

[4] PRAIRIE PLANTING
Exuberant drifts of perennials give rise to contrasting bursts of brightly coloured flowers. Yellow *Rudbeckia maxima* and pink *Echinacea purpurea* and *Verbena hastata* 'Rosea' mingle with grasses such as *Calamagrostis brachytricha* and *C.* x *acutiflora* 'Karl Foerster'. Nudging up to the tall, muted purple accents of *Eupatorium maculatum* 'Riesenschirm', they put on a perfect prairie performance. The drifts of plants are all growing well in the free-draining soil that lies concealed by the unifying, thick layer of gravel at their feet.

Undulations

DESIGNER ISABELLE AND TIMOTHY VAUGHAN
COMPLETED 1990s
LOCATION BRITTANY, FRANCE

GARDENING ON A windswept and inhospitable site can bring a series of disappointments as nature relentlessly destroys the work done. Yet, resistant, appropriate planting can offer plenty of scope for creative projects that will thrive.

Timothy Vaughan, who trained at Royal Botanic Gardens, Kew in England, learned from the distinguished landscape architect Russell Page that structure endures, even faced with the worst winds. When he and his wife Isabelle bought Crec'h ar Pape in 1989, they were aware of the tremendous devastation caused by the well-known hurricane of 1987. Mindful of the words of Page, they opted for a design that would be fully resistant to wind.

The garden is based on the shape of a Celtic cross, with four quadrants divided by paths; at the centre, a diamond-shaped plinth of box brings the garden together. The paths are blue and grey granite setts, reclaimed from French towns no longer wanting them as a street surface. Any severity from the stone is offset by the daisy-like flowers of *Erigeron karvinskianus,* which lolls attractively across the paths, blurring the edges in summer.

Deep hedges provide shelter, and a variety of evergreen plants are clipped into tight, undulating shapes, low to the ground to resist the regular, blustery onslaught. Lounging between the topiaries, shaggy mounds of pale-gold grasses contrast with the evergreens. The result, an impactful array of textures and shades of green, fleshes out and gives energy to a writhing, fluid composition.

It is tempting to infer symmetry from the arrangement, especially in the layout of the box balls, but it is more about balance. Every gap is crammed with plants; the spaces between the topiary are stuffed with perennials that weave through the mounds, working their way out around the whole garden. The colours become more intense as they progress outward, with blue agapanthus, orange crocosmia and yellow kniphofias holding sway.

DESIGN INGREDIENTS

· Juxtaposition of control
  and informality

· Contrast of texture and form

· Rhythm and flow

· Balance

· Unity of colour

[1] HEDGING ENCLOSURE Planted to keep out the salty sea winds, laurel hedging divides the garden into different rooms. Here, the enclosure is circular, with two interruptions, through which other parts of the garden beckon. The hedges are mostly clipped in a traditional, flat-topped shape, but along their lengths are protruding lumps and bumps; these contrast with the geometric hedges and interrupt their regularity. The hedging defines the space within; the enveloping structure gives height to the garden and anchors it to its location.

[2] JUXTAPOSED SHAPES Clipped to look as though they are resting atop groups of topiary balls are four arrowhead-shaped topiaries. Pointing away from the centre of the garden, these pull the eye across to the boundaries. The angular arrowheads contrast with the collection of topiary balls, which do much to give the garden its rolling, undulating appearance – soft, cushiony and comfortable, yet solid and controlled at the same time. The balls vary widely in size, which offsets any tendency towards the formality usually associated with topiary.

[3] BLONDE HIGHLIGHTS

Standing out against the varying shades of green are soft, feathery clumps of the grass *Hakonechloa macra* 'Aureola', which lift the space with their pale gold–green tones. The grass keeps its colour for much of the year, so the owners can rely on it as a near-constant presence. In summer (when this photograph was taken), *Hemerocallis* 'So Lovely' raises the visual excitement a notch further, its creamy yellow trumpets poking out from between the various topiary forms and complementing the grass.

[4] **BOX 'SLUG'** At the far end of the garden, framed by the shoulders of the laurel hedge and an avenue of irregular box balls, are some stone steps with what looks like a fat green slug crawling up, or perhaps descending, their centre. On closer inspection, this organic-looking beast is also formed from clipped box. Its presence is designed to inspire a little chuckle, the more so because it has been allowed to take up most of the room on the steps. Visitors forced to give the feature a wide berth are sure to remember it.

TOPIARY INTEREST

The garden's most outstanding feature is its topiary, variously shaped from common box (*Buxus sempervirens, see right*), the cream-variegated *B. sempervirens* 'Elegantissima', the low-growing *B. microphylla* 'Faulkner' and *Euonymus fortunei* 'Canadale Gold'. Sculpted leptospermums, pittosporums, sages, *Osmanthus heterophyllus* 'Variegatus', *Hebe parviflora* var. *angustifolia*, myrtles, bays, *Quercus ilex* (holm oak) and *Quercus phillyraeoides* (Ubame oak) all supplement and offset the evergreen topiary.

Visual Flow

DESIGNER LUTSKO ASSOCIATES
COMPLETED 2005
LOCATION SAN FRANCISCO, CALIFORNIA, USA

THERE IS NO REASON at all why a garden should not consist of a group of disparate, self-contained elements, each with a different function – but if they are to be pleasing to the eye they should be considered with the concept of 'flow' in mind. No matter how different in form or function the elements might be, the designer can give them a flowing visual unity through the use of common materials, shapes, colours and planting.

This contemporary house in Pacific Heights, San Francisco, was designed in 1990 by architect Joe Esherick. Part of a linked series of historic and modern homes, garden courtyards and a sunken carriage house, and benefiting from superb views out to the city, San Francisco Bay and Alcatraz Island, the property demanded a correspondingly good outdoor area. Lutsko Associates came up with a design that tucks into the location perfectly.

The garden is divided into a series of three rooms (two of which can be seen here). Each one is a discrete enclosed space with its own personality. Different though the elements are, the garden has a strong overall architectural integrity. Viewers in the upper levels of the house can easily appreciate the garden's graphic composition, and at the same time the experience of being in the garden is subtly and creatively informed by the design. When selecting the materials and plants, the designers paid as much attention to their sensory effects on the viewer as to the part they would play in the visual power and beauty of the garden. While mostly enclosed from the urban fabric of the city beyond, the garden acknowledges and makes use of it.

The first room (not visible in this photograph) offers privacy and light and is bounded by translucent reeded glass on the party wall; the opposite wall is clean plaster. The second room (seen on the right here) is almost empty but for a bold bronze wall that curves along its length, terminating in a sheet of falling water. A surprise awaits the visitor in the third room: a breathtaking vista.

The sense of flow is evident, and there is an undeniable confidence in the sweeping use of contrasting materials and finishes to create a bold graphic composition. The planting palette is restrained, giving precedence to form over colour. These strong elements provide an architectural edge as well as a sense of space and time.

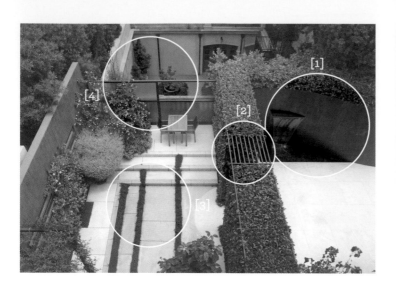

DESIGN INGREDIENTS

· Contrasting materials

· Enclosure

· Graphic strength

· Sense of place

· Strong axis and focal point

FRAMED VIEWS

As the visitor moves between the three rooms, the garden unfolds. Each design element is constantly reframed during the journey, creating a variety of visual compositions and spatial experiences. Emerging from the first garden, the visitor sees an axial view right through to the furthest wall. Here, a lemon tree, espaliered against a plaster wall, terminates a succession of green hedges.

[1] **CURVE OF BRONZE** A huge bronze wall in the form of a curving wave is the most dramatic element in the whole garden. The curving line creates a foil for the otherwise rectilinear space. At one end, a wide outlet releases a sheet of water into a basin cut in the paving below, the straight edge of the basin making a stark, contrasting border. The sound of water is the signature event in this section and creates a sensual experience in an otherwise quiet, introspective space.

[2] **THRESHOLDS** Between the three gardens, the thresholds are defined by gates, walls, arbours and planting. Each threshold is carefully designed to create both a sense of mystery and the excitement of discovery as each space is first concealed and then revealed to the visitor. The walls between the rooms are composed of hedges of clipped *Prunus caroliniana* (Carolina cherry laurel), set within steel frame structures. Mats of groundcover plants neatly conceal the soil in which the laurels grow.

[3] **PALE PAVING** Light-coloured limestone throughout the space not only creates a sense of minimalism and openness but also contrasts with other materials in the garden, such as the dark bronze wall and the bold, graphic bands of low-growing *Thymus pseudolanuginosus* (woolly thyme), two of which are unexpectedly extended to climb up a set of limestone steps. This movement guides the eye up towards a seating area. The limestone has a luminosity, even in the murkiest San Francisco fog.

[4] **TRANSLUCENT GLASS**
Glass with a fine reed pattern has been used throughout to create a sense of separation while still allowing light to flow into the space. Where the glass is used between the rooms, it supports a layered composition of bold foliage forms. In the third space, behind the seating area, the semi-translucent glass frames a view of the Transamerica Pyramid building in the distance. The glass panels are layered behind a Beaux-Arts balustrade, a nod to changing architectural styles.

Curvilinear Trail

DESIGNER IAN KITSON

COMPLETED 2009

LOCATION EAST SUSSEX, UK

ONE OF THE BIGGEST challenges when designing a garden is how to arrive at a motif strong enough to make the garden stand out from its surroundings, without at the same time introducing an element that jars in the landscape. Even if the rules of conservation bodies do not apply to a site, a garden that sits comfortably in its surroundings is much more likely to be a success.

Transformed from a neglected eyesore to a highly designed space, this steeply sloping south-facing garden at Follers Manor in the South Downs National Park has received due celebration in the British press and even won landscape awards. Although relatively new, the garden has already been seen by many Britons because its design and construction were filmed for a TV series.

Ian Kitson's design is a triumph of originality. The surroundings are officially designated an Area of Outstanding Natural Beauty and, in a way, the views were his biggest challenge. But in the event, his vision for the design was formed the moment he first saw the extraordinary setting. The contours of rolling hills inspired the organic design that sits easily in, and borrows from, the larger landscape.

Knowing that the garden needed enough personality to assert itself in the landscape, Kitson also faced some restrictions. The local planning authorities would not allow an old wall to be removed and, to make his task yet more difficult, the client was at first set on keeping a tennis court that stood where the ponds are now.

Kitson created a clear journey from the house to the ponds at the bottom of the slope, introducing twists and turns that hide and reveal different parts of the garden and the views. Remodelling the contours of the slope by cut and fill, he also created a sunken garden. Cleverly, he ensured that both this and the path were hidden from sight in views back to the house from the far side of the water.

DESIGN INGREDIENTS

· Organic informality

· Flow

· Unity

· Borrowed views

· Sympathetic materials

[1] SINUOUS PATH The progression of the sinuous path has a natural feel, as if the designer used the shape of a fallen spiral of orange peel as his template. Controlled yet apparently random, the curves are never uncomfortable or haphazard. Together, the path and walls flow down and morph into a deck that snakes across the billowing, freely shaped pond. William Kent, leading light of the 18th-century English Landscape Movement, argued that nature abhors a straight line, and this garden scheme imitates natural forms.

[2] IRREGULAR STONES While the sensuous curves of the garden are reminiscent of the work of Antoni Gaudí in Barcelona, the way the paving is laid echoes his mosaic work. The floor is self-bedded sandstone, selected from the quarry and used as found rather than cut. Flint – another irregular, non-uniform, 'found' material – was historically widely used across the county and in its buildings, including this property. In the garden, flint is used to make up the retaining walls, but in a contemporary way, providing a strong relationship between house and garden.

[3] WILDLIFE POND After a persuasive campaign by Kitson, his clients allowed a dilapidated tennis court to be replaced by an irregularly shaped pond that would form the terminus of the serpentine path. A narrow bridge crosses the pond without spoiling the close-up view of it from the far side. From the house, the viewer's gaze is able to flow smoothly down the path, over the pond, and into the landscape beyond, rather than being stopped short by the bare rectangle of a tennis court. The pond also offers interest and variety in its colourful planting and the wildlife it attracts.

[4] CURVING SOFTSCAPE Much of the display of herbaceous plants is hidden from the house and terrace, and is only seen from the decking by the pond, looking back at the house. The plant selection was determined by the dry, chalky soil conditions. Sweeps of *Crataegus monogyna* (hawthorn) hedging act as a structural anchor and form a blurred reiteration of the contours of the space above the swathes of perennials. Bursts of colour from scarlet *Crocosmia* 'Lucifer' and vermillion *Achillea* 'Paprika' boost the swaying fronds of grasses *Stipa gigantea* and *Anemanthele lessoniana*.

[5] VIEWING STATION
High up by the house, the circular terrace is a perfect vantage point for the garden and its panoramic views; it is made all the more attractive by being sunken and thus hidden from view and sheltered from the wind. The flint retaining wall provides enclosure and intimacy within the landscape for eating, socializing and gazing. The eye is entertained by planting, some contained by a neat box hedge, and by close-up views of the sempervivums growing on top of the wall. With a turn of the head, the distant hills are thrown into view.

Modern Symmetry

DESIGNER DOMINIQUE LAFOURCADE
COMPLETED 1990s
LOCATION SAINT-REMY-DE-PROVENCE, FRANCE

FORMAL GARDENS used to be designed primarily to complement and reinforce the architecture of the house to which they were attached, with little consideration for the surrounding landscape. Over the years, this tendency has relaxed, the ambition to show control over nature is not so keen, and the value of involving the wider landscape embraced. Here, the formal lines and symmetry echo the geometry of the surrounding farmland, extending into it to make a cohesive whole.

Set in a position that is unusually flat and windswept for the Provence region, the garden at Les Confines is the work of Dominique Lafourcade, who arrived here with her husband at the beginning of the 1990s to find a large house, backed with a row of plane trees, a wheat field, some oaks and little else. She has spent the past twenty-odd years transforming it into a lush, structured space. It is a work in progress, and indeed she has called this part of the garden (pictured) the 'Jardin Experimental'.

The garden is laid out to a formal quadripartite design. A stone-bordered rill, bisected by a pebble and brick path, provides the long axis. Around this central composition, clipped hedging forms little compartments as well as screens, which open up new destinations as the visitor moves around the garden.

Despite reiterating the formal structure of a Renaissance garden, Les Confines manages to retain a sense of relaxed rusticity; this is not the precisely delineated garden of a grand château, but rather the more natural-seeming extension of an 18th-century Provençal farmhouse or *mas*. Here, the structural formality of box hedges is loosened by other elements: olives are used instead of citrus in the oversized pots that edge the rill, and the planting around the *bassin* and rill is relaxed, in contrast to the clipped balls of box that frame it.

Above all, the garden is designed for outdoor living; it is an extension of the house, with different settings in which to walk, take meals and relax.

DESIGN INGREDIENTS

· Light and shade
· Romance
· Structure
· Proportion and scale

[1] WATER AT ITS HEART

The *bassin* or pool with its waterlilies is set in front of the terrace at the back of the house. A wind-driven pump powers an energetic fountain and recirculates water from the pool, along the rill, and back. The pool attracts frogs, birds and insects that bring life to the scene. The Provence region becomes very hot in summer and the purpose of the pool and the rill, which runs off into the distance, is to provide a constant, cooling and reassuring presence of water, making this part of the garden seem like an oasis.

[2] EYE-CATCHING PLOY

Lafourcade uses a classic design tactic by aligning the *bassin* and rill with a large circle fashioned from trained and clipped ivy. From behind the pool, the eye is led straight along the rill, the direction of which is strongly reinforced by the terracotta olive pots, to the ivy circle, which frames the form of a two-dimensional folly standing far in the distance. The effect of the ploy is to make the garden seem shorter by bringing forward the back of the garden. As the folly functions only as a focal point, there was no call for a real structure.

[3] OLIVES IN POTS The double line-up of olive trees in vast terracotta pots, framing the rill, makes one of the strongest design statements in the garden. It is a style that has been much imitated around the world. The arrangement came about almost by accident; because the ground was apparently too wet to plant the olives directly, the plants were containerized. The result is spectacular, with the colour of the terracotta providing gentle relief from the powerfully present viridity, and the pots adding rhythm and a sense of proportion.

[4] CUSTODIAL CONIFERS Standing beyond the olives, *Cupressus sempervirens* (Italian cypress), the most ubiquitous structural plant in the Mediterranean, has been used to reinforce the geometry of the garden by forming symmetrical, parallel rows that extend the lines formed by the olive pots. Clipping the cypresses gives them cleaner, more formal lines. Their considerable height balances the scale of the design. Between them, terracotta pots containing an *Opuntia* (prickly pear) species offer contrasting plant colour and shape.

[5] EVERGREEN PALETTE Green is the dominant colour in the garden, and is present in every shade. Other colours seem washed out in the strong sunlight of the Mediterranean, so the interaction between light, shade and the green surfaces is important in providing an extra dimension of form, pattern and colour. The garden staples are typically Provençal clipped evergreen hedges of box, *Viburnum tinus*, myrtle and rosemary. These protect the space from the mistral wind and also define the different areas.

Sculpted Hedges

DESIGNER JULIEN DE CERVEL
COMPLETED 1860s, RESTORED IN 1990s
LOCATION VEZAC, FRANCE

THERE ARE TIMES when the sheer drama and dense vegetation of a surrounding landscape can make the creation of a garden seem futile: how can any man-made creation compete in such a context? To be effective, a large-scale problem needs a large-scale solution. Here, massed topiary in mostly rounded shapes was used to make a statement in a heavily wooded setting.

Lying along a narrow plateau, and set on sheer cliffs rising 425 ft (130 m) above the valley of the Dordogne River, is the astonishing garden of Marqueyssac. Its panoramic views are extensive, stretching 6 miles (10 km) around and taking in the glinting waters below; several famous castles and villages of the Périgord are visible beyond.

While the topiary extravaganza of the bastion was certainly the work of Julien de Cervel in the mid- to late 19th century, it is thought that the structural terracing, as well as the box allées present further along the ridge, are attributable to a student of the Renaissance master gardener André le Nôtre, whose *terrasses d'honneur* would have featured topiary box hedges clipped into formal structures, rather than the organic shapes of today.

With the spectacular site very much in mind, de Cervel took the idea of the traditional parterre and box garden but twisted it into voluptuous and sensuous shapes more appropriate to the rolling hills than, say, the flat site of Versailles. A lover of Italian gardens, he saw an opportunity to create an Italianate garden that would not look out of place in its environment. Along with 10,000 box plants, he planted cypresses and umbrella pines and built towers and belvederes linked by winding paths.

The gardens were largely neglected from the early 20th century, the box being either overgrown or dead, but rescue came in the form of the current owner, Kléber Rossillon, who bought the property in 1996 and brought the garden back to life.

[1] TWISTED PARTERRES

Following the parterre model, low hedges surround the 'beds' of box forms to create a knot garden with a difference. Although the boundary hedges are clipped into a traditional shape, the course of their progress is a relaxed, labyrinthine ramble through the gardens, not the symmetrical formal arrangement of the traditional box parterre. At intervals, amoebic outcrops of box break out to join their knobbly neighbours, interrupting any strict division of duty between containing and contained forms.

[2] INTERPRETIVE GAME

Lying on our backs, we might watch clouds form recognizable shapes in the sky; and a similar experience may be had by looking at the writhing box forms of the bastion. The hedges might suggest sheep, a reclining musical instrument and some musical notes, Russian dolls, a rabbit perhaps, and some large pieces of furniture; the scope for interpretation is limitless. The random forms sit comfortably, almost like a microcosm, within their surroundings, while the lightly coloured paths around them provide a contrast to the box's deep green.

[3] TALL ELEMENTS The convoluted forms of the topiary are spectacular but appear low-lying in the forested context. To provide height and contrast, a stand of *Cupressus macrocarpa* towers over the hedging, their grey stems providing relief from the monotone green. Despite the limited number of trees, their presence is perceived as a united whole, which helps to establish a sense of perspective. The trees also serve to break up the continuation of the view, while framing different scenes between their trunks.

[4] LEAFY STUDWORK At irregular intervals along the crisp hedge surfaces, hemispherical pimples pop out to add extra interest and texture to an otherwise flat surface. The hemispheres are not of uniform size, which plays with our perceptions and sense of perspective, as distant ones sometimes appear larger than those that are nearby. The effect is unexpectedly modern, with the hemispheres adding an extra playful element to the space and a further layer of interest. Their appearance is slightly industrial, as though the hedge represents a textured metal or rubber surface, like the grip of a tyre.

[5] BOX LOLLIPOPS Rounded 'lollipops' of box have been allowed to sprout indiscriminately out of the green knolls, with spheres of different sizes held aloft on bare stems. In one part of the garden they are everywhere, whereas elsewhere they are scarce. There is a deliberate attempt to avoid the symmetry and uniformity of a Renaissance garden: box lollipops that have grown into irregular shapes have been retained; some are a bit crooked, some have two heads, and all are far from perfect. Yet for all their lack of formality there remains a sense of unity in the way they are gathered together.

Sunken Space

DESIGNER GARY RATWAY

COMPLETED 1994

LOCATION MENDOCINO, CALIFORNIA, USA

A SUNKEN GARDEN is seldom contemplated for aesthetic reasons alone. Creating a garden in a basin or hollow gives the plants permanent shelter from wind, and the sheltered space fosters a microclimate favourable for the cultivation of plants unable to survive in the natural surrounds. Sometimes, time-consuming and expensive excavation is necessary, but it is greatly preferable if a natural hollow can be utilized, as here.

Mention California to most people around the world and they will think of year-round warmth and sun. In reality, California's diverse geography means that its weather varies greatly through the state. The coast of Mendocino County, in the north of the state, is mild all year, but proximity to the Pacific Ocean brings constant, drying winds. Wind is not the only limiting factor for a potential garden; summer fogs, infertile soil, salt in the air and limited water availability must all be taken into account, too.

Moving into a Mendocino cabin with spectacular views over the Pacific Ocean, the owners recognized that there was no garden, just open meadow. But they identified one site that would make a good sunken garden if sheltered by new windbreak hedging and some existing trees, *Pinus muricata* (bishop pine) and *Cupressus macrocarpa* (Monterey cypress). The latter species, especially, is associated with the area, often sculpted by the wind into twisted forms.

Garden designer <u>Gary Ratway</u> used various tactics to cope with the site's challenges. One part of the garden is planted almost entirely with different heathers, the wind-resistant, drought-tolerant, tussocky drifts making dramatic bright purple, orange and lime-green splotches that illuminate the garden, even on the foggiest days. Ratway also added neatly clipped, grey-foliaged *Teucrium fruticans* (shrubby germander) and some *Prunus cerasifera* 'Krauter Vesuvius' (purple-leafed plums), which bring colour at height.

The unusually formal sunken garden was inspired by English Arts & Crafts models. Two *Taxus baccata* 'Fastigiata' yew columns look over a central pond, with a fountain and rill beyond. All around the garden, height is provided in stages: inner walls, planting interspersed with free-standing columns, then more walls with hedges behind, and finally the trees. All serve to create an intimate, enclosed area, protected from the buffeting winds.

DESIGN INGREDIENTS

· Enclosure

· Context of site

· Vertical accents

· Punctuation

· Symmetry

[1] FORMAL FOUNTAIN The head of the garden is dominated by a small, but still imposing, water feature. The design is classic, making use of three height levels to assist the water flow. A lion's-head fountain, on the side of a narrow, raised pool, feeds into a long, slightly raised rill, which then opens into a rectangular pond at the lowest level. The feature's symmetry brings a sense of order and calm, while its formality is softened by relaxed planting and organically contoured hedges. The line of the rill draws the eye towards the fountain.

[2] POND PLANTING Occupying the far end of the pond, *Equisetum hyemale* (horsetail), an upright, prehistoric-looking rush, has its roots contained in an underwater basket because it can spread vigorously. Floating on the water surface are simple, white waterlilies. *Pontederia cordata* (pickerel weed) has an upright form with soft, lance-shaped leaves and deep-blue tubular flowers, which echo the salvia flowers in the foreground. The plants, all suited to aquatic conditions, were selected for their different textures, heights and forms.

[3] BOUNDARY WALLS Creating a boundary within the inner space is a rectangle of retaining walls, and these also provide informal seating. The walls were constructed from rammed earth from the site and topped with stone. The earth surfaces change colour from greenish grey in winter to a warm pink terracotta in summer, their mottled appearance softening the formal lines. Rammed earth walls are ecologically sound; they are made with the site's own soil, anchoring the design into the location, and negating the need for road transportation.

[4] DECORATIVE COLUMNS Echoed by the purple-leaved plum trees on the opposite side of the garden, columns rise at regular intervals from the planting along one side. Like the walls, the columns are made of rammed earth, giving a sense of unity to the whole. Green-painted details make the columns seem less formal; non-functional, their presence is purely aesthetic. As a row, they add rhythm and repetition to the garden. Their dynamic verticality is a counterweight to the assertive horizontal planes of the design.

[5] COOL COLOURS The palette of flower colours beneath the pillars is cool but intense. Ratway chose Mediterranean plants such as chartreuse-green *Euphorbia cornigera*; *Salvia nemorosa* 'Caradonna', with its slender purple spires; and a variety of pink, purple and blue geraniums. In summer, the cool colour scheme is punctuated by hot bursts of orange-yellow in the form of a red-hot poker, *Kniphofia* 'Bees' Sunset'. The plants are mostly drought-tolerant, able to endure the drying winds that sweep in from the Pacific. Ratway added compost to boost fertility.

Patchwork Quilt

DESIGNER PIET OUDOLF
COMPLETED 2004
LOCATION NORTH YORKSHIRE, UK

THE CONVERSION of a large, empty area of land into a place of horticultural interest is a huge challenge. A useful principle to adopt is that of 'divide and conquer'; it can be easier to achieve variety and impact if the space is divided into compartments. In this garden, a 'patchwork quilt' of contrasting design styles and plantings provides constant surprises as the visitor tours the space.

Scampston Hall is an 18th-century English estate, one of the few still owned by the family that founded it. When Sir Charles and Lady Legard inherited it and moved there in 1994, much of the estate was beautifully preserved, but they were at a loss to know what to do with the former kitchen garden. The redundant 4-acre (1.6 ha) space had been used to raise Christmas trees as a cash crop, but then left to fall into ruin. It was a problem: too big to turn back into a productive garden, but really needing to contribute to the estate in some way.

The couple went to a talk by Dutch garden designer Piet Oudolf and liked what they saw and heard. They invited Oudolf to tackle the big space and, undaunted, he came up with an original design idea that works magnificently. Starting with a completely blank canvas, Oudolf divided the empty space into eight compartments, each distinct from the others and divided by beech hedges.

There is a refreshing mix of tempos within the eight spaces. Some parts, such as the Serpentine Garden, are motionless; here, waves of individual clipped yews are set in parallel, fronted by a flat circle of topiary and flanked by two crosses. Other parts, such as the Perennial Meadow, which takes a central position in the new garden, are a riot of movement and colour. Perhaps the most original and arresting sight in the garden, however, is the mass planting of *Molinia caerulea* (purple moor grass), where waves of the tall grass snake diagonally across clipped lawn (see left).

219

DESIGN INGREDIENTS

· Rhythm

· Contrasting atmospheres

· Movement

· Symmetry

· Structural geometry

[1] GRASS STRIPS The relatively new cultivated variety of grass used in this garden is *Molinia caerulea* subsp. *caerulea* 'Poul Petersen', named after the garden designer, who is also a plantsman. Being in among the grass is a sensuous experience. The striking pattern it makes when seen from above seems less important than its ability to capture movement, light and sound in a graceful way. The grass's appearance changes throughout the season but it is the late summer and autumn display that captures the imagination.

[2] WOODEN SEATING Four sturdy timber chairs set on the path that lies between the grass strips offer the opportunity to relax for a while, their solidity making a strong contrast with the feathery planting. The experience of sitting at the centre of the rustling grasses may be likened to resting in a meadow, but one that has been tamed and tailored. Sitting there is extremely restful; the shimmering haze of flower heads is at eye level and the constant movement has a mesmerizing effect. At the same time, the sitter is conscious of the grass's quiet and gentle whispering.

[3] CENTRAL POOL The central aisle that runs between the drifts of *Molinia caerulea* leads straight on into the Perennial Meadow garden. Arriving there, the eye is first drawn not by the planting but by the movement of water. Set in the centre of the quadrants is a simple circular basin from which a single jet of water is thrown to a modest height. The effect is understated yet seems entirely suitable, not only for the surrounding mixed planting but also for the simple, geometric grass planting of the adjacent section.

[4] THE MOUNT Set at the far end of the garden, providing a focal point beyond the Perennial Garden, the four-sided Mount stands in a meadow of wild flowers and bulbs; an orchard of Yoshino cherry trees (*Prunus* x *yedoensis*) is also located there. Stairs enable visitors to climb to the top of the Mount and survey the garden, which adds a fun dimension as the garden is otherwise flat. Diametrically opposite the Mount, on the other side of the garden, a square reflective pool mirrors its form to give the overall design a sense of symmetry.

[5] THE SILENT GARDEN Directly adjacent to the grass drifts, and screened from them by a hedge, is the Silent Garden, a completely different experience. Elsewhere there is constant movement and sound, but here, on the close-cropped lawn, there is a sense of being in a vacuum. A square pool of still, reflective water takes centre stage, while around it pillars of clipped yew are set symmetrically to a precise grid pattern, reminiscent of a baroque garden. The pillars each grow from their own plinth of clipped yew. The quiet is peaceful, yet also slightly unnerving.

Modernist Angles

DESIGNER KRISTOF SWINNEN

COMPLETED 2000

LOCATION ELVERSELE, BELGIUM

THE MODERNIST STYLE of landscaping could be characterized by a single phrase: 'less is more'. Restraint — both in the plant palette and the selection of hardscape materials — is key to creating a sleek, uncluttered look. Clean lines, well-chosen materials and simple plantings bring a welcome sense of calm and order.

Roads slice through the Flemish Lowlands, between Antwerp and Ghent, depositing houses along their margins as they advance through the flat expanses of countryside. One of these houses, an elegant contemporary structure, had a plot of land at its rear that was badly in need of some remedial landscaping. The owners turned to <u>Kristof Swinnen</u>, former protégé of influential Belgian landscape architect Jacques Wirtz (see p. 294), to design a modernist garden that would be in keeping with both the house and the surrounding landscape.

The designer's solution was to create a geometrical layout, mirroring the angular lines of the building. Subtle level changes separate the garden into different areas, thus breaking up the monotony of the flat land. The levels are delineated by low retaining walls of pale French limestone that complement the texture and structure of the house.

The garden is symmetrically formal, with an intimate, cruciform sunken area at its heart, which is occupied by two pools. They run along the central axis of the space, drawing the eye to the rear boundary of the garden, which appears to blend almost seamlessly with the countryside beyond. There is a sense of expansiveness, encouraged by the uninterrupted views of the surrounding fields.

Plants are limited: evergreen structural yew, hornbeam, lawn and some grasses. The sober shades of green do not distract the eye from the essential structure of the garden. There is a single splash of colour from red fibreglass planters that are filled with the fiery blades of *Imperata cylindrica* 'Rubra' (Japanese bloodgrass).

DESIGN INGREDIENTS

· Minimalism

· Symmetry

· Sympathy to genius loci

· Balance of light and shade

· Unity of theme

· Rhythm

[1] BLACK HOLES A black-lined swimming pool and a smaller ornamental pond beyond form the main axis of the garden. Swinnen convinced the owner that positioning them at right angles to the house, rather than along the same axis, would help to connect the garden to the surrounding countryside. In order to prevent the pools from dominating the view from the house, the designer elected to set them on a lower level than that of the main garden and to let the surrounding lawn run right up to their edges.

[2] BLURRED BOUNDARIES There was an existing row of pollarded *Salix alba* (white willow) trees at the end of the garden, to which Swinnen added another to form an allée. From a certain point when one is looking straight out from the house, the trees merge, allowing an almost uninterrupted view of the fields beyond. Move to the left or right and the trunks multiply, offering ever-changing frames for the countryside vistas. The designer has thus blurred the boundary between the garden and the outlying landscape.

[3] MOUNDS AND DOMES

Swinnen has used a carefully controlled palette of greens in the garden. Blocks of common yew, cut into abstract geometric shapes, meander across the lawn and gather around clumps of miscanthus, adding a sense of permanence to the space and breaking up the horizontal plane. Two domed obelisks, covered in climbers, are set at opposing sides of the pattern, presenting an interesting contrast in foliage to the yew topiary shapes. Regular clipping ensures that the outline of the climbers stays clean.

[4] FIBREGLASS CUBES

White fibreglass planters filled with feathery *Pennisetum orientale* (fountain grass) define the dining area. By echoing the form of the dining table and the colour of the limestone paving slabs, they bring unity to the design. Set back slightly from the main garden and marking the entrance to a small outbuilding, the same planters are repeated in bright scarlet. Filled with flame-coloured *Imperata cylindrica* 'Rubra', the red planters offer a flash of vibrant colour against the muted greens of the rest of the garden.

MODERNISM

Modernist gardens are characterized by clean lines – of water, planting or surfacing – which form geometric shapes. Precision-cut hardscape materials emphasize the strictness of the design, while the soft landscaping is organized to keep the space clutter-free. Planting is structured and blocked, with a limited palette of species and colour. Gardens were first designed in this style in response to the advent of modernist architecture in the early 20th century, in a move away from the prevailing Arts & Crafts style of exuberant cottage gardens.

Geometric Pattern

DESIGNER HAROLD LEIDNER
COMPLETED 2009
LOCATION WESTOVER HILLS, TEXAS, USA

PEOPLE ENJOY GARDENS in different ways: they may walk or sit in them and enjoy their scents, colours and other aspects directly; they may take pleasure in appreciating the design from afar. Sometimes a design must take both criteria into account, especially when the garden is predominantly to be viewed from above, when its overall plan will be very clearly perceived.

Located in a historic district just outside Fort Worth, Texas, this garden was created and built in tandem with a large, new house. The dual challenge was to make an inviting space that looked attractive from the upper level of the house overlooking it, and to ensure privacy from neighbouring properties.

The site was awkward to work with, and had to be levelled to eliminate its steep slope. At the same time, Harold Leidner dropped the height to create the impression of a sunken garden. To make the garden intriguing from above, he turned the long and narrow space into a box parterre or knot garden. The design includes a pool with multiple jets, 'infinity' ends and integrated planting; the peaceful trickle of the water fountains counteracts the noise of traffic from outside. There are shady areas in and around the garden pavilion in which to escape the Texan summer heat. The pavilion is equipped with outdoor cooking facilities and space to dine, making al fresco entertaining very easy.

From the vantage point of around the pool, the effect of a sunken garden is enhanced by raised beds set around the pool area. The beds are filled with brightly coloured herbaceous plants and shrubs, such as *Rosa* 'Double Knock Out' and azaleas. These offset the evergreen theme of the rest of the garden.

The parterre, softened only by a ruff of caladiums around a central box ball, accentuates the formality of the space. However, the curvilinear 'knot' pattern of the box does much to liberalize the otherwise strictly linear structure of the garden.

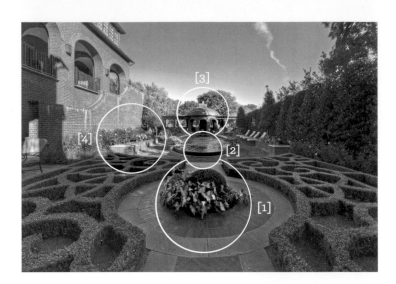

DESIGN INGREDIENTS

· Formality
· Contrasting colours
· Overhead view
· Screening
· Symmetry

[1] COLOUR CONTRASTS Even though the materials used here are not out of the ordinary, the combination of old red brick and Pennsylvania bluestone produces a striking contrast of colour. The bricks are laid out in a traditional herringbone pattern along the paths, and the circular arrangement around the central bed in the parterre is also conventional. The brick is faithful to the building material of the house, while the bluestone is used consistently throughout the space for banding, pool coping and step treads.

[2] RAISED POOL The pool, raised above ground level, makes a dramatic statement in the garden. Water jets arch gracefully from the edges towards the centre – a feature seen in Moorish gardens – to create an ambient audio backdrop. The central sections of the pool sides are coped to provide seating, while planted beds sit at intervals along the pool wall. It is not immediately apparent that, rather than being 'merely' ornamental, the pool is designed for swimming; one end is deep enough to allow diving, and both ends are designed so that water flows over the 'infinity' edges.

[3] SHADY PAVILION With summer temperatures in Fort Worth regularly approaching 100°F (38°C), a shady retreat is essential. The domed roof and flanking wooden pergolas strike an imposing note, and the interior features intricate brick detailing in the arches and columns. The pergolas support wisteria. To one side is an outdoor kitchen space. The pavilion is an important focal element of the design, terminating the garden and separating this section from the rest of the plot. The open structure allows views out beyond the property.

[4] RAISED BEDS The creation of a genuine sunken garden helps to shelter people sitting in it from wind, but it necessitates the expensive removal of a lot of earth. Rather than dig down, Leidner created the illusion of a sunken garden by raising the surrounding flowerbeds significantly above ground level. The raised beds, which are relatively easy to tend, create the intimate feeling of a sunken garden and raise plants closer to eye height, where they are more readily appreciated. In time, the back walls will be covered by climbing plants.

KNOT GARDENS

Dating back to the early Renaissance, the knot garden was a formal design based on a symmetrical motif and set within a square, often as four separate, but not necessarily identical, beds. Knot gardens are now associated with low hedges of box, but in Tudor times herbs such as germander, marjoram, thyme and rosemary were often used instead of box. One of the most famous knot gardens in England is at Hatfield House in Hertfordshire (see right). Over time it has come to feature typical close-clipped box hedges separated by gravel paths.

Concentric Circles

DESIGNERS PETER AND PAM LEWIS

COMPLETED 1990s

LOCATION DORSET, UK

WHAT KIND OF garden design is best for attracting wildlife and insects, especially the insects that benefit organic produce? There is plenty of advice available regarding the plants that attract specific insects – nettles to attract butterflies, for example – but less about the overall plan. Here, a circular design, allowing easy movement from one area of planting to another, was adopted on an experimental basis.

Pam Lewis and her late husband, Peter, came to Sticky Wicket, as the Dorset garden is called, with a dream of founding a smallholding. The project turned out to be a steep learning curve for them. The site is on a north-facing slope, and the soil was not favourable, but through determined effort they managed to create an inspirational garden.

Unhappy with the way that conventional agricultural practices in the United Kingdom were destroying natural habitats, the couple wanted to create a haven for wildlife as well as a garden. On an aesthetic level, Pam saw the design as an outlet for her artistic skills, using plant colour as her medium.

The plan consists of concentric circles of planting, starting tightly in the centre of the plot and gradually becoming looser and more random as the circles move outwards. The beds, containing nectar-rich plants whose heights gradually increase as the garden progresses outwards to the perimeter, are arranged like a dartboard around the central space, with the planting alternating with gravel paths. From the start, the guiding policy in the garden has been deliberately laissez-faire, and every season the garden has looked a little different.

Because the plant list is biased towards nectar-rich species, there is a predominance of single-flowered cultivars; less insect-friendly doubles are not on the menu, although a few exceptions are admitted, like the gloriously scented *Rosa* 'William Lobb'.

The photographed version of this garden (see left) has since been superseded, except for its underlying plan. Since Peter's death in 2004, Pam has moved on to an even more natural approach requiring less day-to-day maintenance. The colour scheme of silvers, pinks, blues and mauves is as strong as ever, but the central camomile lawn has given way to airy, gauzy, naturalistic planting. The garden is still evolving, retaining its essential structure, albeit in a more relaxed form.

DESIGN INGREDIENTS

· Focal point

· Ground structure

· Unity

· Rhythm

· Movement

[1] CAMOMILE LAWN Camomile (*Chamaemelum nobile*) is a good groundcover plant for sunny, open, free-draining areas, and can provide a low maintenance alternative to conventional grass lawns, especially in places where it is difficult to bring in a lawn mower. It will bear some foot traffic and imparts a fresh, appley fragrance when walked on. The cultivar *C. nobile* 'Treneague' is particularly suitable for lawn use; it requires no cutting, is fairly tolerant of dry spells, and it does not flower – an advantage for hayfever sufferers.

[2] CIRCULAR RIDGE At the outer perimeter of the camomile lawn, the planting gives way to low-growing thyme cultivars. A 'mini-dyke', or built-up ring of gravel, provides a freely draining growth area for these plants. In design terms, the circular dyke suggests a miniature ancient landscape, perhaps the imprint of an early defensive earthwork fort – an intriguing element. The 'ripple' of gravel signals a change of height in the planting, from the low-growing camomile in the centre to the taller plants found beyond the encircling path.

[3] GRAVEL PATHS The gravel walkways between the radiating beds provide a natural-looking backdrop to the planting. The plants, rather than being confined, are allowed to escape their bounds, and they easily root in the gravel's substrate. In those areas where escapees (and weeds) are not encouraged, a growth-suppressing, semi-permeable membrane has been laid under the gravel.

[4] MATRIX PLANTING The range of plants is limited, repeated often, and planted randomly, just as the plants might arrange themselves in wild communities. *Allium sphaerocephalon* and *A. cristophii*, violas, silver-grey artemisia, *Eryngium maritimum*, valerian and lilac phlox combine in a painterly mix that is a haven for butterflies, bees and other insects, while also being easy on the eye.

SELF-SEEDING PLANTS

Over the years, nature has increasingly been allowed a free hand in the garden, with Pam Lewis 'editing' the result when it goes a step too far. Many of the plants are self-seeding, which means that some species naturally come to dominate unless they are checked. Plants such as nettles, grown for their attractiveness to butterflies, are firmly confined to their own patch. The garden achieves soft curves, the colours melding as they do in nature. Wildlife is drawn irresistibly to the tangled haven of colour, foliage and scents.

Formal Lines

DESIGNER HELEN DILLON
COMPLETED 1970s
LOCATION DUBLIN, IRELAND

THE EXPRESSION 'formal garden' summons mental images of the classical gardens of Renaissance Europe, their strong axial lines echoing the symmetry of great houses, with parterres, topiary, clipped hedges and pools of water arranged bilaterally around their centre. But formality in gardens does not have to be on such a grand scale; it can be just as effective in smaller spaces, interpreted in a modern way.

Over forty years ago, Helen Dillon and her husband moved from London to live in a sedate Georgian house in Dublin. The new home had the effect of rekindling her appetite for gardening – one of her early jobs had been as an assistant at *Amateur Gardening* magazine. She created a distinguished garden whose design has metamorphosed many times over the years, and this, in turn, led to an illustrious career as author, journalist, broadcaster and lecturer on the subject.

As is the case with many Renaissance gardens, the Dublin garden was designed to be viewed from the drawing room of the house. From that perspective, the layout is clearly suggestive of the Moorish gardens of the Generalife at the Alhambra (see page 105) in Granada, Spain, although it does not feature the Generalife's well-known fountains. Looked back upon from the far end, its formality complements the graceful proportions of the house.

The garden now features a formal canal where once there was lawn. Bisecting the space, the canal is bordered by precisely cut, polished Irish blue limestone terraces, flanked by two wide borders brimming with abundant planting. One of these used to have a hot theme and was a riot of reds, oranges and yellows; the other was blue. Today they are equalized, their colour palette leaning towards cool. At the far end is a shallow, round pool, set before a screen of ivy- and clematis-clad arches that offer a glimpse of more garden beyond.

DESIGN INGREDIENTS

- Rhythm
- Proportion and space
- Symmetry
- Ornament
- Restricted colour palette

[1] AXIS OF WATER The canal, clearly the centrepiece of the garden, brings a palpable sense of drama, and, together with its crisply executed surround, strongly contrasts with the surging waves of plant textures alongside. It determines the basic design of the garden and formalizes its geometry. The change in the width of the channels plays with perspective and visually elongates the garden. The rectangular stepping stone in the centre of the smaller channel is the same width as the cascades linking the pools – an elegant touch.

[2] SHALLOW WATER FEATURE While on a trip to Morocco, Helen noticed the attractive effect of shallow water. On her return, she decided to reduce the depth of the circular pond at the top of the canal – it was originally 3 ft (0.9 m) deep. The water is now contained 3 in. (8 cm) below the surface of the terrace, and a small jet, surrounded by pebbles, causes it to ripple more beautifully than was possible before. The shallower pool is also of much greater use to the local bird population, which uses it for drinking and bathing.

[3] BORDERS Plants are repeated to create rhythm, and placed to get as much drama from the combinations of colour and texture as possible. Pale oriental poppies are pepped up with patches of magenta *Geranium* 'Ann Folkard' and silvery-blue *Eryngium giganteum*. These make way for pastel-pink wands of *Dierama pulcherrimum* and generous towers of cobalt delphiniums. Yellow and orange *Meconopsis cambrica* (Welsh poppies) add zest. Feathery grasses weave through the borders, swaying in response to the smallest breeze.

[4] PLANTERS Galvanized metal containers, sold as dustbins, make unconventional homes for *Allium hollandicum* 'Purple Sensation', with its spectacular pom-pom flowerheads, and clumps of *Hesperis matronalis* (sweet rocket). The plants are also used through the borders to fill gaps, although sweet rocket is best contained as it can be invasive. On a smaller scale, *Iris sibirica* (Siberian iris) sits in terracotta pots in front of the first pool, its azure summer colour bright against the pale paving.

[5] BOX PYRAMIDS On either side of the lower pond there is a box cone, sitting on a topiary square dais. The cones are not reproductions of three-sided pyramids but they provide an appropriate outline behind twin stone sphinxes, closer to the house, that face each other over the pond. In true formal style, these elements are placed symmetrically, with the sphinxes fulfilling the ancient role of such sculptures, that of guarding the terrace. The Egyptian touch is subtly reinforced by the presence in the pond of *Cyperus papyrus* (papyrus) – the sedge once used to make paper.

Lifestyle

Hot-Climate Rooftop

DESIGNER SECRET GARDENS

COMPLETED 2010

LOCATION SYDNEY, AUSTRALIA

ROOF GARDENS are an increasingly popular way of maximizing exterior space, especially in hotter climates where outdoor space is a valuable asset. These additional green spaces make a crucial contribution to the environment: absorbing rainwater, which helps prevent run-off and flooding, cooling down surrounding air, and providing natural insulation for buildings. They are also a welcome destination for birds and insects.

Twenty-nine floors up, spanning three levels, and set against a backdrop of uninterrupted views of Sydney's harbour and city skyline, this penthouse called for a spectacular outside space. The client wanted a low-maintenance place in which to relax, while incorporating ample space for entertaining. The result is striking, with ponds, walkways and a dedicated entertainment level topped off by a hot tub.

The dynamic design by Matt Cantwell of Secret Gardens gave the client everything he wanted and more: lush planting with comfortable seating and eating areas; extensive barbecue facilities; a hot tub; a cooling fountain, and a pond-water feature spanned by a walkway. Powder-coated steel spiral staircases connect the different levels, and a glass balustrade screens the perimeter of the space, providing shelter from blustery coastal winds without spoiling the view. The decking is blackbutt eucalyptus, selected for its hardwood qualities.

Roof gardens offer an excellent way of creating green living environments, important in urban areas, but building at height is never cheap or straightforward. There are some important factors to consider: the cost of an equivalent design at ground level is increased by about a third; wind has a desiccating effect on plants and can make the space uncomfortable to occupy; building regulations and load-bearing limitations can have serious ramifications on the design, and often the only access for materials is by a lift.

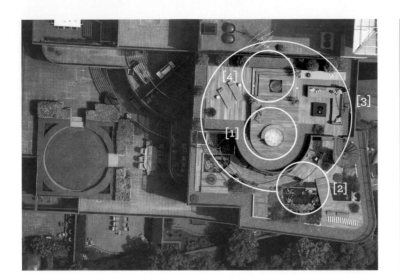

DESIGN INGREDIENTS

· Maximizing views

· Shelter from wind

· Robust building materials
and plants

· Load-bearing and access
implications

[1] ENJOYING THE VIEW With a roof terrace such as this, it is easy to take full advantage of the wonderful views to all sides. The hot tub has been perfectly placed to enjoy the bustle of life around the harbour during the day and its lights at night, as well as the occasional firework display. Other roof terraces may not enjoy such an outlook and screening for privacy may be required. Judiciously placed tall plants such as bamboo and phormium, trellis and screens, or shade sails will provide shelter from wind and the gaze of interested onlookers.

[2] EXPOSED PLANTINGS

The drying winds and overhead sun of this roof garden stipulated plants suited to the conditions. Drought-tolerant species were selected for their ability to survive without constant watering: among them are *Podocarpus elatus*, *Zoysia tenuifolia*, *Dracaena draco*, *Yucca elephantipes*, *Trachelospermum jasminoides*, *Dietes bicolor*, *Lomandra longifolia* 'Tanika', junipers and *Acacia* 'Limelight'. Mediterranean plants such as rosemary and lavender work well along with penstemons, erigeron and wind-resistant grasses.

[3] <u>HIGH LIFE</u> This Sydney city penthouse terrace spans three different levels, with the topmost level entirely dedicated to entertaining. The outdoor space has been comfortably fitted out with stylish all-weather seating grouped around a table, sun loungers in another area and an outdoor kitchen with barbecue which makes living outside a practical and extremely enjoyable experience. The addition of the hot tub, perfectly located on the topmost level to enjoy the stunning view, is perhaps the crowning feature.

[4] WATER ON THE ROOF

Water is always a welcome addition to any garden. An attractive water feature makes an effective focal point, and the sound of running water has a cooling, relaxing effect on the people there, and can help to block out unwelcome external noise. This Sydney roof garden boasts two water features: an elegant granite bowl with a small bubble fountain trickling into the underlying pool, and an informal pond surrounded by abundant planting, its surface scattered with water lilies. Without doubt, it is water that brings this urban roof terrace to life.

PEACE IN THE CITY

Another example of the work of <u>Secret Gardens</u> is this north Sydney roof terrace, which enjoys a superb view of Sydney Harbour Bridge and the city beyond. The garden has been given a completely different treatment. Simple, clean lines contribute to a more formal composition, with a circular grass lawn surrounded by hedging of *Buxus microphylla* (Japanese box). Topiary cones on either side of the circle frame the harbour views, while two lavender plants flank the steps to the raised seating area. The artificial turf is a welcome low-maintenance choice. Abundant planting around the sides creates a sheltered environment, necessary in such an exposed situation, while affording a degree of privacy.

Fireside Entertainment

DESIGNER SARA JANE ROTHWELL

COMPLETED 2012

LOCATION LONDON, UK

THE WORD 'FIRESIDE' immediately suggests a sense of home and family life, with loved ones turning away from the cold and sharing the unifying warmth of a fire. Gardens can seem inhospitable in colder months or at night, but the introduction of a fire makes al fresco living a more tempting prospect. In the past, garden fires were time-consuming to prepare, but today the fireside experience can start with the flick of a switch.

The young couple who own this north London property wanted an outdoor living space with a fireside warmth and focus that would suit their entertaining needs. Designer Sara Jane Rothwell faced a challenge when she was approached by them to 'make the most of what was left' of this small garden after extensive basement excavations had reduced it to a 36 x 16-ft (11 x 5-m) space. Her task was complicated by a need for access to the garden both from the basement, 10 ft (3 m) below the level of the garden, and from the raised ground floor.

An early consideration was that light was needed in the living space of the basement extension. This was achieved by installing a patio floor made of glass that extended over the living space. The glass was individualized with an etched fish motif.

The clients' requirements were met not only by the fireplace but also by a gas barbecue, which is now frequently used by the owners, whether they are entertaining or not. A rendered wall, topped with Balau timber to match the fencing, provides seating and divides the fire and barbecue areas to create more intimate spaces. Seating or dining furniture can be moved in and out of the space in front of the fire as required.

The planting is minimal and evergreen, reflecting the clients' wish for an outdoor room rather than a traditional garden. Maintenance workers, visiting weekly, keep it looking pristine, ensuring that the stone is jet-washed and that leaves are swept.

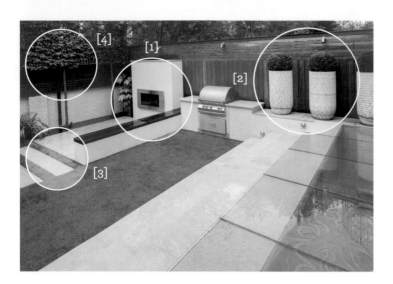

DESIGN INGREDIENTS

· Enclosure

· Demarcation of space

· Balance and scale

· Mass and void

· Economic use of space

[1] FIREPLACE Fire is a focal point in any outdoor space but here, instead of the usual bonfire, it appears in a fireplace, complete with a white 'chimney breast'. This particular product may be installed in any timber-framed construction, wall or masonry cavity. It runs on mains gas, which actually gives off heat, unlike bioethanol fuels, and it does not require a flue. A control panel at the side of the stainless steel fascia enables the user to ignite it at the push of a button, and adjust the flame height to suit the heat requirement.

[2] TALL POTS Three standing pots, each containing *Buxus sempervirens* (box) clipped into a ball, form a row to the side of the kitchen area, marking its border with the glass roof. They match the height and colour of the chimney breast and serve to break up the otherwise oppressive solid wood fencing. Their textured, grey-blue decoration also provides a contrast to the wood behind. The pots are made from glass-reinforced concrete (GRC), a very flexible and practical modern material used for furniture and sculpture as well as containers.

[3] ARTIFICIAL GRASS In keeping with the brief to keep the garden low-maintenance, the lawn is Astroturf. Artificial grass is becoming more popular because improvements in its materials and technology have made it seem more like the real thing. Some owners insist on real grass, but in a small garden of this kind the advantages of Astroturf are manifold: there is no need to mow, weed, feed, water, aerate or scarify it, and laying it in a tight space is a relatively simple matter, as is replacing any patches that have been dirtied or spoilt.

[4] NATURAL SCREEN To prevent the garden from being overlooked, a screen of pleached *Carpinus betulus* (hornbeam) is established along the rear boundary of the property. Local boundary height restrictions apply only to fencing, and the trees usefully grow to 5 ft (1.5 m) above the limit. Hornbeam retains its dead juvenile leaves in winter (though less so than beech), and it needs to be pruned in late August to encourage young foliage. Pleached hedging makes an elegant architectural statement in a garden of any size.

PALE STONE

Sawn sandstone is widely used in the space but Rothwell has prevented it from being an oppressive presence by choosing a light cream colour, which also counterbalances the surrounding dark foliage and green lawn. The treads through the lawn are cut wide to match the width of the bench planks and metal fireplace fascia. The use of broad planks minimizes unsightly grout lines. Directly ahead of the lawn treads is a polished-wood globe water feature resting on pebbles, a striking focal point.

Poolside Panorama

DESIGNER VLADIMIR DJUROVIC

COMPLETED 2001

LOCATION FAQRA, LEBANON

A WONDERFUL VIEW is a tremendous asset for any garden, but for the designer the challenge is always how to place the garden within that landscape to best effect. Here, a pared-back geometric layout neither competes with the landscape, nor attempts to mirror it; rather, it presents a frame from which to admire it.

At just over an hour from Beirut, this spectacular location, 6,500 ft (2,000 m) high on Mount Lebanon, provides extensive skiing during the winter months and enough sunshine for the other nine months of the year to live mostly outdoors. With exceptional panoramic views of the mountains and coastline, it is the ultimate sybaritic lifestyle destination.

The owner of this eyrie, an internationally fêted fashion designer based in Beirut, wanted a space to retreat to, but it also had to work as a venue for large-scale PR events. The designer he turned to was <u>Vladimir Djurovic</u>, whose Serbian father had moved to Lebanon in the 1960s; there has been constant international demand for Vladimir's unashamedly glamorous exteriors ever since he established his business in Beirut in 1995.

At the rear of the property are two terraces of pure white limestone. The upper terrace extends from the house's living areas and forms a strong indoor/outdoor relationship by continuing the internal flooring outwards. The lower terrace (pictured) consists of just two rectangles: one is formed by the pool, which appears as a mirror of water; the other is a platform that drops into two bench-like seating areas set around open fires.

The simplicity and restraint of Djurovic's design is emphasized by the elongated proportions of the terrace, and also by his trademark control of the materials and planting. Given that the view is the principal feature of the garden, he has established a synergy between the natural environment beyond the garden and the man-made one within it.

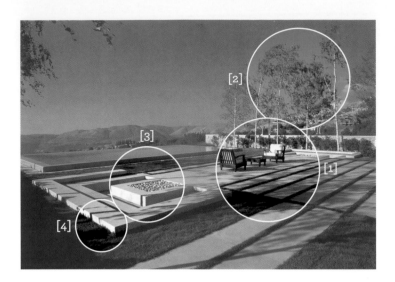

DESIGN INGREDIENTS

· Minimalism

· Rhythm

· Vertical accents

· Proportion and scale

· Context

[1] STONE AND GRASS On the lower terrace, set in front of the pool, bands of glossy white stone paving run the width of the terrace. The bands are separated and outlined by narrow stripes of grass that echo the grass surround of the pool. The transverse bands emphasize the width of the site and give the space rhythm. Aligned with the edge of the pool, they move the eye towards it and the view beyond. On the upper terrace, the bands increase in frequency as the visitor moves away from the house towards the landscape.

[2] PLANTING A key element of Djurovic's style is his moderation in the use of plants and materials. This garden contains no planting other than the rows of silver birch along the fences, the low shrubs used to clothe the walls in green, and the grass. The grass is used to emphasize the geometry of the design – just as box is used in baroque gardens – while the trees provide the only vertical elements, while also directing the eye outwards towards the view and framing it. Both the trees and shrubs soften the hard edges of a design that celebrates restraint at its centre.

[3] FIRES AND SEATING The lower terrace is bracketed by two raised tables containing pebbles. At the pressing of a switch, the pebbles transform into glowing gas fires, which immediately create ambience and warm the air on cold evenings. The fires capture the imagination, conjuring up heroic times and ancient powers; they are like giant beacons, set on the mountain to alert the rest of the world to some portentous event. The seating surrounding the fires is set below the surface of the terrace, which increases the fires' impact.

[4] LOCAL LIMESTONE The entire stone terrace serves as a viewing stage for the mountains beyond. In keeping with his formula of restraint, Djurovic used the local 'kour' limestone outside as well as within the house. While only one material was used, the designer varied the texture of the finish, depending on where it was placed and its function. The space gains much from the elegant, glossy, white stonework and its precise execution. Bordered by dark grass, the stone presents a stylish surface for the play of shadows.

GLOWING FROM WITHIN

At dusk, the garden comes to life with the aid of clever lighting, which creates a remarkably sophisticated nocturnal atmosphere. The lighting installation itself is completely concealed and incorporated into the stonework. Open fires punctuate the space, appearing as pools of light amid the muted glow of the highlighted stone. The different stone levels, including the seating areas, are cleverly illuminated to pick out their contours. Uplighters mark out the trees and boundaries, and lights within the pool create a glass mirror, giving the illusion of a much larger expanse of water.

Open-Air Living Room

DESIGNER WES & PARTNER

COMPLETED 2005

LOCATION HANOVER, GERMANY

THE NOTION OF the 'outdoor room' – a part or whole of the garden that is a useable extension of the home – has been prominent in garden design since the 1970s. But while designers often use common materials to establish visual links between inside and outside spaces, it is quite unusual for 'exterior room' details to closely mimic an interior decor and furnishings.

This penthouse flat in Hanover and the outdoor space attached to it are so similar in appearance that probably their greatest difference is the lack of a ceiling outside. The idea of executing the exterior room as literally as possible came from landscape architects WES & Partner, who like to work according to conceptual artistic principles. The garden furnishings closely mirror those of an interior living room: curtains, a white polished marble floor, a carpet and a wardrobe.

The original personnel at the WES practice in the 1970s came from an art background and focused on designing sculpture and art installations for commercial companies. They gradually moved into landscape design, with the team altering to include landscape architects. Today, the four partners who lead the outfit all contribute to projects, knowing that this will add a creative frisson to their work. Their projects are varied, but attention to the central concepts always distinguishes their landscapes.

The client in this case was an art collector who found the previous confusion of planting unsuited to the display of his sculptures. He liked the concept of an outdoor living room with a ceiling of starry sky, not just because it would make a perfect backdrop for his art, but because it would feel like an art installation. And indeed, the limited colour palette suggests a modernist painting, nearly monochromatic but with just a splash of bright paint. Extending the living space, the outside room acquires a new spatial and aesthetic dimension.

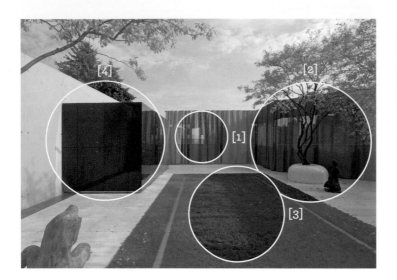

DESIGN INGREDIENTS

· Simplicity

· Humour

· Limited colour

· Allegory

· Unity

[1] **CURTAINS** At the back of the garden, half-screening the landscape beyond, are curtains that slide along poles, just as they would inside the penthouse. Moving gently with the breeze, they bring a kinetic dynamism to the space. Gaps in the wall behind them form 'windows' whose outlines are visible through the translucent, silvery material. The screening provided by the curtains is flexible, offering a filter between the environment and the garden space. As in an interior room, the curtains can be opened and closed as mood dictates – a rare facility to have available in a garden space.

[2] **SNOWY MESPILUS** The only horticultural detail that clearly demonstrates the garden to be an exterior space is a collection of multi-stemmed *Amelanchier lamarckii* (snowy mespilus) trees, set into bulbous, white planters. The tree species was chosen for the big contribution it would make at different times of the year. Producing a shower of white blossom in spring, it has bright green foliage that provides plenty of colour in the spring and summer, turning bright red in the autumn; in winter, the open habit of the twisting stems and bare branches provides sculptural, architectural shapes.

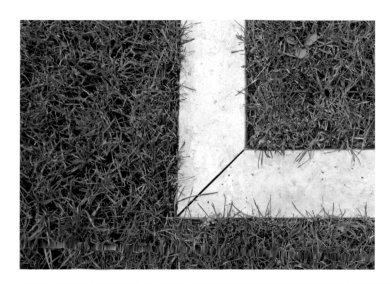

[3] GRASS CARPET The rectangle of turf contains an inner frame of stainless steel, which cleverly and instantly transforms it visually from an area of turf to an exterior carpet. At the same time, the steel rectangle suggests the markings of a simplified tennis court, leaving the viewer wondering what game the grass might be intended for. Like the trees, the grass is a horticultural element, but here it seems to belong in an interior space. The ambiguity of the grass is the central pivot of the concept of an outdoor interior space.

[4] CABINET A dominating feature in the garden, and one that adds the only colour apart from the natural greens, is a large cabinet set at the back in a far corner. The panels are painted with glossy red acrylic, which reflects light and offers a coloured surface for shadows. The sharp lines make a modernist statement, with the doors standing flush except for their 'handles'. The cabinet affords storage space that is accessible from the garden, while part of it is given over to a small bathroom, this time accessed from inside the apartment.

255

WHITE FIXTURES

Although the garden is not expressly designed as an extension of the interior, more as a separate room, its white crystal quartzite pavers link visually with the white marble flooring and window paintwork of the interior, providing continuity between the inside and outside spaces. The floor outside seems to swell upwards to accommodate the specimen trees, but the planters are actually made of glass-reinforced plastic (fibreglass).

Night Gallery

DESIGNER STEVEN KOCH

COMPLETED 2010

LOCATION GLENEDEN BEACH, OREGON, USA

WHEN NIGHT FALLS, most garden users are happy to seek indoor pursuits and return after the next sunrise. But a garden may be designed with the night in mind; it will still be a pleasant location in the daytime, but clever use of lighting and reflective materials transforms it into an exciting space, either for night-time socializing or, as here, as an innovatory showcase for sculpture. For the designer, the key was to exchange daytime colour and texture for a dramatic play of light and shadow.

This contemporary Oregon beach house is perched 200 ft (60 m) above Siletz Bay and commands far-reaching views of the Pacific Ocean beyond. To the rear of the house, nestled into the topography and sheltered from onshore winds, its courtyard is designed to showcase sculpture. The courtyard was given virtually no coastal outlook, but that difficult decision was made necessary by another overriding factor: the owner wanted to borrow the coastline's qualities of light, wind and water to display the sculpture in a fresh and stimulating environment, one that remained so after the sun had gone down.

The sympathetic and functional scheme by Steven Koch has as its pivotal design element a 60-ft-long (18-m) glass and stainless-steel gabion wall. By day it captures the sunlight and creates a glowing brilliance. At night it acts like a theatrical scrim: the wall appears opaque when objects in front of it are illuminated, but transparent or translucent when it is illuminated from behind. The dominating wall is balanced by several pieces of contemporary Asian sculpture, and a row of three maples also draws the eye away from the wall.

The cleanness of the space is emphasized by its being on a single level. Interest is created by contrasting surface textures and colours, with dark slate paving giving sharp, straight edges to a shallow pool and an area of crushed white granite. In contrast, a wavy-edged planted border seems to flow from the wall like a tide over the white granite.

Intriguing by day, the space comes alive at night when featured elements of the garden are lit from within, or uplit from below, casting shadows around in theatrical gestures. In rainy weather, the lights inside the property are reflected by the wet black slate. The property owner is an optical surgeon, and Koch was inspired by this fact to make the play of light the catalyst for the project.

DESIGN INGREDIENTS

· Enclosure

· Appeal to different senses

· Minimalism

· Mass and void

· Referencing the location

[1] WALL OF LIGHT For this design, Koch used a gabion wall consisting of slag glass kept in place by an open metal framework. By day, as the sun moves around the garden, light is captured by the glass and reflected out across the courtyard in prismatic splashes. The designer likens this effect to the sun reflecting off the breaking surf below the house. At night, lit from within, the wall seems to throb with light. The wall's mass appears to be suspended in the air, the result of its support structure being offset to the side.

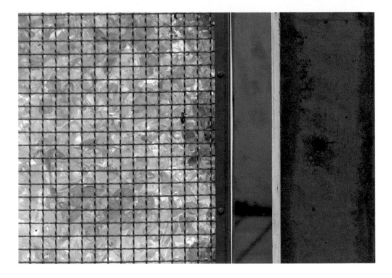

[2] FLUID VEGETATION The planted beds seem to flow into the gravelled area, carving a sinuous boundary like surf on a beach; they appear to freeze a moment in time. Only one species is employed. *Pachysandra terminalis* (Japanese spurge) is a useful, mat-forming, evergreen plant able to cope with most soils, even in exposed situations; although it prefers shady sites it can tolerate some sun. It has attractive foliage and produces tiny white flowers in early summer. It can be used, as here, to 'paint' areas of bare earth a vibrant green.

WATER AND LIGHT

At the far end of the space, illuminated water trickles down a copper-clad textured screen into a pool (see below), suggesting the sound of cascading waves. Three small jets punctuate the pool, bubbling up to different, low heights; they create white water that both looks and sounds like surf. Lit at night from below, the jets look like incandescent liquid candles floating on the water's surface. Combined, the waterfall and fountains help to instil a sense of serenity.

[3] **JAPANESE MAPLES** Three Japanese maples (*Acer palmatum*) were carefully selected as the architectural trees of the garden. Because they occupy isolated, conspicuous positions, it was important that they were good specimens and deserved to be highlighted. They were chosen for their graceful habit and richly coloured foliage, which, when illuminated at night, glows as if on fire. Thus, especially at night, the hot red of the acers brings a splash of colour to the otherwise muted palette of the garden. The acers, no less than the sculptures, are showcased by the neutral backdrop; indeed, visitors are likely to notice them first of all.

[4] <u>OUTDOOR GALLERY</u> The simplicity of the showcase garden design means that the works of art are housed and viewed in the most advantageous way. Here, two heavy, abstract, bronze sculptural forms are given a dramatic backdrop by the glass wall. Their reflective finish captures shafts of light of different colours, some of it from the wall and some from other sources, all playing on their curvaceous surfaces and ricocheting around the space. This was the artistic intent of the owner: to release the sculptures from the static lighting of a typical indoor gallery.

Kids' Play Area

DESIGNER BLASEN LANDSCAPE
ARCHITECTURE
COMPLETED 2005
LOCATION SAN FRANCISCO, CALIFORNIA, USA

CONVERTING A GARDEN or a backyard into a play area for young children usually entails the installation of unsightly plastic structures that the parents look forward to seeing removed one day. However, there are ways in which fun facilities for children can be provided without having to sacrifice garden style.

With the imminent appearance of twins, the owners of this three-storey, modernist house, set on the steep slopes of San Francisco's Buena Vista Heights, decided it was time to undertake the overhaul of their precipitous, weed-clogged garden. Their decision to bring in the husband-and-wife team Blasen Landscape Architecture was timely – the pair had just encountered the work of Japanese architect Tadao Ando and were inspired by his clean, smooth concrete walls and minimalist treatment of space.

The site was challenging, though: a steeply sloped wedge, 25 ft (7.6 m) at its widest point. The owners agreed that minimalism would work best with the house style and their interior design. The answer was to use every inch of the limited space, making any features an intrinsic part of the design and limiting the range of materials and design elements – colour, texture and form. It was key that the garden should look good from above. It was a breakthrough when they realized that the slope could be incorporated into the useable space.

At the lowest level, the children can race around, or build sandcastles in the sandpit. Laid mostly to lawn, this area also has a flowerbed for digging and planting edible herbs. To get up to the next level, the kids can climb a rope up a grassy bank or take the steps; to get back down, they can roll down the slope or use the polished concrete slide (there is a soft landing pad). Above, a bench cantilevered into a concrete wall provides an observation spot for the parents, but it is set back far enough to give the children a sense of their own space.

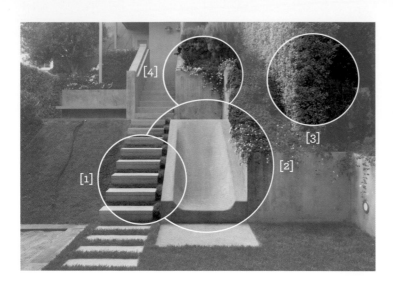

[1] **STEPS AND SEATS** Italian granite steps are sunk into the slope individually and appear to float, so the turf between each one causes a visual 'stop' and emphasizes the spacing of the paving on the lawn below; what results is a positive/negative optical effect. Viewed from above, the two features form a strong continuous axial track. Increasing the width of the treads meant that the steps could do double duty as seating, so there was no need for separate, space-consuming chairs or benches.

[2] **CONCRETE** This material has a continuous presence through the garden, ensuring that the different areas are connected. Walls support raised beds on the lower and middle levels, as well as up the slope. On the upper level, concrete bannisters turn a corner and form the back of a cantilevered stone bench. The polished slide is intrinsic to the concrete formwork wall, which gives it a basic, unrefined, architectural presence. The concrete is coloured to match the render on the house.

[3] VEGETATION SCREEN

Privacy from the neighbouring houses on both sides is provided by a double layer of evergreen plants, and this vegetation also helps to muffle noise from the surrounding streets. Two varieties of *Pittosporum tenuifolium*, one of them variegated (see in the left foreground) are arranged in stepped hedges up the slope; they rise to a height of 9 ft (2.75 m) and are kept well manicured all year round. On a larger scale, a tall yew and an architectural palm terminate the screen, adding contrast and interest.

[4] PLANTING

While concrete and grass are the main materials in this garden, the tops of the walls are softened by beds of trailing bedding plants and perennials. Their blooms – in a palette restricted to dark reds, purples and whites – and their differing foliage colours and shapes are set against the blue-green of rosemary and the pale grey-greens of the two varieties of *Pittosporum tenuifolium* that make up the hedge. The floral accents are minimal, yet in this predominantly green context they have an important role to play.

SOCIAL SPACE

The property's renovation is topped by a sunny roof deck that offers panoramic views of San Francisco. The smooth concrete used in the garden covers the boundary wall, too, and this is fitted with a fire and chimney to warm guests; logs for the fire are stored on either side of the fireplace. Low, wide benches, made out of a wood that matches the decking, offer plenty of room for people to sit back to back. Sculpted box plants and containers of dwarf olive trees and lavender soften an elegant setting that is designed for grown-up entertaining.

Outdoor Comfort

DESIGNER DANIEL KEELEY

COMPLETED 2012

LOCATION FAYETTEVILLE, ARKANSAS, USA

MOST PEOPLE LIKE to be comfortable in their gardens, but not everyone chooses to bring all the comforts of home outside. Living in a humid, subtropical climate, however, blurs the distinction between inside and outside; exterior spaces can function as interior recreation rooms, made all the more comfortable by TV and other facilities; but even here, garden plants still have a role to play.

At the heart of the city of Fayetteville in Arkansas lies Fayetteville Square, a charming English-style marketplace surrounded on all sides by listed buildings. Benefiting from this popular location is a luxury condominium that has almost as much space outside as inside, thanks to its large roof terrace.

The owners of the residence wanted to increase the appeal and functionality of the terrace, and transform the empty space into something really special; essentially, they wanted to maximize its potential for plush outdoor living. In addition to furniture for sunbathing, they envisaged facilities for cooking, dining, lounging in front of the television, and socializing. They called on Daniel Keeley, who appropriately describes himself as an 'exterior designer' specializing in making spaces for 'entertainment, escape and enjoyment'.

Logistics are always challenging when building gardens at a height. Equipment, materials and plants had to be brought in through the front door of the building, or be lifted up by crane.

Keeley addressed the issue of privacy by erecting fencing panels between the terrace and neighbouring properties; he also installed a long planter of box hedging to screen an unwanted view and lift up the sightline towards the distant Ozark mountains. Multi-stemmed trees in timber planters were set in the line of hedging to break it up and increase the sense of intimacy. The condo is a second residence, so maintenance had to be kept to a minimum. Even though the planting was restricted, the extreme exposure to sun and wind made an automatic drip-watering system essential.

Lighting is an important transformative tool, for both aesthetic and practical reasons. The floor of half the space was raised by a step to define different areas, and LED rope lighting was used to alert users to the step. Uplighters were incorporated into the planters, and spotlights were hidden in the hedging.

DESIGN INGREDIENTS

· Enclosure

· Multi-functionality

· Maximum use of space

· Reproduction of interior styling

· Screening

[1] SPACE DIVIDER Cleverly sited at the junction of two floor levels is a multi-purpose cabinet that helps to define the two distinct spaces. The cabinet is made of ipe wood and backed with semi-translucent plexiglass; lit from within, it provides a dramatic effect for night-time gatherings. For users on the lower, living level it houses a special, extra-bright, fully weatherproofed television; usefully, the cabinet is at drinks-bar height at this level. For users on the upper, dining level, the cabinet is at counter height.

ALTERNATIVE STYLING

Keeley was also commissioned to style the adjacent terrace. The brief was the same, but the execution completely different. The television is housed on a wall inside a cabinet; artwork by Fayetteville photographer Jake Aslin, printed on aluminium to withstand the elements, fronts the cabinet. The 'interior styling' is further emphasized by two exterior standard lamps; these are anchored against high winds by large granite bases.

[2] FURNITURE AND FABRICS

Because the design comprises more hardscape than plantscape, edges and surfaces are tempered by soft furnishings. The furniture was designed to be multi-functional: wooden sun loungers (see left) fold flat and serve as benches when not in use. Chairs swivel to allow television viewing, and the sofa cushions can be configured in different ways. The sofas are from the outdoor furniture specialist Ego Paris and are covered in 'sharkskin' marine vinyl material to withstand the elements.

[3] **FIREPLACE** In the lower, living area, a fireplace of innovative design forms a centrepiece between two sofas. Made of concrete and operated by remote control, it runs on natural gas and easily generates enough heat to take the chill off the evening air when socializing or watching television. Like several of the garden's facilities, it is adaptable and multi-purpose. In the warmer months, when heating in the evening is no longer likely to be required, it is converted into a coffee table by means of a custom-made stone top.

[4] **STONE PAVERS** Floating, loosely fitted quartzite pavers offer a cool and elegant walking surface. The variation in stone colour – with yellow hues mixing with blue, grey and white – changes the overall aesthetic, and visually stone offers possibly the nearest equivalent to an exterior carpet. The floating system is easy to install over an existing deck and allows water to pass quickly through to the drainage system below. Stone pavers require less maintenance than a wooden deck, and there is no risk of picking up a splinter when walking over them with bare feet.

Compact Kitchen

DESIGNER LUCY WILLCOX

COMPLETED 2010

LOCATION LONDON, UK

OWNING A TINY city garden would seem to be incompatible with the ambition of growing fruit and vegetables. When space is at a premium, few people are prepared to sacrifice it to store bamboo canes, fleece and other unsightly garden-allotment paraphernalia. But not all plants need such equipment, and some may be cultivated without the sacrifice of space needed for other purposes.

In rural areas, where sprawling gardens are far more common than in the city, space allocated to growing vegetables and herbs tends to be tucked away out of sight, with pride of place going to showpiece areas in which aesthetics takes precedence over practicality. City dwellers, even those who formerly grew their own food, rarely make food produce the focal point of their exterior space; mostly, they forego the edibles because they assume they do not have room.

The couple who moved into this Victorian cottage in south-west London previously lived in a flat. They had discovered a love of growing their own vegetables in window boxes, and they wanted to grow more. However, the back garden was a tiny plot, measuring only 20 x 13 ft (6 x 4 m), and they also wished for a comfortable environment for entertaining, with a barbecue and seating. Further, the pair had a young child, then still a toddler, so a safe space for play was also a top priority.

The couple asked garden designer Lucy Willcox to help them reorganize the garden into a more sophisticated space that would flow out from their sleek new kitchen and give the whole a harmonious, contemporary and airy feel.

Willcox could see no reason why fruit and vegetables should be banished; indeed, she made them into a prominent feature of her design. She installed staggered wooden planters, in which her clients now grow a wide variety of different crops. A sturdy shelf was also erected to hold pots of herbs and strawberry plants.

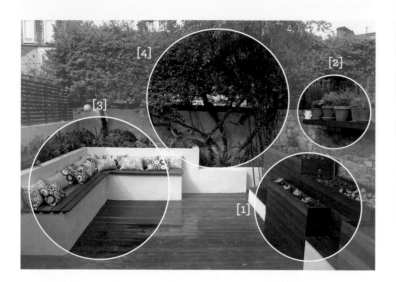

DESIGN INGREDIENTS

· Proportion

· Maximizing space

· Perspective manipulation

· Multi-functional

· Limited materials

[1] STAGGERED PLANTING

Planting boxes are established along the full length of the garden's right-hand wall. Willcox maximized the planting space by placing the planters in tiers and staggering them on several different levels. Rather than looking disjointed, they appear as an integrated unit, running seamlessly along the stretch. There are spaces for different crops, like salad leaves, aubergines, tomatoes, beans and beetroot, and near the house there is a bin in which potatoes are cultivated in sacks of growing medium.

[2] TERRACOTTA POTS On an

upper shelf, terracotta pots are filled with herbs, including rosemary, chives and parsley. Terracotta is ideal for planting herbs, as, unlike plastic, it is porous and allows the soil to breathe, while retaining the warmth of the sun. Here, among the pots of herbs, strawberry plants offer a splash of colour. Strawberries are an easy fruit to grow in a kitchen garden; they do at least as well in containers as in the ground and, elevated to a sunny spot, they will thrive if supplied with plenty of water. Nets may be required to protect the fruit from wildlife.

[3] BUILT-IN SEATING The seating on the left-hand side is an integrated extension of the raised beds, a brilliant space-saving tactic. Breaking up the vertical boundary planes, the planting behind the seats has been lifted into the light. The construction is deliberately simple, with white, rendered walls and ipe timber seats that reiterate the decking. The timber seats may be lifted to access storage areas beneath. Bright cushions introduce contrasting highlights into the scheme and invite visitors to take their ease.

[4] LIVING SCREEN At the foot of the garden, existing pyracantha shrubs were tidied up and shaped to provide a dense evergreen screen for privacy from overlooking houses. The trunks of the trees twist and weave across the white back wall, making a contrast with the dominantly horizontal planes of the rest of the newly renovated garden. On either side, slatted screens are erected above the boundary walls. The open slats allow more light into the garden and promote a sense of privacy without turning the garden into an oppressively enclosed space.

OPTIONS FOR CHILDREN

In an easily supervised spot just outside the kitchen door, there is a small, sunken sandpit. When not in use, it may be covered by a flush-set lid, fitted so cleverly that it practically disappears into the deck. The lower steps beneath the vegetable beds are at a perfect height for young children to sit, and one is slightly higher than the others to give flexibility as the children grow. The clients, hoping that the children will come to share their interest in growing plants, let them stand on the steps to 'help' with the vegetable and fruit production, so there is an educational element to the garden as well.

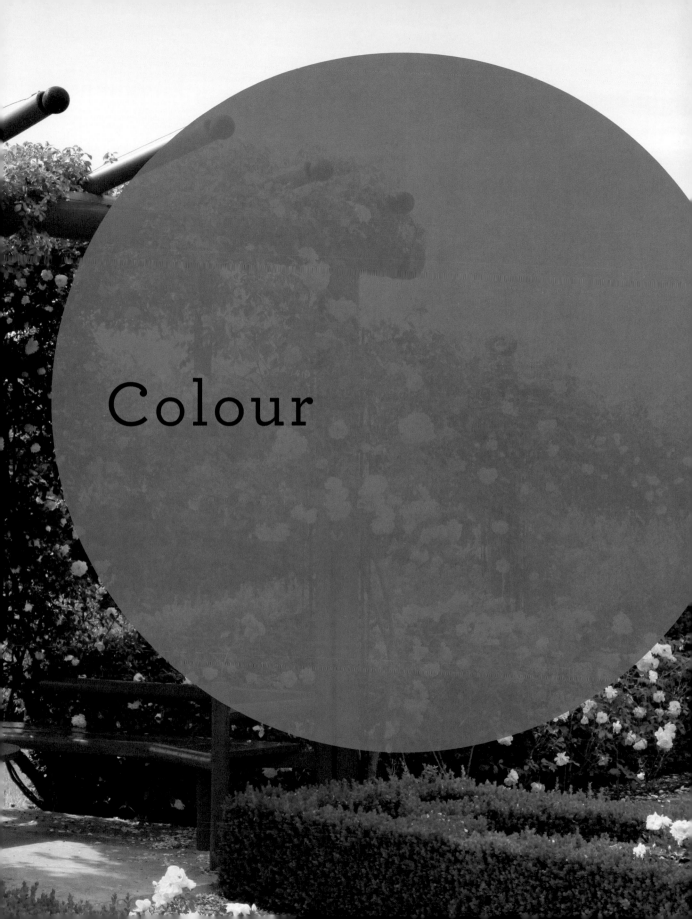

Colour

Pure White

DESIGNERS GILLES AND PATRICK SERMADIRAS

COMPLETED 2004

LOCATION SALIGNAC, FRANCE

WHAT IS COMMONLY called a 'white garden' is usually created with a palette of white flowers offset by a variety of foliage colours: green, blue-green, grey or silver. The effect is calming and restful, and uplifting, too. In the West, white flowers are associated with purity and innocence, births and weddings, and those ideas undoubtedly influence how white gardens are perceived.

Over five centuries, twenty-two generations of the same family have lived at Le Manoir d'Eyrignac, and during that time the 10-acre (4-ha) garden around the handsome 17th-century stone manor house, nestling in the heart of the Périgord Noir, has undergone many changes. Today, the garden is best known for its elegant topiary sculpture.

Designed in the 18th century in the French style, the first gardens were completely revised in the 19th century as an English landscape park. But in the 1960s, Gilles Sermadiras, father of current owner Patrick Sermadiras, decided to restore the original style; pride of place was given to topiary in the spirit of the Renaissance, with forms shaped from yew, box, hornbeam and cypress tracing the site's original layout. There are *parterres de broderie* (intricate, embroidery-like parterres), garden chambers and box enclosures; formal avenues of sophisticated topiary reveal enticing vistas.

As in many traditional French gardens, the palette is subdued; instead of borders bursting with colour, evergreen planting offers a year-round presentation of a great many shades of green. Patrick Sermadiras seeks to preserve traditional methods of clipping by hand, and shears and lines are used to maintain the gardens precisely.

In 2004 a further colour was added to the Eyrignac palette, in the shape of a new White Garden It is the perfect complement to the existing garden, whose green topiary is a contrasting backdrop to the white floral abundance. With its lively water features and bridal gaiety, the White Garden brings charm and a change of pace to its corner of the estate.

In gardening, as in painting, white is hard to mix with other colours because it jumps to the fore and overpowers everything else, although less so if it is kept light and frothy. It is a romantic colour, especially when used as it is at Eyrignac, and it is perfect for evenings or shady spots because it is the last colour to fade out of sight in the dusk.

DESIGN INGREDIENTS

· Unity

· Contrast

· Structure

· Year-round interest

· Formality

[1] WHITE ON WHITE The compartments of the parterre are filled by the compact, spreading *Rosa* 'Noaschnee' (in France: 'Opalia'). Beyond, the climber *R.* 'Iceberg' reaches above the timber posts set around the garden and clambers over the chain catenaries slung between them. Further into the summer, the later-flowering *R.* 'Albéric Barbier' carries on the show. Roses maintain the white theme for most of the summer, while in spring the white is provided by bands of snowy tulips, hyacinths and narcissus.

[2] FROG FOUNTAINS Five ornamental ponds representing the five senses are set in a quincunx (four points set in a square with a fifth point in the centre). The central pool features four large bronze frogs, with water gushing high in the air from their mouths. The sculptures were inspired by the famous frogs at the Latona fountain at Versailles. The angle of their water jets is particularly impressive and brings a great energy to the space. The four corner ponds are contained by star-shaped topiary hedging and each has a single water jet effervescing at its centre.

WHITE AT SISSINGHURST

Probably the world's most famous white garden is at Sissinghurst Castle in England (see right). Designed by Vita Sackville-West in the 1930s, it is a romantic enclosure crammed with English cottage-style planting. As with many white gardens, the commitment is not just to plants with white flowers, but also plants with silver leaves. Although the eye is met everywhere by white flowers, the effect is not overwhelming. It is generally true that simple colour themes produce less visual 'stress' than mixed colours.

[3] ANDUZE VASES The central pond is approached by four allées or paths, laid to a cross design. A pair of tall terracotta Anduze vases stand at the junction of each path with the path encircling the pond, one at each side. Since the 17th century, the vases have been made near Alès in the Gard region. The role of the vases here is to bring a clear visual close to each approach path, while also supporting displays of white flowers at a raised height. In season, the urns overflow with white surfinias and frothy, shell-coloured *Gaura lindheimeri*.

[4] RED LACQUER Providing a strong contrast with everything else in the White Garden, all the timber in the space – the uprights for the rose catenaries and the furniture at the end of the paths – is lacquered red. The theme is set at the top entrance to the garden by a giant red Japanese torii gate, traditionally a marker of the transition from the profane to the sacred. The red is a reminder of the sort of objects to be found in gardens in the 18th century, when 'Japonisme' was fashionable. The bright colour injects visual gusto and lifts the space from being just 'an elegant garden'.

Jet Black

DESIGNER CHARLOTTE ROWE

COMPLETED 2007

LOCATION LONDON, UK

COLOUR COMBINING can sometimes be tricky to get right in the garden. Do the various shades complement each other? Is it tending towards gaudy? It is easy to see the appeal of stripping back the paint chart and keeping things simple. Black may seem a radical choice of colour scheme for a garden, but here is an example of black working extremely well with natural planting.

This residence in Fulham, south-west London, belongs to a fashion designer and it was important that the aesthetic of the garden equalled that of the house. Flowing out from the minimalist interior of the living area, the garden echoes the interior palette of jet black and dark grey. This creates continuity and establishes the garden as another 'living' room, only outside.

Charlotte Rowe utilized a combination of dark-coloured hardscape materials and planting to form the background of the garden. Granite surfaces, tongue-and-groove boundaries and stained oak decking mimic the interior, while the planting palette was limited to keep the effect uncluttered. The choice of materials and plants also means that the garden is low-maintenance and provides interest throughout the year.

The garden would not work without some relief from the dark tones, so highlights were introduced in the form of silver-leaved, clear-stemmed olive trees (which also contribute vertical structure), loose tussocks of the acid-yellow grass *Hakonechloa macra* 'Alboaurea' and white flowers: *Hydrangea arborescens* 'Annabelle' and the climbing evergreen *Trachelospermum jasminoides*. Purple-flowered *Salvia nemorosa*, *Allium* 'Purple Sensation' and *Tulipa* 'Queen of Night' reinforce the black theme.

The relaxed planting around the boundaries also serves to soften the edges of the hard landscaping, presenting a pleasing contrast. The garden particularly comes alive at night with clever lighting, a combination of subtle spotlights and dramatic uplighting.

Choosing a black colour theme for your garden is a bold decision. The fact that the garden is small, 42 ½ x 16 ½ ft (13 x 5 m) means that it could have felt sombre, even gloomy. However, elegant lines and restrained planting have contributed to a well-proportioned and stylish space.

DESIGN INGREDIENTS

· Restricted planting palette

· Proportion and balance

· Well-positioned lighting

· Contrasting forms

· Complementary materials

[1] ACID-YELLOW ACCENTS

The black elements of planting are brought by *Phyllostachys nigra* (black-stemmed bamboo) and *Ophiopogon planiscapus* 'Nigrescens' (black mondo grass), the latter carpeting the beds around the olive trees. Punctuating the density of this darkness, bursts of lime green and acid yellow achieve a fantastic contrast. Rowe fulfils this with the frothy, yellow flowers of *Alchemilla mollis*, the bright gold grass *Hakonechloa macra* 'Alboaurea', and the lime-green stems of *Cornus stolonifera* 'Flaviramea'.

[2] MATERIALS

The minimalist palette – a combination of dark-stained oak decking, lighter grey granite paving and polished black pebbles – works admirably. If Rowe had used one type of material, of one colour only, the result would have been relentlessly dull. The juxtaposition of the varying shades of greys and blacks, together with the different textures of the materials, provides the garden with added interest as well as depth. The materials reinforce the black foliage of the planting, and effect a near seamless transition from house to garden.

[3] <u>SEATING</u> The oval terrazzo table and the matching curved benches are carefully chosen for their colour and simplicity. Their solid build sets the tone of the design, grounding and balancing it. The pieces are also reassuringly heavy, which instantly suggests quality. Terrazzo is a mix of reconstituted marble, granite, cement and water, and this table was produced by Cadix UK. The weather-resistant terrazzo furniture can stay in place year round, providing an opportunity for spontaneous outdoor dining.

[4] BALANCED PLANTING
In this small garden, the planting, although restrained, works really hard. Everything is there for good reason. The olives have been chosen to add repetition and vertical accents to the space, as well as for their silver leaves, which stand out from the darker background. The black mondo grass in the beds beneath anchor the trees and reinforce the blackness, while the looseness of the planting behind, as well as the contrasting colours it provides, sets off the formal lines of the trees perfectly.

281

MUTED BLACK GARDEN

Rowe's black palette is not for the faint-hearted – something more subdued might be preferred. Another creation from the designer (see right) is contemporary with clean lines and a fairly formal structure, but it is not as extreme. Here, Rowe has used polished black pebbles and a similar type of paving, but in this instance the drama is modified by lusher planting, more understated furniture and willow-hurdle fences. A clever detail may be seen in the exaggerated gaps in the paving, planted with *Soleirolia soleirolii* (mind-your-own business).

Glowing Ochre

DESIGNERS ERIC OSSART AND ARNAUD MAURIERES

COMPLETED 2000

LOCATION UZES, FRANCE

OCHRE IS A CLAY pigment that occurs naturally in sand; its colours vary from yellow to deep orange or brown, although the word commonly refers to a warm, reddish yellow. In the vernacular architecture of countries such as Morocco it is often seen in the colour of walls of rammed earth. Whether or not true ochre clay is used, the colour of ochre can be a beautiful backdrop for a garden.

The owners of this property in southern France commissioned Eric Ossart and Arnaud Maurières to transform 2½ acres (1 ha) of orchard into a contemporary space where they could enjoy their sculpture. It is now one of the best-known contemporary gardens in the country, full of opulent planting, pools, rills, shady courtyards, perfume and colour. The minimalist backdrop of ochre-coloured cement and gravel brings a glow to the garden, even when the skies are overcast and dull.

The property was named 'Noria' after an ancient Arab irrigation device, a sort of water wheel, that turned up in a nearby field. Learning of this was possibly the starting point for the design. Ossart and Maurières were moved to capture the spirit of Islamic paradise gardens and the courtyard garden architecture of Moorish Andalucía – as seen at the Generalife in Granada, for example. But the Islamic approach is brought firmly into the present with a definite nod to the modernist gardens of Luis Barragán, the celebrated Mexican architect.

The garden has an oasis-like quality with cooling water and lush plantings. A grove of pomegranate trees, lavishly underplanted, lines a long pool that is connected to a rill. At its opposite end the pool is fed by another rill that descends vertically down a concrete wall. A series of linked rooms provides a succession of sensuous spaces through which the visitor can wander. The garden is symmetrical and formally arranged, but softened with relaxed, exuberant planting that fills the air with scent.

Vibrant Blue

DESIGNERS JACQUES MAJORELLE, THEN
YVES SAINT LAURENT AND PIERRE BERGE

COMPLETED 1930s

LOCATION MARRAKESH, MOROCCO

IN BRIGHT SUNLIGHT, green and blue-green plants can be offset to electrifying effect by buildings and hard landscaping painted in a bold and zingy blue. Even on a dull day there is something uplifting about the combination of two colours that, according to an outmoded dress code, should never be seen together. Supplementary hard-landscaping colours can intensify the effect.

Visitors experience a sense of excitement when entering the hidden world of Le Jardin Majorelle in Marrakesh. It is like returning to the exoticism of the Arabian Nights, a tranquil haven, realms away from the dusty pandemonium of the streets outside.

In the 1920s Jacques Majorelle, a respected and successful artist, moved from Paris to Marrakesh, where he created the dazzling garden that would become his most famous work. His passion for plants was all-consuming and he filled the space with collections of cacti, exotic plants and trees, setting these against a backdrop of vibrant ultramarine that he formulated and patented as 'Majorelle Blue'.

The garden proved to be a financial drain, so in 1947 he was forced to sell off parts of it and open the remainder to the public for an entrance fee. After he left in 1961, the garden was abandoned. It was in a state of disrepair by the time the fashion designer Yves Saint Laurent and his partner Pierre Bergé bought it in 1980 and set about restoring it.

The garden covers nearly 2½ acres (1 ha), and, apart from a formal square fountain and its long rectangular canal, it has a very relaxed structure. Colour is the overriding feature. Blue, easy on the eye yet bold and dramatic, dominates the scene, from the walls, fountain and ponds to the villa-studio. There is relief in the flashes of yellow from planters and details on the building. The garden experience is very sensuous, with the ultramarine backdrop absorbing the sharp Moroccan light and throwing all the elements into soft silhouette.

DESIGN INGREDIENTS

· Inspiration from surroundings

· Bold use of colour

· Retreat from the bustling exterior

· Exotic planting

· Islamic motifs

[1] MAJORELLE BLUE The culture of Morocco was the inspiration for Jacques Majorelle to create and trademark the colour 'Majorelle Blue'. Perhaps he was influenced by the cobalt-blue Moroccan tiles or the intense pigment of lapis lazuli. He used it first to paint his studio (now a museum), but he gradually went on to paint everything – gates, pergolas, walls, ponds and fountains – in this vivid colour. The luxuriant green foliage stands out against the blue, which almost vibrates with energy.

[2] LAVISH PLANTING Majorelle was an enthusiastic amateur botanist and he introduced new varieties of plants from all around the world. Cacti, palm trees, bamboos, coconut palms, thujas, weeping willows, carob trees, jasmines, agaves, white water lilies, daturas, cypresses, bougainvilleas and ferns all combine to create a 'cathedral of shapes and colours'. Stumps and towers of spiky cactus offset tall, waving fronds of palm and showers of flamboyantly coloured bougainvillea.

[3] OASIS ATMOSPHERE Water has always been an essential factor of Islamic garden design, and in dry countries the lavish use of water was clearly symbolic of a ruler's power and generosity. Islamic gardens are often characterized by long rectangular pools, connected by channels from which the sounds of rushing water can be heard. Here, a raised rectangular pool and fountain are set within a much larger rectangular pool at ground level. Echoing the fountain, a little water trickles from the upper level and splashes into the large pool.

[4] YELLOW HIGHLIGHTS
Le Jardin Majorelle was designed as a garden of contrasts. Paths meander into cool, shady sanctuaries overhung by soaring palm trees and lush tropical foliage, then open out into bright spaces filled with cacti. Here, blue-painted groundwork is offset by a flamboyant group of bright yellow planters. The choice of yellow gives an impression of sunlight entering the shady space. Yellow is also used to highlight details of the villa-studio, notably ornamental pillars and exterior ceilings.

VILLA-STUDIO AND PERGOLA

The juxtaposition of the blue-painted villa and the garden gave Majorelle and his modern successors opportunities to establish vistas of contrasting colour and texture. Here, a small, ornate window with a bright yellow surround is set off by a white plaster frame carved into lacy patterns – a Moroccan technique known as *gebs* – and then by the blue of the villa wall. The window looks out onto an adjacent pergola, built from brick piers and surmounted by a turquoise-painted open wooden roof supporting wisteria. Between the villa and the pergola are large floor tiles in deep red. A bed of *Monstera deliciosa* (Swiss cheese plant) that runs beneath the full length of the pergola provides further colour contrast.

Warm Orange

DESIGNERS PATRICK WYNNIATT-HUSEY
AND PATRICK CLARKE
COMPLETED 2007
LOCATION BRIGHTON, UK

THE INTRODUCTION OF ORANGE into a garden always has the psychological effect of making it seem warmer than it actually is. But orange can have another useful effect, this time on a more visual level. In small gardens, where the design challenge is to disguise the lack of space as much as possible, vivid orange can be used as a form of distraction, to trick the eye and create the illusion of something much larger.

This project offered a lot of challenges to the designers, Patrick Wynniatt-Husey and Patrick Clarke. The site was a steep, scrubby, unuseable slope carrying ancient brick walls that were in very poor order. Then there was a specific brief from the client: she wanted an extra 'room' that made a strong statement and reflected the interior of her house; the garden had to be somewhere sheltered where she could relax; the space needed to be robust enough to withstand the enthusiastic attentions of her dog, and it should require only minimal maintenance.

What the duo managed to achieve was to turn the small space – only 16 x 20 ft (5 x 6 m) – into everything she wanted. The use of orange was just one of several clever visual tricks that they used to make the garden seem much larger. Breaks in the vertical and horizontal surfaces were introduced to act as visual punctuation, slowing down the passage of the eye around the site. By forcing the viewer to take a longer time in considering the space, the designers artificially extended it. The planted area in the centre also interrupts the visual flow by creating a vertical axis in the central section.

The garden boasts a clever, space-saving design feature that is unsuspected by the onlooker. The garden was raised to a higher level than the house, with its rear level being extended towards the house. In the void below the garden there is useful storage space, accessed via a trapdoor in the deck.

Steps leading from the house to the garden level were made steep to prevent them from intruding too far out into the space. The risers were painted black instead of being clad in stone or wood, to conceal the steepness and make them recede from the eye.

The level of the garden is raised to a perfect height to make it fully visible from the kitchen window. Orange tiles on the kitchen walls link visually with the external orange walls, providing a satisfying link between interior and exterior.

[1] BURSTS OF ORANGE

The garden faces east and is not particularly sunny, so the bright panels of orange add flashes of colour that really brighten up the space. Orange also serves as a brilliant foil for the planting (mostly evergreen black and green), while in winter the leafless branches of the feature tree, *Aralia elata*, stand out starkly against the colour. Having orange panels breaking up the wood-clad walls was one of the designers' tactics to cheat the eye into perceiving the space as bigger than it actually is.

[2] CONTRAST PLANTING

Near the centre of the garden is a colour contrast that stands out from the greens and orange of the rest of the garden. Against the brown of a rusted-steel water feature, itself a unique element in the garden, is a bed of *Ophiopogon planiscapus* 'Nigrescens' (black mondo grass). The black leaves and violet-to-white blooms of this species are increasingly popular with gardeners, although sometimes it is confused with cultivars of *Liriope muscari* (monkey grass or lily turf). Black mondo grass turns a deeper black during winter.

[3] VERSATILE FEATURE

This little water feature has several aesthetic functions in the garden. Its simple cube shape sits well within the surrounding geometrically clean lines, while its rusted Corten steel flatters the orange walls and the hardwood decking, also linking the two. When it is activated, a water spout provides a soothing sound and creates ripples, resulting in plays of light across the water's surface. Without the fountain, the surface becomes a still mirror for everything around it, most noticeably the orange walls.

[4] **VARIED SEATING** Very simple and effective, two concrete blocks that may be used as seating are arranged in a staggered fashion on the decking. They tuck in behind the water feature (see at top) and mimic its shape. Each seat has a corner sawn diagonally from its base, giving it 'edge' and turning it into a strong graphic statement. Supplementing the blocks, there is a bench at one side of the garden (see right). Its steel frame is covered by wooden slats that seem to replicate those of the decking beneath it. The effect is pleasingly neat, uncluttered, connecting and harmonious.

SURFACE DETAILS

The garden surfaces, both vertical and horizontal, are cleverly designed to make the space seem larger. The decking on the ground frames square blocks of sawn Yorkstone paving. The hardwood decking is continued vertically as a screen for the boundary walls. Rectangular openings in the hardwood slats reveal large expanses of orange-rendered wall. As the eye travels along the surfaces, its movement is slowed by these disruptions to the continuity; the brain interprets the slowed pace as an increase in physical space. The hardwood boards are split into smaller widths than usual, both on the ground and on the walls – another optical slowdown device.

Calming Green

DESIGNER JACQUES WIRTZ
COMPLETED 1989
LOCATION ANTWERP, BELGIUM

GERTRUDE JEKYLL (1843–1932), garden designer and lover of colourful borders, once wrote that 'green is also a colour', a reminder that the green structures that support flowers are as significant as the flowers themselves. Indeed, green is not a single colour but a multiplicity of tones and hues, from olive to chartreuse, that are versatile enough not to clash when they are combined.

Green, a colour associated with calm, comfort and rest, is known to be more relaxing than any other. This garden, the work of landscape gardener Jacques Wirtz, is, in its marked neutrality of colour, a nod to the style of 17th-century virtuoso landscape architect André Le Nôtre.

The structural basis of the garden is a *patte d'oie* or goose-foot design, with allées radiating from a central point. In between the paths are 'wildernesses' of verdure, and at each corner of the rectangular garden space are beds laid out with embroidery scrolls of clipped beech.

The garden has a Renaissance character on paper, but 17th-century gardens are symmetrical and formal, and this garden does not entirely conform. Patrick Taylor, author of *The Wirtz Gardens* (2011), writes of the 'wild regularity' of this garden, saying:

'Pure symmetry in a garden can be oppressive. In gardens it is the general suggestion of symmetry, challenged here and there by irregularity, which so often gives excitement and tension.'

The property, sited in woodland, is surrounded by *Quercus robur* (English oak), *Q. rubra* (red oak), beech and Scots pine. A canal runs around the boundary, enclosed by stepped hedges of clipped beech, and a path backed by pleached hornbeam. Where the canal turns at a right angle, the beech ramparts form a circular island, towering up and topped by hornbeam, like a great green wedding cake. The play of light and shade emphasizes the tiers and their different leaf textures.

· Perspective trickery

· Limited colour palette

· Twist on history

· Texture

· Symmetry

· Theatre

[1] **CIRCULAR ISLAND** Bordered by water, an extraordinary island of tiered beech hedge is the climactic feature of the garden. It is set on a circular plot, with mown turf covering the shore and meeting the water. The outer side of the beech hedge is sculpted into four tiers with inwardly sloping sides. A circle of pleached hornbeam trees stands high above, the trunks pruned clean to give the joined canopy a surreal, floating appearance. The formal elements of the island are countered by beds of reeds in the water, a modern touch.

[2] **PARTERRES OF GRASS**
Ornamental grasses – the low, pinkish *Pennisetum alopecuroides* and the tall, golden *Molinia caerulea* – offer a textural contrast to the adjacent mown grass lawns and the shaped trees. In the traditional Renaissance garden, between the radiating 'toes' or allées of the goose-foot design, there would have been either parterres with clipped box edges or *bosquets* (lines of clipped trees). Here, Wirtz has introduced a modern twist on the Renaissance garden; the structure is formal, but the planting is loose and has a slightly tousled appearance.

[4] **STILL CANAL** It is in Wirtz's use of water that he comes closest to the work of André Le Nôtre. The formal canal that runs through the property is straight-edged; its precisely angled shoreline emphasizes that the waterway is man-made. The use of water, bordered by closely mown turf, pays homage to Le Nôtre's masterworks of baroque garden design, such as the Grand Parterre of the Château de Chantilly, where two enormous parterres, consisting of only grass, gravel paths and pools, are divided by a broad expanse of water.

[3] <u>DOMES OF BEECH</u> Bringing a full stop to the apex of each bed, at the point where all the paths come together, is a beech clipped into the shape of a tall dome. The beeches' symmetrical regularity affirms the formality and equilibrium of the design. Their foliage provides another green hue in the summer; during the winter months, the leaves turn golden-brown but stay on the branches, becoming a completely different focus of interest, not only for their contrasting colour but also for the filigree openness of their structure.

CLOUD-PRUNED BOX

In 1969 Wirtz bought a brick house for his family, alongside which was an abandoned vegetable garden bordered by badly neglected box hedges. Rather than replace them, Wirtz cut out their dead wood and encouraged new growth by judicious pruning. Using the Japanese technique of *niwaki*, or cloud-pruning, he transformed the broken-down hedges into cloud shapes (see right). The garden is now an awe-inspiring fantasy of topiaries, billowy box and meandering, curved hedges.

Shocking Pink

DESIGNER STUART CRAINE
COMPLETED 2006
LOCATION LONDON, UK

THE NOTION OF USING bright colours for some or all of the hard landscaping in a garden has gained favour in the 21st century. Painted backdrops might not be to everyone's taste, but they make a bold statement. There is really no limit to which hues can be chosen, as long as the completed garden is a pleasure to contemplate.

The shocking pink that gives this London garden an almost tropical air was actually the idea of the client. A regular visitor to Morocco, she was smitten by the vibrancy of the colours used there. She had fallen in love with the cobalt theme of Le Jardin Majorelle in Marrakesh (see p. 286) and was inspired to make an equally striking statement in her own garden.

Bold colour is normally reserved for sunnier climates than that of England, but here the leftfield choice works brilliantly. The principal reason is that both the plants and the additional hard landscaping materials have been expertly chosen to complement the pink; the execution of the construction is also faultless, and the overall design is practical, contemporary and dynamic.

The client wanted to divide the garden into distinct areas, each with its own function and character, and Stuart Craine found a perfect design solution. Immediately beyond the house is a very grown-up and sophisticated space; the upper level is hidden from view from below and offers the benefit of a separate area for entertaining; and beyond that is a children's play area. Craine maximized the use of space with a layout and design that finely balances each of those different elements.

While rural gardens often 'borrow' from the landscape beyond, urban gardens can work better as a continuation of the interior of a building. In this case, the colour theme extends from that of the internal furnishings. The uplifting and useable space cleverly overcomes its rather gloomy east-facing and shady situation. Above all, it cries 'welcome!'

DESIGN INGREDIENTS

· Different levels

· Maximizing available space

· Continuity with interior

· Multi-functional

[1] POWERFUL BACKDROP The pink used for the walls is probably the brightest that a colour can be in a garden, and some would avoid it for fear that it would overwhelm the planting. But this design demonstrates that it can work well on at least two levels. Firstly, it provides a brilliant backdrop for the plants, causing them to 'pop out' and display their various forms and textures to best advantage; secondly, the colour flows out from the house, taking its cue from the interior fabrics and upholstery and extending the interior outwards.

[2] HARMONY AND DISCORD As if the pink of the stonework were not shocking enough, Craine has introduced more pinks in the planting, both to clash and harmonize with it. Placed in planters bounded by dazzling white stone, *Azalea* 'Hinomayo' mimics the paint, while *A.* 'Orange Beauty' bravely clashes to good effect. Evergreen plants line the walls and sides of planters while emphasizing the different levels. When the hard landscaping is potentially so prominent, plants have an important role in balancing, softening and drawing the eye away.

[3] GEOMETRICAL SHOWPIECE

Against a bold expanse of pink wall, only lightly obscured by a trailing rose and other plants, the vibrant green of a large cube of *Buxus sempervirens* (box) punctuates the central space. The box cube has almost the status of a free-standing sculpture, and, with pink above, below and all around, it seems to float in the space. The crispness of the styling is reinforced by the transparent screen of steel and glass behind. Evoking the glass case of a museum, this gives the cube the appearance of an exhibit.

[4] WATER FEATURE

For such a small garden, this water feature might seem outsized and disproportionate. Designers tend to shy away from including large features in limited areas for fear of making them seem cramped, but here the vivid pink might overwhelm if there were nothing strong to balance it out. This large silver rectangle does the job very well; laminated with silver leaf, the vertical metal façade really comes into its own at night, shimmering and glowing as a thin veil of water flows over its textured surface.

[5] LINKING STAIRCASE

There is a 6 ft 6 in. (2 m) difference in height between the garden's levels. To negotiate this, the staircase cunningly takes two 90-degree turns. The stairs are hidden to prevent them from becoming too prominent, with risers painted pink to help them blend in with the walls. The stairs link an upper level that makes the most of the available light levels – the garden is east-facing and shady – with a lower level that is generous enough not to feel claustrophobic. The stairs provide separation between the various practical functions of the garden.

Hot Red

DESIGNER HASSELL STUDIO
COMPLETED 2013
LOCATION MELBOURNE, AUSTRALIA

THE TRADITIONAL complementary pairings of primary colours with secondary colours, described since at least the early 18th century, are red–green, yellow–violet and blue–orange. In a garden context, where green naturally predominates, red hard landscaping is a logical choice, both for its complementary status and for its power to attract attention, as long as it does not overwhelm.

This garden, part of a network of living roofs at the Burnley Campus of the University of Melbourne, was created as a dynamic demonstration for students of the possibilities of rooftop gardens. What might be unexpected is that the space is at the cutting edge of garden design. It is true that its primary function is to demonstrate planted-roof techniques, but it is also a pleasing space to experience. The designers, Hassell Studio, made the bold design decision of using red, realizing that interest in the garden would help to spread the university's eco-message.

The University of Melbourne started researching 'green' or 'eco' roofs in 2006. Up until then, most of this sort of work had been conducted in cool parts of Europe and the United States, rather than in Australia, where water-shortage issues prevail.

The benefits of green roofs, especially in urban environments, are manifold. The most pertinent is their effectiveness at slowing down storm-water run-off from buildings, which helps to prevent flash flooding during sudden downpours. Excess water can then be collected and recycled usefully. Their insulating properties improve the environmental performance of buildings by reducing their energy consumption. Another attribute is that each one essentially creates a new habitat.

This roof garden is not only a demonstration area, but a place of ongoing research into plants, substrates and water behaviour. Visitors can observe the performance of the plants at close range, thanks to a timber walkway that circles around the space.

DESIGN INGREDIENTS

· Unity

· Colour

· Symbolism

· Multiple levels

· Journey of the senses

[1] CLOSE-UP PLANTING

The randomly shaped planters, bordered by glossy, red painted steel cladding, appear to float above the other planting in the garden. The red tallies with the red ribbons wandering around the space. Hassell Studio designed the space to be interactive, with numerous opportunities to engage with the planting and the ecological concepts that it represents. The central islands increase these opportunities by raising the planting to more accessible levels, as though on the stage of a microscope.

[2] RED RIBBONS

The network of bright red lines threads whimsically through the garden, sometimes tying together certain experiences, other times highlighting particular experiments. The pattern formed by the powder-coated, custom-fabricated steel ribbons and central islands was inspired originally by the shapes detectable in a cross-section of a plant's cell structure. The bright ribbons and their unpredictable courses combine with the snaking wooden paths to slow down the visual and physical experience of the garden and encourage closer examination.

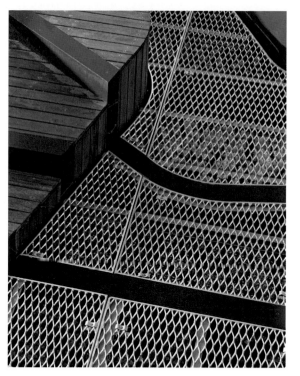

[3] HORTICULTURAL POSSIBILITIES
The garden explores the potential of sustainable roof-garden planting in Australia. Roof gardens must accommodate not only a layer of growth medium but also facilities for watering and drainage. The roof level changes by increments of 2 in. (5 cm), which increases the depth of the substrate. The success of different species grown in different substrate depths can be quantified, taking into account the often hot and dry conditions.

[4] GRATING WALKWAY A steel open-mesh walkway provides a durable, permeable surface for walking, while simultaneously allowing light to pass through to a protected area of low-lying succulents and other mat-forming plants beneath. The material reinforces the industrial character of the garden, as well as being a functional component. Just as the red elements of the garden contrast with the green planting, so too the red ribbons make a graphic statement against the silver of the mesh.

[5] UNDULATING PATHWAYS
The raised areas of the walkway provide different opportunities for impromptu classes about the garden's ecology. The varied width, depth and vertical cladding of the pavement delivers integrated seating for students in front of areas that might be discussed. Predictability is avoided by introducing a section of steps on one side of the garden – their changes in height highlighted with red – while on the other side, changes in height are achieved by gentle ramps. The overall aesthetic effect of the garden is that of an abstract work of art.

Primary Colours

DESIGNER MARTHA SCHWARTZ

COMPLETED 1991

LOCATION SANTA FE, NEW MEXICO, USA

GARDEN DESIGNERS tend to be concerned with creating spaces that sit well in the surrounding natural environment, both in the materials used for the hard landscaping and in their choice of plants. For most clients, though, to blend in completely leaves something missing. What they require is a strong personal reference that shows the garden to be an expression of their identity.

The client's modern adobe house sits on the brow of a hill, with spectacular, panoramic views of the New Mexico Badlands and the Sangre de Cristo Mountains. The surrounding desert landscape radiates warmth, the bare terracotta soil littered with juniper bushes and pinyon pines.

An artist and collector, the client wanted a garden concept that made a statement about her artistic sensibilities, but at the same time expressed something of the local Spanish vernacular. She commissioned landscape architect Martha Schwartz to draw up the plans. Responding to the location, Schwartz came up with an outward-looking series of relaxed spaces for taking advantage of the views, together with a contrasting and conspicuously ordered sunken courtyard area (see right).

Golden gravel covers the floor of the courtyard, whose details are informed by the colours of the landscape and the house itself. The space is divided by an orthogonal series of rills, each clad in different coloured tiles. Where they intersect, they disappear beneath four square fountains; nine crab apple trees in square or round beds occupy the voids in between. Geometry is the story here: a series of squares, circles and lines arranged in a simple grid.

The garden, while contemporary in style, draws on the ancient Islamic tradition of paradise gardens. Enclosed to exclude the wild lands beyond, these often feature water moving around the garden in geometrically arranged rills – just as it does in this garden's crisscross, multi-coloured framework.

DESIGN INGREDIENTS

· Enclosure

· Pattern

· Non-conformism

· Drama

· Geometry

[1] COLOURED RILLS

Intersecting the sunken space are four rills, tiled in the three primary colours of red, blue and yellow, together with green (which in some colour systems replaces yellow as a primary colour). In each of the rills, a contrasting colour is used for the tiled inner lining. The colours raise the design to a conceptual level by introducing an apparently artificial element into an environment where flowering plants would normally provide colour. The primary colours thus provoke an emotional reaction.

[2] LIGHTING

At night, when the bright colours of the tiles are obscured, their role is taken over by exterior lighting. Most magical in their effect are the fountains, which are lit from within. Like the rills, each is a different colour, with the metal sides of the pools appearing as blocks of blue, red, yellow and green light. The effect is bold but strangely soothing. In addition, the nine trees are lit from above, each by its own 'shepherd's crook' downlight. A set of steps are defined by lights, the lamps casting a welcoming flood of light from beneath the veranda.

[3] MARBLE COVER A collection of large, white, marble rocks covers the soil at the base of each tree, defining the bed in which it grows. Even though the rocks are randomly shaped, they are arranged with a pristine, geometric edge to form either a circle or a square. Because there is no pattern to their placement, they resemble a giant game of tic-tac-toe. By day, the up-pointing white rocks contrast strongly with the golden gravel surface, and at night they appear to glow.

[4] RUNNING WATER Four raised brick plinths, their colour echoing the adobe walls of the house, each contain a square water feature consisting of a single jet of water. The warm red brick picks up the colour of the gravel surface, while contrasting with the coloured rills. The coloured metal panels that line the pools (and which feature strongly in the lighting scheme at night), enhance the sound of the tumbling water. The wide plinths provide useful seating on social occasions.

[5] ILLUMINATED STAIRCASE A series of lights set at ground level in a blue-washed wall signal the presence of the only stairs that lead out of the sunken garden. The single access point gives a sense of confinement, reinforced by a metal grid fixed to the inside edge of the staircase. There is no way of seeing out of the garden, and the design is completely detached from any exterior influence. The atmosphere is not oppressive but there is an elicited tension, which serves to enhance the sense of drama experienced during the climb to the upper areas.

Urban

Compact Front Garden

DESIGNER ELLEN KNOEFF-VRIEND
COMPLETED 2006
LOCATION TILBURG, NETHERLANDS

URBAN FRONT gardens are often hard to turn into spaces to enjoy because of their lack of privacy. Where privacy is not an issue, however, the main design task becomes to maximize the functionality of the space. If the front garden is compact, the focus should be on meeting the client's practical needs in a way that does not compromise the integrity of the design.

Part of a new development in southern Holland, this residential property is set on a rectangular plot. The area is divided in two lengthways, with the house occupying one long half. The remaining half comprises two areas of garden, front and back, separated by a central section of living space that is part of, and juts out from, the residence. Sliding glass doors on both sides of this extension give access to the two gardens, and the living space can be opened up to take advantage of both garden areas. The arrangement creates a blurring of the internal and external boundaries.

The task of styling the two gardens fell to landscape architect Ellen Knoeff-Vriend. She saw the appeal of being surrounded by garden on two sides, and therefore decided to treat the two gardens as one. This would provide continuity and a feeling of being within a green space when indoors. To compound that impression, she included plenty of plant material, creating vertical layers of contrasting textures and colours.

Deep red detailing on the vertical walls and a number of free-standing planters lifts the dominating scheme of black, grey and brown surfaces. Bluestone paving is used throughout, promoting the 'living inside and outside' ethos.

Marking the boundary to the street in a subtle, unobtrusive way are tall, narrow, translucent etched-glass panels. With gaps between them to allow light through, they add to the feeling of space without a significant loss of privacy.

DESIGN INGREDIENTS

· Unity

· Rhythm and flow

· Vertical accents

· Limited colour palette

· Balance of mass and void

[1] TWO WATER FEATURES

Behind a rectangular raised pond, which mirrors the sky between the waterlily leaves that float on its surface, there is a fish-filled canal at ground level. The canal appears to run directly from the front garden, under the living-room extension, and out into the back garden. The device connects the two spaces visually – especially when the fish are seen on both sides. Next to the canal, a raised, red-painted concrete wall mimics the surround of the raised pool; it houses three simple pipe spouts that empty into the canal.

[2] PERGOLA

A single-span steel pergola stretches across the garden, dividing the space and framing the dining area. The black finish of the steel looks contemporary and is picked up by the black of the chair-seat material. Knoeff-Vriend has grown *Wisteria sinensis* up the pergola from both ends. The climber's attractive leaves shroud the metal during the growing season, while in early summer the overhead beam drips with its gloriously scented, lavender-coloured blooms. The pergola creates a 'room within a room' that offers additional seclusion.

[3] BOLD PLANTING White, snowball flowerheads of *Hydrangea arborescens* 'Annabelle' look stylish against the backdrop of a gabion wall. In the context of this small garden, the hydrangea makes a strong, confident statement, the more so for the closely planted, shiny-leaved grass beneath. The wall consists of basalt rocks crammed into metal gabions (cages), which are wired together to make a relatively instant and inexpensive boundary. Here, the basalt-filled gabion wall is similar in appearance to a dry stone wall, but gabions are flexible and any heavy filler can be used in them.

[4] CLIPPED TREES Two specimens of *Fagus sylvatica* 'Atropunicea' (a copper-beech cultivar) stand side by side, their laterals clipped to make neat column shapes. On the opposite side of the garden, *Catalpa bignonioides* 'Nana' is grown as a standard tree, just like the back-garden specimen (see below, right), its crown pruned into a tidy sphere. Although space was tight, Knoeff-Vriend managed to introduce a few trees to provide height and depth of field, especially when viewed from inside the living-room extension. Contrasting leaf colour distinguishes the vertical planes of planting.

THE BACK GARDEN

By opting to treat the two gardens as one, Knoeff-Vriend has achieved a flow through the living space and established a cohesive relationship between them. In the back garden (see right), a standard catalpa tree mirrors a specimen on the other side of the house. Other elements are repeated in both gardens, creating harmony but not symmetry. For example, a raised bed with red sides reflects the raised, red-sided pond in the front garden.

Industrial Roof Garden

DESIGNERS SUZIE GIBBONS, MHAIRI CLUTSON
AND JULIE WISE

COMPLETED 2012

LOCATION LONDON, UK

WHEN SEEKING to buy a property with a roof terrace, almost the first consideration is the view. Why spend money renovating a rooftop when the reward is to endure an ugly vista? There is, of course, the option of screening out the view entirely, but that detracts from the enjoyment of an outside space. The ideal is to find a view that is appealing, and a terrace space that is large enough for family or friends to enjoy the view together.

The views of London from this roof terrace garden, sitting atop an early Victorian house, were straight out of *Mary Poppins*. In addition, there was a constantly changing, 360-degree spectacle of sky, clouds, weather and light. Although the terrace space itself was flat, it was awkwardly pierced by three chimney stacks. In its favour, the roof terrace was large (60 x 30 ft/18 x 9 m), structurally sound and able to take the necessary load. Seeing the roof garden's potential, photographer Suzie Gibbons and her husband disregarded its nasty roof tiles and bitumen blisters and bought the house.

The couple tackled the renovation themselves, with help and advice from two garden designer friends, Mhairi Clutson and Julie Wise. The first job was to make the space safe for themselves and their small child by installing a hedge of *Prunus lusitanica* (Portuguese laurel) backed by galvanized steel-mesh fencing. They built a conservatory with access from the floor below, and disguised an ugly sloped roof with sedum planting. Timber decking was laid over the old roof tiles, and the chimney stacks were painted brick red to provide a vertical contrast with the sky. An ingenious water feature was designed around the central stack, with a cascade feature on one of its wide faces.

Exposed areas of mesh fencing are screened with an upright grass, *Calamagrostis* x *acutiflora* 'Karl Foerster', through whose stems the light now filters attractively. Timber furniture, which tones in with the decking, is arranged around the space. Planters full of evergreen plants, such as *Trachelospermum jasminoides* and *Magnolia grandiflora*, occupy the more sheltered corners for year-round presence.

The garden is now a natural extension to the rest of the house. The screening prevents it from being overlooked, without blocking the views altogether – a compromise that makes the terrace a very comfortable and sheltered place in which to relax.

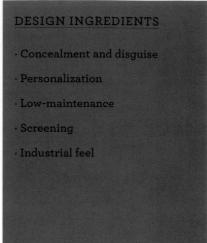

· Concealment and disguise

· Personalization

· Low-maintenance

· Screening

· Industrial feel

[1] SEDUM SLOPE Disguising the sloping roof of the access stairwell presented a challenge. Gibbons was told that the angle was too great for a green roof to work properly, and that anything over twenty degrees would cause problems. But with the planting area properly framed with ridges to prevent slippage, and with adequate drainage and irrigation, the oblique bed of sedums has been a success (such slopes should always be oriented towards the light). The unusual and eye-catching feature helps to balance the expanse of deck.

[2] WATER FEATURE The chimney stack in the centre of the terrace has been fitted with rusted steel cladding, which conforms to the industrial styling of the other landscaping materials in the garden. The stack now stands in a rectangular reflective pool, and Gibbons designed an unusual zigzag of runnels to cascade water down one of the faces. The angle of the runs mirrors that of the adjacent stairwell roof slope, with its planting. The water feature was inspired by one seen by Gibbons years ago in a garden at RHS Hampton Court Palace Flower Show.

[3] FOUND OBJECTS The terrace's hard edges and industrial detailing are softened by found objects that personalize the space and add interest. An old ship's bell hangs from the steel mesh fencing, and a collection of marine debris – driftwood, pieces of coral and a rusted ship's hurricane lamp – decorate the table. Random rusted metal objects have been made into sculptures, complemented by metal planters and a weathered watering can.

[4] SPECIMEN PLANTS Variation in the boundary height, set by the mesh fencing, is introduced by tall plants such as this *Betula utilis* var. *jacquemontii*, a silver birch variety that is fairly resistant to the exposure of the open and elevated site. The species was selected for its particularly good bark which, before it peels, is very white. The young tree is underplanted with a robust sedge, *Carex comans* 'Frosted Curls'.

[5] UPVC CONSERVATORY
Locating it by the opening of the access stairwell, and painting it gunmetal grey for an industrial feel, the couple installed a conservatory made from UPVC (unplasticized polyvinyl chloride – a rigid, chemically resistant form of PVC). UPVC is a practical choice for structures such as this because it is light, requires little maintenance and offers good insulation. UPVC is not normally chosen for its aesthetic properties, but Gibbons cleverly concealed the 'plastic' look of the building; the grey paint suggests a metal construction.

Concrete Basement

DESIGNER MASAYUKI YOSHIDA

COMPLETED 2000

LOCATION TOKYO, JAPAN

BASEMENT GARDENS are notoriously awkward, especially for growing plants. The lack of light is an obvious problem, but areas adjacent to houses also tend to sit in a rain shadow, limiting their exposure to natural rainfall; the building itself often imposes further limits on irrigation. However, cheerful planting is exactly what is needed outside the windows of a dark basement, and there is no need to be stuck with a bare wall.

The owners of this Tokyo house had been using their dimly lit basement room for storage, but they had come to think that it was time for the room to be converted into an attractive and practical space. The pivot on which the project depended was whether the ugly space outside could be reworked into a pleasant, inviting one.

The tiny basement space was bounded to the rear by a slope, albeit an extremely sheer one, rather than a vertical wall. The owners thought that this offered some possibilities, so they called in landscape designer Masayuki Yoshida to undertake the challenge. The designer transformed the space by creating a staggered, stepped arrangement of beds to maximize their exposure to light, especially in the upper garden, and allow as much light as possible to reach the lower levels.

In total there are nine different planting areas on seven levels. Simple materials are assembled together; concrete, timber and plants are presented to each other in ways that generate contrasting textures and colours. At the base of the steps there is a drainage trough, covered by a grating concealed with a collection of white quartz pebbles; the white stones add another distinct material to the mix.

On entering the basement room, the view out is immediately engaging, although the top tiers are hidden by the frame of the large glass door. Moving closer to the glass reveals the upper scene, which is overlooked by a crowning cherry tree.

DESIGN INGREDIENTS

· Seasonal themes

· Contrasting materials

· Simplicity

· Unity

· Structural balance and interest

[1] WOODEN SUPPORTS

Reclaimed railway sleepers define the stepped beds and create a definite, sculptural shape. The sleepers are not only laid horizontally to make the ledges and borders of the beds, but also driven vertically to separate different areas on the same level and give some verticality to the design. Most of the uprights are set in pairs, one tall and one shorter, which gives a sense of three-dimensional depth to the beds. The arrangement is at once solid and elaborate.

[2] **SPRING BLOOMS** In spring, the flowering cherry at the top of the slope dominates the look of the planting. To complement the pinky-white blossom, the designer picked the early-flowering *Astilbe* x *arendsii* 'Venus' for its perky pink floral plumage; this was placed in the topmost tier of the step garden. Further down the steps, a caladium leaf blushes in tribute. Japanese gardens are generally not known for their use of flowers, but here the designer decided to challenge traditional horticultural practices.

323

[3] JAPANESE TRADITION High above the garden, a reed screen creates a traditional Japanese backdrop for the flowering cherry, defining its shape. It also acts as a lighter-hued climax at the top of the steps. In spring, *Prunus* 'Shogetsu' bears clusters of pink blossoms so heavy that they present their faces downwards towards the room. The height of the planting in the top bed is deliberately restricted so that the plants do not compete with appreciation of the cherry tree. *Hanami* – the viewing of cherry-blossom – is an important part of the Japanese cultural calendar.

[4] WALLS OF WHITE CONCRETE
Bordering the garden, the tall walls were made of white poured concrete, which retains the indentations of its formwork. The concrete may seem a stark, industrial frame for the restrained planting, but in design terms the walls stand in a simple vertical plane, offering a counterbalance to the visual complexity of the stepped, horizontal and vertical timbers. The garden has a strong dynamic; the weighty structural arrangement of walls and timber is balanced and softened by the planting, which looks delicate in its forceful context.

SEASONAL PLANTINGS

Masayuki Yoshida provided designs for each of the four seasons. At the start of each new season, most of the old planting is lifted and replaced with completely new plants, just as bedding plants are replaced in the West. The pinks and whites of the spring planting are replaced in summer by stronger hues (see left), with scarlet *Ixora coccinea* making a splash among begonias. In autumn the garden becomes purple, while in winter it is an evergreen show with red highlights.

London Modernist

DESIGNER TOMMASO DEL BUONO
AND PAUL GAZERWITZ

COMPLETED 2008

LOCATION LONDON, UK

THE DEPARTURE of children from a family home is usually, for the parents, a signal to revisit parts of the house and garden previously given over to them and find interesting new ways to use the space. The process may require a radical and total transformation, but more usually the changes are moderated to preserve some reminders of the family phase just passed.

St John's Wood in north-west London is a sought-after area of Victorian stucco villas lining leafy streets, and spacious, stylish terraces. Few of the gardens are correspondingly spacious, however, and most conform to a standard rectangular pattern.

The design duo Tommaso del Buono and Paul Gazerwitz were asked to assess an overgrown garden that had long been abandoned as a play area, but which the owners now wanted to transform into a chic sanctuary in which to relax with friends. This garden was an ungainly shape, 115 x 30 ft (35 x 9 m). It required a balanced design that prevented the garden from looking long and narrow. As their children had left home, the clients felt at liberty to ask for an adult space that reflected their own taste for contemporary elegance.

Challenges came in the shape of several existing trees that the clients wanted incorporated into the design: a *Betula pendula* (silver birch), an evergreen *Magnolia grandiflora* (southern magnolia) and a large London plane (*Platanus* x *hispanica*). The garden also sloped quite substantially, a factor that the designers addressed by introducing stepped levels rather than by levelling the slope entirely.

Perhaps the most important element of the design was a new pavilion. Inspired by the design of Mies van der Rohe's Barcelona Pavilion – one of the most iconic examples of modernist architecture – it is located at the end of the garden to serve as a flexible working or living space. The designers were aware that the garden needed to reflect both the style of the house and the new garden pavilion, effectively drawing the two together.

The design exemplifies restraint throughout: the geometry is uncomplicated, and the simple plant palette is deliberately restricted to hardy, reliable plants with a strong, evergreen structure to minimize fuss in such a constrained space. The evergreen components make sure that the garden looks as good in the winter as it does in summer.

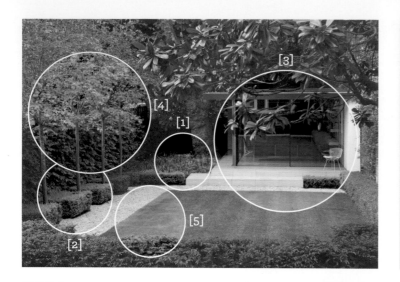

DESIGN INGREDIENTS

· Limited palette

· Strong geometry

· Unity

· Rhythm

· Asymmetry

[1] FLOWERING CARPET Del Buono and Gazerwitz wanted to create a green, flowering carpet that would appear as a calming 'sea' when viewed from the pavilion. They specified plants that would thrive in the consistently inhospitable, dry and shady conditions beneath the plane tree. These included *Pachysandra terminalis* 'Green Carpet', *Galium odoratum* (sweet woodruff), *Helleborus orientalis* 'White Lady' and *Epimedium* x *youngianum* 'Niveum'. The key factor in the choice was that they are all woodland plants.

[2] GREEN FRAMEWORK Hedges form structure and delineation in the garden without impeding the view. Different plants are used to achieve contrasting colour and texture. Yew at the end of the terrace creates an intimate space for entertaining, while a long, low and continuous box hedge on one side balances low cubes on the other side, between the trees. Behind the trees, deciduous hornbeam hedging provides contrasting seasonality; its structure is also looser than the close-clipped box and yew. These green elements provide unifying scaffolding for the space.

[3] MARBLE STEPS The terrace by the house, the wall behind it, the plinth surrounding the pavilion and the steps leading down from the pavilion to the garden are all paved with travertine marble. This material provides a clean, contemporary finish, and the repetition of its use at both ends of the garden pulls the design together. The steps were necessary as a means of eliminating the garden's pronounced slope. More than just a practical expedient, they make a strong, attractive, horizontal feature. A modern touch is introduced by replacing part of the lower step with low box hedging.

[4] SCREENING TREES Seven tall *Amelanchier arborea* 'Robin Hill' trees provide a screen on the south side of the garden, which was overlooked. The cultivar was selected for its multi-seasonal interest: spring blossom, attractive summer foliage and autumn colour. Planting them at an equal distance one from another has given a rhythm to the space, and their forms lead the eye down towards the end of the garden. The rhythm is emphasized below the trees by cubes of box set between them; the gaps left between the trees and the box cubes help to make the garden look more spacious.

[5] CONTEMPORARY LAWN Normally Del Buono and Gazerwitz would not specify a lawn for such a small garden, as the grass is difficult to keep looking good year round in an urban environment. But the client specifically requested it, and because it is really pristine, it appears as an inviting, smooth, green carpet that complements the formal lines of the planting. The pearly quartz gravel path harmonizes with the travertine marble but is distinctly lighter in colour, and it also contrasts well with the evergreen planting and the lawn. The whole look is harmonious and unified.

Natural Rock

DESIGNER PETER BERG

COMPLETED 2008

LOCATION ETTELBRUCK, LUXEMBOURG

WHEN A GARDEN site is scattered with rocks, people often build a rock garden to take advantage of that natural asset. However, rocks may be brought to a garden for reasons that have nothing to do with gardening – their weight and bulk may be needed to stabilize a slope and prevent slippage. Here the rocks offer a fine opportunity to create an interesting, unusual-looking garden.

The town of Ettelbruck lies at the centre of the Grand Duchy of Luxembourg, a small country landlocked between Germany, Belgium and France. Within the town, the owners of this contemporary property excavated into a hillside to build their house; when they were finished, they were left with nothing at all in the way of a garden. The site was extremely steep, a drop of around 36 feet (11 m) from the top level at the back to the front of the house. The land, especially at the rear, required stabilizing to prevent heavy rain from causing slides.

For landscape architect Peter Berg there was only one solution: to use natural rock to shore up the slope and provide a stable foundation for terraces built on different levels. Berg's grandfather was a stone quarryman, and also a gardener, and this may explain why he has employed stone, specifically basalt, in 90 per cent of his gardens.

The project was challenging – 500 tons of basalt had to be craned in, and the team required all their muscle power to wrangle the individual rocks into place. Having established a stabilizing layer that obviated the need for further foundations, the couple had the basis for a striking, natural-looking, low-maintenance garden. Gaps were left between the rocks to offer spaces for planting, as well as to allow water to percolate naturally into the earth below rather than gushing down a solid surface. The rock garden is sympathetic to the landscape beyond, blending into its surroundings and becoming more natural-looking as it progresses outwards.

DESIGN INGREDIENTS

· Unity

· Scale

· Contrasting textures and forms

· Repetition

· Strong axis

[1] STEEL SPAN A steel bridge crosses the steep gully at the back of the house, providing direct access from the second floor to the upper part of the rear garden. The grey steel sits well with the basalt boulders and concrete walls, and the clean lines complement the contemporary styling of the house. The bridge forms part of an axis on the master plan, which leads from the front door, up steps through the house interior, and up further steps on the rear slope (see above). The continuous axis unifies the house and the patio set at the top of the slope.

[2] ROCK GARDEN The rocks, far from being a random collection, were selected at the quarry for their aesthetic qualities. Berg had to decide which of their 'faces' would be uppermost, and how they should be arranged to sit well with their neighbours. Formed during the rapid cooling of lava in periods of volcanic activity, basalt is characteristically fine-grained and dark coloured. Freshly hewn rock looks black when wet, and dark grey when dry. Exposure to the elements causes the surface to assume a reddish-brown hue.

[3] BASALT STEPS A set of steps ascends through the rock, connecting the patio to the house. The lines of the sawn basalt are unrefined enough to appear as though they were cut from the surrounding stone. Basalt has been used in various forms in the garden – firstly, in its natural state as boulders for the rock garden; then as gravel, lining the gully below; and finally, as rock sawn to make steps and paving for the terraces. The sharp edges of the sawn elements contrast with the amorphous boulders, but planting softens the junctions.

[4] SEMPERVIVUMS Hollows in the surfaces of rocks may not seem a hospitable habitat, but plants of the sempervivum genus are adapted to survive there. Known as houseleeks, and also 'hen and chicks' and 'liveforever', they can live in shallow dips and crevices because of their ability to store water in their leaves. Their rosettes form mats that may eventually cover dry, exposed areas. Their fresh-looking leaves and bright flower colours make them a natural choice for breaking up a grey, rocky expanse, as here.

[5] ROCK PLANTS Berg favours green plants for his rock gardens. Examples are *Euonymus alatus* and *Amelanchier lamarckii*, which provide autumn colour. Grasses, ferns and shrubs were selected for their height, shape and ability to fit into the scale of the rocks, as well as provide a variety of forms, textures and shades within the green spectrum. The client has added a red, cut-leaved acer to the planting, flouting Berg's rule of having only green plants. The acer certainly stands out, but it adds subtle colour through the year, and its rounded habit mimics the form of the boulders.

Secluded Courtyard

DESIGNER RUSS CLETTA
COMPLETED 2006
LOCATION LOS ANGELES, CALIFORNIA, USA

A VERY EARLY STYLE of garden, first appearing in medieval times, was the courtyard (known in Latin as *hortus conclusus*, or 'enclosed garden'). Its solid walls kept out the dust, noise, animals and even potential marauders from the street, and provided welcome sanctuary from the hubbub outside. Today, a courtyard garden still fulfils those functions.

An enclosed courtyard is a welcoming place to venture out of doors, especially when space inside is at a premium and the weather is generally favourable for outside living, as it is in Los Angeles.

For this courtyard garden, landscape architect <u>Russ Cletta</u> was faced with a 35 x 18-ft (11 x 5.5-m) plot and a long list of requirements. The client's wish list included outdoor seating and dining, a water feature, a fire, a barbecue, an outdoor shower and planting for privacy, all while retaining a Zen-like atmosphere. Knowing that a cramped and cluttered space rapidly becomes oppressive and claustrophobic, Cletta had to think laterally and include multi-tasking features that would fulfil the client's needs while conserving space.

First of all, Cletta paved the surface so that none of the useable entertaining space was wasted. He incorporated a water feature into a bench, and tucked the barbecue out of the way, in a corner by the steps. The firepit was cut into the paving. Keeping the layout simple ensured that the space was as uncluttered as possible, and simplicity ruled the colour scheme, too: silver and green plants, one colour for the concrete elements, and a dark grey render for the walls. The garden's colours are sympathetic to those of the modernist residence.

Cletta found the greatest challenge he faced was keeping the stainless-steel barbecue inconspicuous within the scheme. Instead of using more steel for the housing, he gave it a concrete enclosure. The ipe-wood countertop has a hidden hydraulic arm for accessing the interior storage area from above.

DESIGN INGREDIENTS

· Proportion

· Restraint

· Multi-tasking elements

· Screening

· Flow

[1] LARGE PAVERS The use of large pavers changes the optical perception of the size of the space, paradoxically making it seem larger (the same effect is achieved by using large feature plants). The gaps between the stones are a little wider than normal, with the spaces in between filled with *Ophiopogon japonicus* 'Nanus' (dwarf mondo grass). The grass forms a grid that discreetly breaks up the horizontal plane, subtly adding interest. The grass is hardy and reliable, and is able to withstand some foot traffic.

[2] POURED CONCRETE
Concrete was poured in situ to form the bench and its integrated water feature, as well as the barbecue enclosure and the large pavers. The light sand finish of the bench, barbecue housing and pavers creates a unified presence, which means that no single part stands out. This unity of appearance soothes the eye and prevents the space from feeling cluttered. Concrete is a fashionable and flexible material for use in gardens; if made using alternatives to cement, it becomes an ecologically friendly option as well.

[3] PLANTING Privacy and shade are afforded by *Archontophoenix cunninghamiana* (king palm), planted in key positions along the boundary wall. Between its slender stems are evergreen shrubs, such as *Astelia chathamica* 'Silver Spear' (see above) and *Pittosporum crassifolium* 'Compactum'. At ground level, glaucous fingers of the succulent *Senecio mandraliscae* gesticulate from the boundary beds. The planting combination adds variety and interest without overwhelming the space.

[4] FIREPIT Close to the dining area, where its effect will be most appreciated, but tucked away in the far corner where there is no throughway, a simple, recessed gas firepit provides warmth on cool evenings. The firepit has a cover of recycled glass that is fitted flush with the surface of the patio when the fire is not in use. The firepit was kept at ground level, rather than raised as a permanent feature, to prevent it from taking up room and being an inconvenience during large social gatherings.

WATER FEATURES

Aside from the outdoor shower, not one but two water features are squeezed unobtrusively into the garden. Outside a guest bedroom, there is a lounging area with a small, circular, Asian-style bubble fountain at ground level (see right). The other water feature is at knee height; incorporated into a concrete seat, its single jet provides a subtle and soothing aural backdrop for the main part of the outside space.

Japanese Hybrid

DESIGNER TODD LONGSTAFFE-GOWAN

COMPLETED 2010

LOCATION ZURICH, SWITZERLAND

THE APPEAL OF TRADITIONAL Japanese gardens lies in their disconnection from their environment; they exclude the external world. They are individual but at the same time universal, representing ideas of aesthetic perfection and symbolic meaning. Today, gardens created in the Japanese manner may not have the spiritual depth of the originals, but they recapture their sense of order and timeless calm.

In his book, *Quiet Beauty: The Japanese Gardens of North America*, Kendall H. Brown remarks that:

'In contrast to the cacophony of cities, the anonymity of suburbs, and even the anxiety of deserts or forests, these gardens can provide beautifully controlled environments.'

Japanese-inspired gardens now exist in far-flung corners of the globe, and it is therefore unsurprising to find this one in a leafy suburb of Zurich.

The worldly and aesthetic British client wished to indulge in a little of what Van Gogh called 'Japonaiserie'. She briefed gardener and historian Todd Longstaffe-Gowan that it was not to be a pure Japanese garden but an informed hybrid that reflected her cosmopolitan lifestyle and interests; it also had to incorporate a large, abstract, bronze nude (not seen here). Given a free hand to respond imaginatively to the Japanese theme, Longstaffe-Gowan created a garden with what he describes as an 'illusory appearance of Japanese artifice'.

The rattan fences, bamboo gates, boulders, stepping stones and wooden decking, along with maples and parrotias, create an atmosphere that is reminiscent of a Japanese *roji,* or tea garden. Yet this is a modern, miniature Anglo-Swiss city garden, designed to complement a stylish 1970s house with a Japanese feel. Its plan is simple, laid out to provide a sequence of spatial impressions within a very small area. This is a garden that reinvents Japanese style for a 21st-century city lifestyle.

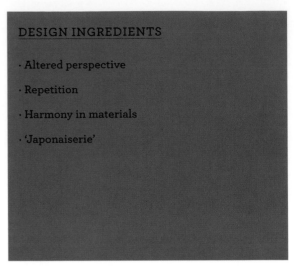

· Altered perspective

· Repetition

· Harmony in materials

· 'Japonaiserie'

[1] BOX BALLS The Japanese technique of *niwaki* – the art of sculpting 'garden trees' into cloud shapes – involves clipping trees and shrubs to create a perfect plant aesthetic. The formula has been tweaked here to achieve a more restrained, contemporary shape in the form of balls of box. The rounded shrubs are mimicked by five globe-shaped lights, which nuzzle up to the box and tuck under the other planting. The lights, in the 'Moonlight' range by Nostraforma, are just over 22 in. (56 cm) in diameter. Brilliantly, they do double duty, as sculptural features during the day and providers of magical atmosphere at night.

[2] JAPANESE MATERIALS Longstaffe-Gowan has used a variety of materials to give weight to the Japanese theme. He sourced rattan fencing and bamboo gates from Japan in order to provide an authentic rustic backdrop. Pale grey limestone boulders, paving stones and gravel were selected to contrast with black house detailing, and white globe lighting picked up on the pale grey theme. A timber deck provides a place to take tea in the afternoon. Using a wide variety of materials normally carries the risk of sending a confusing visual message, but here the design is so simple that the materials take their places and work perfectly in harmony.

[3] JAPANESE MAPLES *Acer palmatum* (Japanese maple) is synonymous with Japanese gardens, and here a light green cultivar contrasts with a purple form. Maples are very popular all over the world for their broadly spreading forms and delicate leaves, which produce spectacular colours, especially in autumn. Some of the finger-leaved variety, *A. palmatum* var. *dissectum*, have been used elsewhere in the garden. Larger specimens near the house create an increased sense of depth in the garden.

[4] LIMESTONE BOULDERS The garden's limestone boulders and paving stones make a very important contribution to the design. Known as 'glacial erratics', the stones were deposited by glaciers on what are now the alpine meadows of Braunwald in the Swiss canton of Glarus. The stones were handpicked by the designer and set into the surface, as they would be in a Japanese garden. Their presence recalls both Japan and their Swiss area of origin.

JAPONAISERIE

Before opening up to the West in 1868, Japan had existed in self-imposed political and cultural isolation from the rest of the world. Within thirty years of its emergence, the West was hooked on 'Japonaiserie', a trend fuelled by the publication in 1893 of *Landscape Gardening in Japan* by Josiah Conder, a young British architect. Japanese gardens were built in Europe and the United States, especially in the early 20th century. By the 1950s the trend was over, only to be revived later in the century. The Japanese Garden at Tatton Park in Cheshire, England, (see below) designed by Tatton's head gardener, Sam Youd, is a modern reinvention of the classic Japanese tea garden.

Small Formal

DESIGNER DANUTA MLOZNIAK

COMPLETED 2008

LOCATION KOMOROW, POLAND

[3] CIRCLES AND SPHERES

Round shapes of all kinds are plentiful in the garden. Box balls – some raised in tall pots and some nestling in the beds at ground level – are scattered around, along with standard trees, also in pots. Silver-mirrored balls, embedded among the groundcover plants, reflect the light, and there are also various globes of dark wood, granite, terracotta and glass decorating different parts of the space. Młoźniak calls such features 'garden jewellery'. Even the large hydrangea flowers follow the spherical trend.

[4] TOPIARY SHAPES

Large, beautifully sculpted yew cones contrast with much smaller, spherical box shapes. The cones work well in this small garden, anchoring the design while providing height and arresting focal points. A frequent visitor to the RHS Chelsea Flower Show in London, Młoźniak first saw box and yew clipped into shapes there in 2004 and was inspired to use them herself. To the rear, standard yew lollipops continue the theme of formal structure. Młoźniak is a particularly enthusiastic advocate of yew topiary for its elegance, longevity and ease of maintenance.

ILLUSION OF SPACE

Visitors often do a double-take when they come across the large mirror set behind the waterlily pond. What first appears to be a long pool passing under a pergola is revealed to be a short pool reflected by a wall-mounted looking glass. Młoźniak has strengthened the deception by disguising the top of the mirror wall with ivy. Mirrors feature in other places around the garden, acting as both eye catchers and visual extensions of the garden.

Harbourside Roof Terrace

DESIGNER ANDY STURGEON

COMPLETED 2009

LOCATION HONG KONG, CHINA

HOWEVER BUSY a city may be, a roof terrace set high above its noise and bustle can offer peace, detachment and relaxation, with the occupants still able to see and enjoy the movement and spectacle of their urban environment. Perhaps most stimulating of all is a garden view of water, which alternates between a sparkling blue in fine weather and a dramatic grey on dull days.

Located high above the South China Sea, and overlooking Tsing Yi Island and Hong Kong harbour beyond, these terrace gardens sit behind a large infinity pool on a cantilevered terrace, part of a tower of high-end apartments. It was the job of <u>Andy Sturgeon</u> to create an impressive but restful space with intimate areas for recreation.

Sturgeon designed the space as a continuation of the interior decor, seeking to provide a seamless transition from indoors to outside, and then onwards to the pool area. His design combines classical and contemporary elements, and he paid close attention to the quality of the detailing, which is crisp and elegant. Throughout the garden, a range of materials and finishes, such as dark- and mid-grey granite, ceramic tiles and Alpolic aluminium, offer contrasting colours and textures.

Timber-decked walkways create paths and routes to different secluded areas of the gardens, and visitors are drawn into the space and introduced to areas concealed by carefully sited planting.

The gardens sit on a concrete podium, which presented limitations on the design. Raised planters give added depth for tree roots, and steps and levels were built to create diversity, as well as balance the heights of the planters. The water features are shallow because of the constraint on excavation.

The large planters and pavilions block strong winds blowing in from the open sea, helping to keep users sheltered and comfortable, and all the structures are battened down to withstand typhoons.

DESIGN INGREDIENTS

· Balance

· Mass and void

· Flow

· Repetition of detailing

· Unity

[1] GREENERY The planting is suited to the subtropical climate and offers architectural interest. Large plants, including *Bambusa multiplex* (hedge bamboo), *Bucida molineti* (spiny black olive) and *Plumeria rubra* (frangipani) are used to frame views. Small shrubs, such as *Jasminum grandiflorum*, *Duranta erecta*, *Nandina domestica* and *Callistemon viminalis*, give structure at a lower level and ensure colour and texture through the year. Palms provide shade, and evergreen plants surrounding the pools give privacy.

[2] WATER FEATURES A water channel runs beneath the glass screen towards the swimming pool, providing a visual link to it, as well as to the harbour beyond. Rather than duplicate the colour of the floor of the pool, Sturgeon has introduced variety by choosing a greener shade. At the side of the pool, stepping stones cross the channel, breaking up the large expanse of sunbathing terrace. Fountains and other water features create movement and promote a sense of tranquillity, with soft water jets bubbling out of a cluster of nine square platforms (see box, right).

[3] PAVILIONS Seven roofed structures dot the area in an irregular fashion. They provide shady places to enjoy a conversation, or to relax away from the tennis court and the social areas; the roofs give privacy from the apartments above. The frames are constructed from marine-grade stainless steel and are resistant to the salty winds; the roofs are louvred with tropical hardwood slats. At each corner is a light that casts shadows of the slats at night. The styling of the pavilions is clean and uncluttered.

[4] GRID STRUCTURE The linear design is set to a grid and takes its lead from the geometry of the main pool. All the lines relate to each other, with wooden walkways leading to small pools, paved sunbathing areas and water features. In design terms, square and rectangular features combine to make up larger squares. The design creates a sense of flow but pulls the garden together at the same time. Some of the walkways, pavilions and pools are set at a different level, one step up or down.

LOUVRED ELEMENTS

The louvre, a screen with slats angled to admit light or air, is a running theme throughout the design. Dark aluminium louvres run vertically up the building's walls and extend out into the garden, making a link between the architecture and the landscape, while providing a strong visual backdrop to the space. Louvres also feature on the roofs of the pavilions, protecting users from direct sunlight. The detailing on the sides of the planters echoes the louvre theme.

Living Wall

DESIGNER PATRICK BLANC

COMPLETED 2005

LOCATION PARIS, FRANCE

ANYONE WHO HAS struggled to cultivate a patch of flat ground will appreciate how hard it would be if the plane were turned by ninety degrees, making it necessary to garden vertically. Success in vertical gardening depends on the planting medium, how it is secured to the wall, the kind of plants used, and the effectiveness of the irrigation system in supporting all the plants equally.

Creating a garden that defies gravity might seem an impossibility, yet a green roof system was first demonstrated as a realistic idea and patented by Professor Stanley Hart White at the University of Illinois, Urbana-Champaign in 1938. Botanist Patrick Blanc, although he would not claim to be the originator of the concept, is credited with developing it in the modern era. His 'Vertical Garden' (see right), at the Musée du Quai Branly in Paris, is one of the best-known examples of its kind.

With a surface area of around 8,600 sq ft (800 sq m), Blanc's 'living wall' is an imposing presence on the banks of the River Seine. When planning the planting, Blanc had to select species capable of surviving on a facade with northern exposure, and which was also swept by air currents from the river. The result is a rich carpet of vegetation in different textures and shades of green, punctuated by occasional bursts of colour.

Blanc had been experimenting with vertical gardens since the age of fifteen; he has since remarked that growing tropical plants on his bedroom wall resulted in many watery and malodorous mishaps. But he perfected his system and used it for the first time on an exterior wall in 1991. He has since brought his living wallscapes to buildings all over the world, and his system has been much imitated and adapted by others. Commenting on the number of vertical gardens at the RHS Chelsea Flower Show one year, he said, 'It is good. I cannot cover all the walls of the world by myself!'

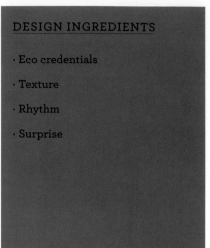

DESIGN INGREDIENTS

· Eco credentials

· Texture

· Rhythm

· Surprise

[1] PLANTING SUBFRAME Blanc's method of establishing a vertical garden requires, first, a durable metal frame that is supported a few inches away from the wall, allowing air to circulate behind the plants and dry the wall as necessary. The supports distribute the garden's weight evenly across the wall. PVC slabs cover the frame, and those in turn are covered by a non-biodegradable felt, into which the plants are inserted. Irrigation containing plant nutrients is pumped through the felt. The increasing popularity of living walls has brought a number of other types of vertical planting systems onto what has become a competitive market.

[2] PLANTING SCHEME One of Blanc's favourite plants is *Iris japonica*, whose spear-like leaves make clumps that droop downwards. Surprisingly, vertical planting is not restricted to plants with a low-growing form, and Blanc regularly uses shrubs in his designs. When planning a wall, he places the plants that require most light at the top; plants that are more shade-tolerant, like ferns and saxifrages, are placed at lower levels. In this way, the planting mimics the way the plants would be found in nature. The fact that the foliage of large plants hangs downwards means that small plants are not overwhelmed by large ones.

[3] SHADES OF GREEN Plants are arranged in great swathes, with ribbons of varied greens running both vertically down and diagonally across the wall. From emerald to lime green, every shade is used. The juxtaposition of tonalities and textures creates a real sense of tactility, rather like a tapestry made from different threads. Blanc has discovered that a wide selection of mosses, ferns, ivies and grasses are able to thrive in a vertical, soil-free environment. Maintenance of green walls requires lifts or temporary scaffolding for the gardeners.

[4] COLOUR ACCENTS The planting combination, although mostly of varied greens, offers splashes of vivid colour. The vivid purple *Campanula portenschlagiana* (Dalmatian bellflower), for example, is a low-growing perennial that establishes itself quickly to form an evergreen mat of small, rounded leaves. When it flowers in late summer, its delicate, bell-shaped flowers offer a pleasing contrast to jaunty red geraniums and yellow saxifrages. With the aid of scissor or spider lifts, gardeners can replace or supplement plants that have flowered with later-flowering varieties.

GREEN TRANSFORMATION

One of the largest-scale living walls completed by Blanc is this residential building facade in the Rue d'Alsace, Paris; it has a surface area of over 15,000 sq ft (1,400 sq m). Set in a narrow street, it transforms the view from the flats opposite; an overbearing building of grey concrete is masked by a striking design of fresh greenery.

Environment

Desert Modern

DESIGNER STEVE MARTINO

COMPLETED 2009

LOCATION PHOENIX, ARIZONA, USA

INHOSPITABLE, hot and dry, the desert is not often chosen as the backdrop to human habitation – once they are home, many people prefer not to be reminded of it. But gardeners know that paying close attention to the native flora is essential to long-term success, and from there it is but a short step to creating a whole garden environment that acknowledges the dry climate and its effects.

The Sonoran Desert, one of the largest and hottest in North America, covers parts of the south-western United States and continues across the border into Mexico. Its landscape is varied: endless miles of sand dunes, scrubby plains with groves of giant cactus, and rugged mountain ranges.

Landscape architect Steve Martino designs modernist gardens that celebrate the desert landscape rather than resist it. The owners of this house in Paradise Valley, on the outskirts of Phoenix, asked him to transform their shallow backyard, with its lawn and collection of boulders, into something more sophisticated that established more of a sense of connection with the landscape beyond.

Believing that boulders are too easy an option in desert-garden design, Martino removed them and altered the levels, creating a functional space that was easier to navigate. He then arranged the elements in the garden to establish clear visual associations between the house and the desert.

There is something of the Mexican architect Luis Barragán in Martino's design, particularly in the retaining walls, which appear to be free-standing, and the colours, which complement those of the surrounding hills. A wall supports a row of cantilevered steel beams, whose terracotta colour reappears on the wall at the far end of the garden, creating a visual unity. Limestone paving and gravel harmonize with the exterior terrain. The result is an uncluttered space, with many multi-tasking elements that keep the garden clean and simple.

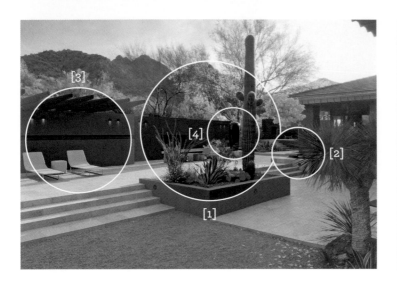

DESIGN INGREDIENTS

· Rhythm

· Unity

· Simplicity

· Sympathy to genius loci

· Site-appropriate planting

[1] REPRESENTATIONAL PLANTING

The planter in the centre of the space represents a microcosm of the desert, with a specimen of the arborescent cactus *Carnegiea gigantea* (saguaro cactus) effectively pinning down all the horizontal planes. The tall cactus looms above and dwarfs brittlebush, agave, prickly pear and creosote bush. In the desert, these plants are adapted to deal with high temperatures, low rainfall and intense sunlight. Martino has limited his planting scheme to native species to maximize their chances of survival.

[2] INFINITY POOL
A large water feature is situated little more than 1 ft (30 cm) from the glass doors of the sitting room. When the doors are open, the water feature appears to be part of the interior. At the far end, a cascade installation with a stainless-steel lip pours water into a black-tiled pool with an infinity edge. The water overflows constantly into the pebble-covered drain set around the pool's base, creating a splashing noise and a refreshing ambience. Siting the cascade where the surface height changes emphasizes the varied levels in the garden.

[3] MULTI-FUNCTIONAL WALLS

The taupe-coloured, stuccoed walls appear as a continuation of the distant mountains, bringing the far landscape into the garden. They work hard functionally as well, supporting a cantilevered limestone bench, a large fireplace and wall lights that are set in pairs for optimal effect. The walls are staggered, with the gaps in between offering glimpses through to the desert beyond. The forward wall is divided in two horizontally, which amplifies the horizontal planes and breaks up the wall's vertical mass.

[4] CERAMIC CENTREPIECE

Occupying a prominent position, a blue ceramic sculpture by Japanese artist Jun Kaneko is placed on a plinth for maximum effect. One of the client's biggest motivations for remodelling the garden was to gain appropriate spaces to display two large, ultra-contemporary pieces of sculpture, which had been incompatible with the previous garden. Elsewhere, a large piece by Fletcher Benton is set on a rotatable base so that it can be turned and fully appreciated from all sides.

LIGHT AND SHADE

For Martino, good design takes full account of the light, both during the day and at night. Light is, of course, important to him in his sideline as a photographer. To the west side of the garden there is a fence made of overlapping panels of frosted glass (see left), which throws reflections around and is lit to great effect at night. In the sharp desert light, walls create shadows and shade, making the site feel open and spacious.

Drought Resistant

DESIGNERS RUTH BANCROFT
AND LESTER HAWKINS
COMPLETED 1970s
LOCATION WALNUT CREEK, CALIFORNIA, USA

PARCHED SOILS are perhaps the greatest challenge to a gardener. In some locations, water supplies may be brought in, but increasingly – in the face of water shortages, and as a result of greater eco awareness – gardeners are seeking plants that naturally flourish in drylands, without a constant helping hand from irrigation. Growing drought-tolerant plants does not mean settling for a bland assembly of greys and browns, either. A collection of succulent plants can provide a combination of colours and shapes that is just as brilliant as those found in other types of garden.

Veteran plant collector <u>Ruth Bancroft</u> is well known in horticultural circles for demonstrating to the world the potential of dryland gardening. She first started collecting succulent plants in the 1950s.

By the 1970s she had an extensive collection, but it was all confined to pots. The family had run a walnut business, and she decided to use some of its land, owned since 1880, for planting the collection. A drought-resistant garden was a radical undertaking at that time, but people were already noticing water shortages in California and Ruth suspected that the problem would get worse; she

was proved right. California is experiencing the worst droughts of its history, and now, more than ever, her garden is recognized as a shining example of what can be grown in drought conditions.

Local landscape designer Lester Hawkins laid out the original network of circuitous paths enclosing mounded beds. He also added a number of architectural shade plants to protect certain specimens from the unyielding summer sun.

Succulents are plants that have evolved to survive drought conditions by storing water in their leaves and stems. Agaves, aloes, aeoniums and

sedums, all with fleshy leaves, are all examples. Botanists often exclude cacti from the group, but technically most fall into this classification.

Bancroft's garden was the US Garden Conservancy's first project and now contains around 2,000 different species. Important collections of aloes, agaves, yuccas and echeverias, collected from Africa, Australia, California, Chile and Mexico, are arranged in an informal style, with trees like pines and mesquites providing overhead shade. *Aeonium* 'Glenn Davidson', the very first succulent of the collection, is still growing in the garden.

· Balance of vertical
  and horizontal

· Texture

· Contrasting colour

· Height and depth

· Focal points

[1] MIGHTY AGAVE For its sheer size and intimidating form, the giant *Agave salmiana* is undeniably the eyecatcher of this grouping within the garden. This agave can reach 10 ft (3 m) in height and flowers at around fifteen years of age. It propels a single, dramatic flower stalk more than 20 ft (6 m) skywards to produce a candelabrum of yellow flowers; after that, the plant dies. New plants grow from seed, and they also develop from offshoots. In Mexico, the fermented sap of *Agave salmiana* is used to make *pulque*, a milky, viscous drink with a sour, yeast-like taste.

[2] SHADE TREE It might be thought that there is no place for a deciduous tree in this demanding environment, but *Parkinsonia aculeata* (palo verde) fits the brief admirably. Native to the deserts of the south-western United States and northern Mexico, this member of the pea family has a light canopy that screens the vulnerable plants beneath it from the effects of the sun. In aesthetic terms, its graceful, spreading form and ferny leaves provide a foil for the jagged spikes and thick leaves of the succulents around it. Its feathery look implies that it is harmless, but it is covered in spines.

[3] <u>CROWN OF YUCCAS</u> Towering above the huge agave are the spineless glossy spears of *Yucca gigantea*. The colour and form of the yucca's round brushes give the neighbouring agave a distinct outline. This is the tallest yucca, growing up to 30 ft (9 m) high. The heads gain architectural impact as they become branched with age. It would be easy to think that one spiky succulent plant looks very much like another, but there is a wealth of different forms, colours and shapes – plenty to give the gardener a good variety of contrasting textures.

[4] <u>ALOE COLOUR</u> As *Agave salmiana* produces only one inflorescence in fifteen years, it is fortunate that the aloes clustered beneath the palo verde tree can be relied upon to brighten up the shadier spots in the border. Once they mature, usually within four or five years, aloes bloom annually. The inflorescences tend to open gradually, providing a long season of colour. Here, the colour is an electric scarlet, but other aloe species flower in yellow, orange and pink. Their leaves vary, too: grey to bright green, and sometimes striped or mottled.

[5] <u>SUCCULENT CARPETING</u> Balancing the sizeable, architectural specimens in the garden, low-growing succulents form a mat on the ground, straying onto the paths and escaping the confines of the border. These plants may be small, but they are no less intriguing in form. The glaucous leaves of *Euphorbia myrsinites* (myrtle spurge, or creeping spurge) cluster around coils of snake-like stems, giving it an otherworldly appearance, more suggestive of an animal than a plant. *E. myrsinites* originated in Turkey, a country of temperature extremes, and it is hardy enough to cope with the garden's dry conditions.

Subtropical Space

DESIGNER RAYMOND JUNGLES

COMPLETED 2009

LOCATION MIAMI, FLORIDA, USA

DEFINING THE CLIMATE of a place by its location alone can be inaccurate. Proximity to the equator is one factor, but others come to bear. Miami, for example, technically lies in a subtropical region of the United States, but Florida is surrounded on three sides by water, which raises the temperature of incoming cold fronts. Its climate therefore leans towards a classically warm and wet tropical one.

Although there is an ongoing debate about the climatic status of southern Florida, the character of this Miami garden by landscape architect Raymond Jungles is subtropical. Indeed, most of the plants selected for the garden are able to withstand the occasional winter dip in temperature.

The clients were planning to update their rather unexciting 1960s home and wanted a garden to go with it. The architect who was commissioned to work on the house suggested Jungles as the man to tackle the garden, which meant that the landscaper and architect were able to work on their plans simultaneously. In this way, the house plans could be adjusted to achieve an optimal marriage of house and garden, rather than making the garden fit around a finished house.

Firstly, the forecourt needed to be altered to move the parking away from the house. The drive is now lined with *Quercus virginiana* (live oak), whose branches reach across and cast shadows over the gravel surface. The house is framed by these trees, and the transfer from street to house is cool and shady. Lawned spaces were added to balance the densely planted areas, and the pool was relocated and enhanced with a barbecue and dining area, as well as a place to lounge.

The new rectilinear setting is both modernist and in keeping with the restyled house. Jungles kept his hard landscaping deliberately simple in style to provide a strong and effective backdrop for the colours and textures of his planting.

DESIGN INGREDIENTS

· Manipulation of light

· Sensory appreciation

· Texture and form

· Proportion

· Sculptural simplicity

[1] LUSH PLANTING Palms make a big contribution to the sense of place in Jungles's gardens. He uses them as they grow in nature: small palms as understorey, large ones for canopy, and cluster palms at different heights. Glossy-leaved *Philodendron* 'Burle Marx' fills gaps between larger plants at ground level, and strappy bromeliads provide focal points. Jungles's designs are always bold and rich in different plant types. The interaction of foliage form, scale and texture is a predominant element in his approach to garden design.

[2] CASCADE Water runs across the surface and down the sides of a simple square construction of stacked slate. The progress of the water is gentle as it trickles over the nooks and crannies of the rough-textured stone, but the movement provides soothing, watery sound effects that enliven the environment for those reclining close by, and counters any noise from outside the garden. The water feature comes alive at night, when the droplets sparkle in the beams of uplighting. The shimmering surface of the slate top echoes that of the long, rectangular pool behind.

[3] **SWIMMING POOL** Beyond the water feature, the swimming pool is asymmetric in design. The water is raised above ground level, with one long side bordered by a limestone wall and walkway. On the other side, the water flows over an invisible edge, like that of an infinity pool. The side over which the water flows is constructed of stacked slate, which establishes a visual connection with the water feature. For those relaxing on the timber deck between the two cascades, the splashing sounds come from two directions. The contrasting edge detailing of the pool is original and eye-catching.

[4] **TRAVERTINE LIMESTONE** The walls at each end of the space, the pool's side wall, and all the walkways are faced or paved with creamy travertine. This is a natural form of limestone that has been popular for exterior landscaping since Roman times. The stone has a characteristically pitted surface that is especially attractive when it is honed, although it is often used in its natural state as well. The stone is pale enough to lighten the area, but the texture ensures that the surfaces are soft in appearance. The stone is restful to the eyes in that it does not reflect glare from the sun, unlike polished marble.

[5] **TERMINAL WALL** At the top of the imposing, travertine-veneered wall that terminates the garden is a concealed planter containing drought-resistant plants and hanging creepers. A timber infill partly blocks the space between the wall's two stone uprights, leaving a central window and a view of the foliage beyond. The width of the ipe timber screen matches the width of the pool, and that of the ipe sunbathing deck that separates the pool and the water feature. The wall is less dominating for its timber screen and window, and yet it still provides a visual full-stop to the space.

Tropical Jungle

DESIGNERS JIM THOMPSON, THEN BILL
WARREN AND OTHERS
COMPLETED 1959, RESTORED IN 1990s
LOCATION BANGKOK, THAILAND

SOMETIMES IT TAKES the fresh eyes of an
outsider to fully appreciate ancient, traditional
ways of doing things – practices that the local
people may have turned away from – or to see ways
of presenting old things in a new light. Coming
from different cultures, travellers are often well
placed to discern the qualities of a place or
environment that make it unique.

Set on the edge of a *klong*, one of a network of
waterways that runs through Bangkok, this
traditional Thai wooden house was the home of an
American, Jim Thompson, who came to Bangkok in
1945, fell in love with the culture of Thailand, and
decided to stay. He later became famous for
regenerating the ailing Thai silk industry and for his
collection of Asian antiquities.

Thompson constructed the house from the
salvage of six other houses. His home would not
have appealed to any well-heeled Thai or *farang*
(European visitor), but he was able to appreciate
traditional design for the cool shade it offered. For
Thompson, the natural setting for such a house was
the Thai jungle, which would provide shade and
screen out the city. The jungle-like garden he created
is renowned today for its feel of a tranquil sanctuary.

In 1967, however, Thompson mysteriously
disappeared on a walking trip in the Cameron
Highlands. The house was neglected, and the
garden quickly grew into dense, impenetrable
jungle. It was not until twenty-five years later that
Bill Warren, a friend of Thompson, and a team of
local landscape architects set about reinstating the
paths and beds. The house and garden were made
into a museum to showcase Thompson's artefacts.

The restored jungle planting was brilliantly
accomplished, despite the constant battle with the
rapid rate of plant growth. The garden is now a cool,
lush oasis, a haven from the chaotic city outside.

Shady Woodland

DESIGNER JUDY PEARCE

COMPLETED 2008

LOCATION SOMERSET, UK

IN A TEMPERATE climate, with plenty of rain and sunshine, garden vegetation will naturally revert to woodland. Dense forest makes gardening impossible, but tree species that cast a dappled shade allow a wide variety of plants to be grown beneath. Woodland plants are self-sufficient and naturally fertile, making a woodland garden a good, low-maintenance option.

When Judy Pearce and her husband arrived at Lady Farm over forty years ago, it was a complete mess. An overflowing slurry tank stood undesirably close to the farmhouse and there were bits of discarded farm machinery strewn everywhere. The 'tidy-up', as Pearce put it, led to the removal of outbuildings and almost 4 acres (1.6 ha) of concrete foundations.

With help from distinguished horticulturalist Mary Payne, Pearce transformed the farmyard into 8 acres (3.2 ha) of much-admired garden. She did not want to scrabble around on her hands and knees in flowerbeds, so it was important to choose plants able to thrive without too much attention, but which also made a strong statement visually. Payne introduced her to grasses, and together they have created very successful prairie and steppe plantings.

Pearce's discovery of a natural water source facilitated lakes on two levels, linked by a stream. When an ornamental waterfall was made for the lower lake, a garden conduit was required to entice visitors down to see it. Having seen the value of year-round interest with minimal input (the steppe and prairie gardens give their all from late spring to early winter), Pearce decided to create a shade garden. There were a few *Betula pendula* (silver birch) at the edge of the field alongside the watercourse, so she augmented that group while adding planting below. The shady woodland walk performs all year round, from the first winter hellebores to *Hydrangea arborescens* 'Annabelle', whose snowball flowers last into the autumn.

[1] SILVER TREES The birch variety with which Pearce chose to augment her wood was *Betula utilis* var. *jacquemontii*; its bright white bark is guaranteed to stand out in winter. She arranged the saplings in a random fashion to resemble a natural copse, and laid a rolled-gravel, bark-covered path in between the trees, aiming for the look of a natural wood. The birch variety has a light canopy and does not grow very tall; it retains the dainty air it has when young, throwing lightly dappled shade onto the ground beneath.

[2] HOSTA COLLECTION Pearce calls this part of her garden the 'Hosta Walk', for good reason. There are around six hosta (plantain lily) types, all planted en masse for maximum effect. Many, like *Hosta* 'Frances Williams', *H*. 'Gold Standard' and *H*. 'Albomarginata', are variegated (with contrasting leaf margins). Hostas are, of course, very attractive to slugs and snails. Pearce admits that she does suppress the pests with slug pellets, but only once a year, and always on Valentine's Day, a little tip learnt from the eminent gardener Beth Chatto.

[3] PURPLE POMPOMS Alliums are an incomparable choice for providing dramatic, contrasting shapes above groundcover plants. Being on opposite sides of the colour wheel, purple and lime green are naturally harmonious partners, and here the purple flowers complement fresh green spring foliage . *Allium hollandicum* 'Purple Sensation' and the paler *A. hollandicum* (aflatunense) are used; the related plants are similar in form but with a subtle variation in tone that adds depth.

[4] FERN FRONDS *Matteuccia struthiopteris* (shuttlecock fern) has attractive, bright green foliage as it uncurls in the spring, and its lacy fronds are a foil to the broad leaves of the hostas. The fern is a good choice because it is hardy and able to survive in fairly extreme site conditions, ranging from waterlogged quagmire to parched ground. Pearce established ferns elsewhere as part of her show of bluebells, and she transplanted some of the plants to replicate their effect at the Hosta Walk.

[5] FORGET-ME-NOT *Myosotis arvensis* (forget-me-not) was introduced into the garden for its ability to create a glorious, misty, sky-blue carpet. The original inspiration for this effect came from some woodland on the property that in May is covered by native bluebells (*Hyacinthoides non-scripta*). Bluebells would not have done here because they spread rapidly and their flowers are short-lived. Forget-me-nots flower later and longer than the bluebells and are very tenacious. They are cleared yearly, as they would smother the hostas into extinction if left.

Windy Hilltop

DESIGNER ANTHONY PAUL

COMPLETED 2007

LOCATION PROVENCE, FRANCE

FREQUENT EXPOSURE to wind is a strongly limiting factor in the establishment of a garden. In colder months, wind chill can make an environment intolerably cold for many plants, while wind-driven rain and snow has a severely battering effect on them. In summer, scorching winds burn foliage and dry out the soil. Very few garden plants thrive in wind-dominated sites.

Surrounded by apricot and almond orchards, fields of lavender and olive trees, this property in the Vaucluse region of northern Provence enjoys magnificent views of Mont Ventoux, which dominates the eastern horizon. The mountain (*venteux* means 'windy' in French) is so called for two raging winds that drive through the region, the chilly mistral from the north and the stifling sirocco from the Sahara Desert. These can reach speeds of 60 miles per hour (100 km/h), especially in the winter and spring. In summer, temperatures average 95–104°F (35–40°C), and in winter regularly plunge to 14°F (–10°C); torrential rains are seldom far away.

This onslaught of extremes calls for inventive planting. Designer Anthony Paul has succeeded in making a garden that settles a stone farmhouse comfortably into its setting. One of his most inspiring solutions was to plant dramatic blocks of billowing lavenders in diagonal lines across the banks to the side of the terrace; the effect is of a hazy, billowing purple carpet. The corduroy-like look of the planting reflects that of the surrounding agriculture and blurs the boundaries between the garden and its environs. Traditional materials and skills were used throughout the garden to create an established appearance. The dry-stone walls, made with salvaged stone, are informal structures but are still able to confer a degree of formality, with their strong geometry and precise lines. A planting palette that draws on limited colours bolsters the minimalist, architectural character of the garden.

DESIGN INGREDIENTS

· Simplicity

· Contrasting textures

· Dramatic planting

· Limited colour palette

· Strong architectural lines

[1] IMPRESSIONIST PLANTING

Much of the planting here has the character of an Impressionist painting, with layers of deep greens and silver greys balanced by sweeping brushstrokes of purple and blue, rippled through with the caerulean ribbons of *Iris pallida*. Tender plants had no place in the planting scheme; tough, low-growing Mediterranean plants, like lavender, cistus, santolina and rosemary, are arranged in dense masses to help them resist the battering winds. Every plant had to be robust and wind resistant.

[2] SERPENTINE WALLS

Dry-stone walls mark divisions in the planting, snaking through massed plantings of perovskia and lavender, for example, in a way that seems random and playful, despite the walls' solidity. By using the local stone, Anthony Paul linked the garden to the house while pulling it into the landscape. Each wall terminates with a pier, shaped like a finger pointing at the sky; the features unfailingly draw the eye upwards. The abundant walls, weaving across the property, help to shelter plants (and visitors) when the winds are blowing strongly.

[3] <u>REFLECTIVE WATER</u> The rectangular swimming pool is designed as an infinity pool, and when viewed from the house it runs off the far edge, seeming to blend with the view of the sea and the sky beyond. The interior lining of the pool is painted a forest green to increase the reflective qualities of the water and intensify the colours mirrored in it. The pool is an integral part of the design; its role is to reflect the surroundings during the day, and to provide a dramatic illuminated feature at night.

[4] <u>WINDBREAK TREES</u> On a windy hilltop, one of the first tasks of a garden planner is to identify sites in the garden that would most benefit from obstacles able to slow down wind speeds without creating potentially damaging vortices. In time, this row of young trees will grow into a significant wind barrier. Other trees on the site include apricots and evergreen oaks. On a raised terrace at the back of the house there is an ancient olive tree, one of many originally imported from Italy.

[5] <u>SPA POOL</u> At the corner of the swimming pool, next to its infinity edge, is a whirlpool bathtub with a wide circular deck surround. This feature brings some punctuation to the rectangle formed by the pool. Its position and shape reinforce the strong geometry of this part of the garden. The location maximizes the clients' enjoyment of the spa bath; it receives the full benefit of the sun on hot days, yet is cooled by the proximity of the swimming pool. A descending bank of lavender nudges up against the surround, filling the air with its relaxing scent.

Contemporary Water

DESIGNER WAGNER HODGSON LANDSCAPE ARCHITECTURE

COMPLETED 2011

LOCATION VERMONT, USA

IF A PROPERTY is located in a region with above-average falls of rain and snow, it does not follow that its owners will come to love running water, or want to surround themselves with water year round. But with today's ecological call to adjust to the natural environment, gardens with a strong water component may yet become more common in predominantly wet-weather locations.

This site in Vermont commands magnificent views over Lake Champlain and the Adirondack Mountains, but it was occupied by a forty-year-old, energy-inefficient, awkwardly sited residence sitting with its back to all that beauty. The clients, an art collector and an entrepreneur, fell in love with the site, one where they could also fulfil their ambition to breed shires, an old English breed of draught horse. Having acquired the property, they replaced the house with a modern, environmentally sound home. The couple commissioned Wagner Hodgson Landscape Architecture to create an arrival court with a strong water component that would dramatize the approach to the house while acknowledging the property's beautiful lakeside setting.

Originally, the house and land were a small part of a much larger concern. Established in 1886, Shelburne Farms was created as a model agricultural estate. The gardens around its main building were designed by Frederick Law Olmsted, co-creator of many well-known municipal parks with his senior partner, Calvert Vaux. The farm grew to 3,800 acres (1,540 ha) and pioneered innovative practices in agriculture and land use. In 1972, the descendants of the original farmers established a non-profit organization for the practice of sustainable farming and forestry, with a heavy stress on conservation. The clients' 10-acre (4-ha) site was one of the parcels of land that were sold off during the reorganization.

The history of the estate and the beauty of the outlook inspired the design team. They framed views of the lake and mountains with sugar maples, and the natural slope of the site provided an opportunity to build at different levels. Locally available materials like steel, slate, stone and wood were used, as well as Corten steel. Particularly important, though, the designers celebrated the site's relatively wet climate, integrating water into the design rather than treating it as an inconvenience.

DESIGN INGREDIENTS

· Sustainability

· Sympathy with surroundings

· Multiple levels

· Function

· Local materials

[1] RAIN CHAIN The wet-climate area was the inspiration for many design features. Rainwater runs off the roof valley into the pool below via a chain of industrial size. Such a chain is an unusual but functional alternative to traditional downpipes from a gutter. This is an area of heavy snowfall, and guttering is not used due to the potentially destructive weight of snow and ice. Rain chains have been customary in Japan for centuries, and can also be found in parts of the world where chain is easier to source than machined downpipes. Guiding water visibly down a chain is a novel way of replacing a nondescript downpipe with a water feature.

[2] MODERN MOAT From beneath the eaves, rainwater descends to a shallow pool made from Corten steel and lined with pebbles from Lake Champlain. A series of Corten steel and stone weirs and waterfalls then guides the water around the house and down to a lake. Originally, the clients wanted a seasonal water feature that would collect water from the roof whenever it rained or snowed and guide it around the house into a collection tank; this would reduce the home's dependence on water supplied from elsewhere. Once they saw the system in action, they decided they wanted it to operate all year, so a pump was fitted to circulate the water.

[3] LUSH FERNS Planting beds alongside the pools are mostly occupied by ferns, and these will keep their bright green foliage for much of the year in this favourably wet environment; in a hotter, dryer habitat the foliage would shrivel in summer. The beds of ferns appear as a swathe of uniform green that complements the uncluttered coloration and modern styling of the house. Adventurous visitors to the entranceway are invited to seek an alternative vantage point by the presence of two stepping stones set in the water.

[4] STONE BRIDGE A lilac bluestone slab forms a bridge over the pool to the main entrance. The bluestone was sourced locally in a New England quarry. It was given a thermal finish and now has a patina, but it retains a little 'tooth' or rough texture to make it non-slip. Linear LED lighting is installed under the bridge; at night it looks as if it is floating in the pool. People crossing the water gain a sense of entering the house via a drawbridge over a moat, and the bridge calls attention to the importance of water in the garden.

'GREEN' CREDENTIALS

Much has been done in the garden to reduce its environmental impact. The pump that circulates the water is driven by solar power, which substantially reduces electricity required from the national grid, and the garden lights are individually solar powered. Materials, such as stone flooring (see right), came from sustainable sources and are recyclable; they were gathered and moved with minimal impact on the environment. Some of the water from the roof is contained, which reduces the environmental effects of run-off.

Rain Garden

DESIGNER NIGEL DUNNETT

COMPLETED 2010

LOCATION LONDON, UK

LEARNING TO COPE better with the effects of climate change has become a priority in the world at large, and garden designers have a potentially huge role to play. Because areas are either getting too much rain or not enough of it, effective water stewardship is becoming a key criterion worldwide in judging whether a garden is truly a success.

Nigel Dunnett, Professor of Planting Design and Vegetation Technology at the University of Sheffield, crusades for greater awareness of ecology and sustainability in garden design. He wants garden spaces to be functional, and he also knows how to make them look good, as evidenced by his four medal-winning show gardens at the RHS Chelsea Flower Show in London.

Dunnett's Rain Garden is located at the London Wetland Centre, an important nature site owned by the Wildfowl and Wetlands Trust, near the River Thames in West London. His garden was opened in 2010 as part of the tenth-anniversary celebrations of the Trust. The Wetland Centre, occupying 104 acres (42 ha) of former water treatment works and redundant reservoirs, encourages the public to explore and appreciate the natural wetland habitat.

Dunnett designed an interactive garden that demonstrates water conservation and inspires people to try out water-saving techniques at home. His design centres around a stream and is loosely based on a series of concentric circles, like the radiating ripples created by drops of rain on a pond.

The circles define linked, raised 'bog' beds and a pond filled with aquatic plants. The beds soak up rainfall run-off collected from the roof of a building in the garden. Some of the garden's water is drawn up and transpired by moisture-tolerant planting; some percolates down to the water table. Excess water is passed along a series of wooden rills into other beds, set at a lower level. Stepping stones enable nimble visitors to cross the stream.

DESIGN INGREDIENTS

· Ethical aesthetics

· Environment-appropriate planting

· Organic structure

· Recycled materials

· Focal points

[1] BOARDWALK A series of wide, curving boardwalks provides access right into the garden and raises footfall above the soggy ground beneath. The sweeping arcs follow the lines of the circular beds and trace the flowing movement of the space. Visitors moving along the paths see the curves disappear intriguingly ahead among the grasses, an invitation to explore further. Planting in the adjacent beds is neatly separated by sections of pebbles with low wooden dividers. The plants are laid out in large groups, and their heights are allowed to vary.

[2] WILDLIFE TOWER Fashioned from recycled tiles, bricks, bits of wood and found objects, a 'creature tower' provides a multi-storey habitat and feeding station for a wide range of insects, invertebrates, small mammals and birds. Just as the garden's primary purpose is to provide a model of the natural flow of water, so the design also endeavours to make as much room for nature as possible. The dramatic wildlife tower makes a conspicuous sculptural statement, while reminding visitors of the need to conserve garden wildlife.

[3] RECYCLED CONTAINER

The building within the garden is an old shipping container that was converted for use as an information centre. A prime example of recycling, it has a green roof carpeted by a variety of plants; these provide yet another surface to absorb rainwater, helping to reduce or slow down potentially damaging run-off. The container also incorporates wildlife habitats in its walls. It was a matter of principle in the building of this garden that as many as possible of the materials sourced were reclaimed.

[4] REED FILTERING

Growing in the pond, *Phragmites australis* subsp. *australis*, a variegated form of the common reed, purifies the pondwater by consuming the excess nutrients washed into it and removing its carbon dioxide. The plants, rooted into the gravel bed, absorb oxygen into their leaves and draw it down and out through their roots. The oxygen around the roots supports micro-organisms that digest pond pollutants. Amongst the reeds, swathes of *Lythrum salicaria* (purple loosestrife) offer a contrasting pop of vivid colour.

BEAUTIFUL AND PRACTICAL

An important message of the Rain Garden is that the pressing environmental or 'green' need for plants that perform well in a watery environment does not imply that gardens can no longer be beautiful. Its boardwalks swing through drifts of perennials like *Gaura lindheimeri* and *Aster* x *frikartii*. Erect ranks of the grasses *Calamagrostis* x *acutiflora* 'Karl Foerster' and *Molinia caerulea* subsp. *arundinacea* 'Skyracer' provide a contrasting backdrop. Further back, a screen of mid-sized trees provides shelter.

Winter Colour

DESIGNER NORMAN VILLIS AND PETER ORRISS

COMPLETED 1976

LOCATION CAMBRIDGE, UK

IN TEMPERATE CLIMES, gardens tend to be left alone in winter, with gardeners waiting for life to reassert itself with the first bulbs of spring. It is true that winter is mostly a time of dormancy, but certain plants can take on a magical quality in the low-angled sunshine that prevails during the cold months. In the cold, their coloured bark or stems, powerful fragrance, berries, or evergreen, architectural form make a powerful impression.

One of the oldest botanical gardens in England, Cambridge University Botanic Garden was opened in 1846 as a teaching resource. Its winter garden, created by garden superintendents Norman Villis and Peter Orriss, was added nearly forty years ago to showcase the remarkable effects that can be achieved with plants that are at their best in winter. The winter garden is one of the most applauded examples of its kind in the United Kingdom.

Two deep borders on either side of the path provide constant entertainment in their colours, scents and structures. No unsightly patches of died-back perennials are allowed to blight the show. The overall impression of life, colour and energy is not so different from an equivalent June display; it is just as interesting, just a little quieter.

On bright afternoons the space comes to life, the sinking sun igniting the colours and backlighting the plantings with a golden glow. Conversely, those lucky enough to witness an early-morning frost are treated to a spectacular, ice-glazed wonderland.

At ground level, cushions of colourful heathers and a black grass, *Ophiopogon planiscapus* 'Nigrescens', weave a tapestry beneath the taller plants. *Prunus* x *subhirtella* 'Autumnalis' (autumn-flowering cherry) covers its leafless stems with pinky-white blossom on and off from November to March, and a brief spell of warmth brings out the flowers of *Lonicera* x *purpusii* (winter honeysuckle), which attracts the early bees of the season.

[4]

[3]

[5]

[2]

[1]

DESIGN INGREDIENTS

· Colour

· Structure

· Scent

· Contrast

· Shelter

[1] BORDER FIRE Winter borders benefit from brightly coloured stems. Dogwoods, such as the acid-green stemmed *Cornus sericea* 'Flaviramea' and the vibrant crimson *C. alba* 'Sibirica', perform best in sunshine, or at a water's edge. New stem growth produces the finest colour, so in this garden the plants are 'stooled', or cut back to the ground, in March. Other options for coloured stems include the orange-pink *C. sanguinea* 'Midwinter Fire', the flame-stemmed willow, *Salix alba* var. *vitellina*, and the pale white bramble *Rubus cockburnianus*.

[2] MEANDERING PATH The wave-like path and the swelling beds of groundcover plants that flank it create the impression in miniature of a stream winding through a valley, banked by generously attired hillsides. Beckoning the visitor forward by its promise of things to come 'just around the bend', the path knits the two borders together at its vanishing point, which makes the display seem still more abundant. The path's course is reinforced visually by margins of turf on either side. The effect is reminiscent of a Japanese woodblock print.

[3] **BEAUTIFUL BARK** As a spectacle, *Betula pendula* (silver birch) is always an asset in the garden long after its leaves have dropped, with its ghostly stems catching the light and brightening dull corners. Another birch that is highly valued in the winter garden for its bark is *B. albosinensis* var. *septentrionalis* (Chinese red birch); its pinky-grey bands respond beautifully to the low highlights of the winter sun. Peeling furls of the satin-textured, coppery-red bark of both *Prunus serrula* (Tibetan cherry) and *Acer griseum* (paperbark maple) make a show as they filter the light.

[4] **ARRESTING SHAPES** Architecture is important in any winter garden, whether from overarching specimen conifers or from evergreen shrubs such as mahonia, with its arresting form breaking down into attractive toothy leaflets and cockades of perfumed, yellow flowers. Other architectural plants include the aptly named corkscrew hazel (*Corylus avellana* 'Contorta'), with its wildly twisted stems. *Garrya elliptica* suspends a dense display of silvery tassels from its evergreen branches; the male cultivar *G. elliptica* 'James Roof' has the longest catkins.

[5] **SCENTED BLOOMS** Winter-flowering plants might not produce the most conspicuous blooms but many make up for this with their scent. *Viburnum* x *bodnantense* 'Dawn' (see right), *Chimonanthus praecox* (wintersweet), *Sarcococca confusa* (sweet box) and *Daphne bholua* 'Jacqueline Postill' all generate intensely sweet fragrance. The spidery yellow flowers of *Hamamelis mollis* (witch hazel) and its cultivars are possessed of a surprisingly beguiling scent, too. The scent of all perfumed plants is most likely to be noticed when the sun is shining.

Atmosphere

Secluded Grid

DESIGNER ADAM SHEPHERD
COMPLETED 2011
LOCATION LONDON, UK

ONLY A SMALL minority of people would choose
to be overlooked by surrounding properties while
using their garden. In such circumstances, the eye
is compulsively drawn outside the garden towards
the overlooking windows, and that experience is
neither relaxing nor rewarding. The design
solution is to draw the eye back from the
boundaries and focus the garden in on itself.

This garden, measuring a little over 2000 sq ft
(185 sq m), sits behind an imposing, stucco-fronted
Victorian villa on an elegant leafy street in Belsize
Park, a well-heeled area of north London. Previously,
the lower floors of the house were divided into two
dwellings, and the garden was split to give the
owners of each some exterior space. The current
owners reunited the interior spaces and wanted
to do the same in the garden.

The clients wanted a contemporary space for
the family to use, one that provided some seclusion
while being easy to maintain. The design, by
landscape architect <u>Adam Shepherd,</u> was in keeping
with the refurbished villa interior. He used a
minimal palette of cool, neutral colours and a style
that tallied with the owners' quirky art collection.
At that point, the owners requested minimal
planting; Shepherd agreed, suspecting that they
could be persuaded later on.

Shepherd has created a multi-faceted garden of
events and journeys. A grid of different levels is
filled with planting spaces, steps, seating and dining
areas, all rewarding an exploratory trip around the
garden. The plants are mainly a simple selection of
perennials and grasses, with the exception of a
dramatic 'living wall', the focus of the garden. Box
balls contrast with the the linear ground plan.

The hard landscaping is simple, too. Brick walls
are rendered and painted pale grey; this tones with
large slabs of riven black slate, and both contrast
with decked areas of ipe hardwood.

DESIGN INGREDIENTS

· Unity

· Journey for the senses

· Enclosure

· Multiple levels

· Vertical elements

[1] LAYERED HEDGES The garden is bordered by a low, inner hedge of box, with a much taller, outer hedge of yew behind it. The owners wanted a private space but the fencing was not in good shape. Rather than go to the large expense of replacing it, Shepherd masked its deficiencies with a dense barrier that gave a feeling of seclusion without drawing attention to itself. The double hedges were inspired by the garden for Laurent-Perrier in the RHS Chelsea Flower Show of 2009, designed by Luciano Giubbilei (see box opposite).

[2] SPLIT LEVELS When, in the past, the garden was split in two to serve flats within the villa, the two halves were set at different levels. Now needing to re-combine the two halves, Shepherd took advantage of the unusual situation by designing the garden as a series of different levels connected by steps. Areas of planting, some of them behind integrated seating, are set at different heights. The lower levels have the feel of a sunken garden. Down there, the atmosphere is more sheltered and private; the hedge enclosure feels high up, embracing and protective.

[3] **PIN OAKS** Three *Quercus palustris* (pin oak) trees are set into the paving in a staggered arrangement that adds depth to the space. Disregarding the possibilities of the varied garden levels, Shepherd planted them all at the same height, which gives their crowns some consistency. The canopies join to form a band of verdant shading across the garden. The species was chosen for its upright, pyramidal form, its suitability for the shady conditions, its attractive leaf shape and the wonderful red of its foliage in the autumn.

[4] **LIVING WALL** The garden's most striking single feature is a living wall, planted with fatsias, heucheras of various leaf colours and ferns. Because the floor space was limited, the client wished to keep the available flooring useable and uncluttered by additional planting. That restriction led to the idea of transferring planting to a vertical wall; in this way, the garden could benefit from additional green texture and a softening of the hard landscaping without reducing the footprint. The living wall is 7 ft (2 m) high and just over 16 ft (4.8 m) long, and is planted on both sides. Its presence is felt especially strongly when coming through the garden entrance on the wall's far side. Because the wall is nearby, the visitor encounters its eye-level planting and damp, earthy atmosphere at close quarters.

LUCIANO GIUBBILEI

Italian garden designer Luciano Giubbilei, twice a gold-medal winner at the RHS Chelsea Flower Show, in 2009 (see below) and 2011, and winner of Best in Show in 2014, favours a confident, uncluttered style. Here, his streamlined tiers of hedging emphasize the proportions of the site and provide a three-dimensional continuity. Box hedging, *Calamagrostis* x *acutiflora* 'Karl Foerster' (feather reed-grass) and *Paeonia* 'Buckeye Belle' form layers of contrasting textures and colours. The result is an elegant garden with an atmosphere of quiet calm.

East–West Fusion

DESIGNER JEAN-CHARLES CHIRON
COMPLETED 1996
LOCATION LOIRE ATLANTIQUE, FRANCE

SINCE THE 1970S, the notion of 'fusion', in which elements from the traditions of different parts of the world are combined into new 'global' entities, has been an important factor in cuisine, music and the visual arts. While some critics decry 'fusion' as a threat to specific regional identities, others celebrate its potential for generating new experiences undreamt of in the original cultures.

Some 9 miles (15 km) north of the French city of Nantes, overlooking the broad River Erdre, perches the hamlet of Le Perdrier. It is here that the landscape gardener Jean-Charles Chiron bases his business, and where he has brought East and West together to make an extraordinary garden.

The space around his modern house and studio was just a field of roughly 4 acres (1.6 ha) when Chiron moved there in 2000. Unfarmed for some time, its soil was good, and he had an empty space for trying out his ideas. His aim was to create not only a family garden but also a showcase of his work. It embraces the considerations that most clients call for in his designs, namely year-round interest and low upkeep.

Chiron has not visited East Asia, but the Eastern influence on his design is palpable. The garden melds with the bucolic Nantes countryside and is punctuated by strong architectural ingredients. The layout has a strong rectilinear format, with the space bisected by a long avenue that leads down to a red 'moon gate' at the end. Visible through the 'gate' are schist rocks arranged in a group of three – a traditional number in Eastern gardens. Such rocks variously represent Buddha and his two attendants, or the mountain peaks of the three islands of the immortals, the reputed location of the elixir of life.

Offshoots from the main axis lead to areas for contemplation, walking or play. In autumn, deciduous trees shine among evergreens. Here, the traditional French garden is boldly contrasted with Eastern architecture and horticulture.

[1] PARTITION WALLS Red and black freestanding walls create architectural impact in the space as well as separation between different areas. Their presence is aesthetic as well as functional, creating vertical planes to offset the horizontal, especially alongside the long axial path. Shadows play across their faces, and their graphic shapes and smooth monotones provide a dramatic foil for the planting set before them. Here, a tight group of box balls cluster beneath a black monolith, while a red monolith sets the scene ablaze.

[2] PATH BORDER Progressing towards the distant moon gate, the path is bordered on the left (only) by large cubes of clipped box alternating with plantings of a smooth hydrangea cultivar, *Hydrangea arborescens* 'Annabelle'. In the spring, the bright green young foliage of the hydrangea makes a feathery foil to the geometric blocks of box. In summer, its white flowers contribute to the basic colour palette of red, green, white and black. In autumn (see right), the blowsy flowerheads gradually die to brown, one by one, while still contributing to the architecture of the garden.

[3] MOON GATE Off to the right of the path, behind the monoliths, is a moon gate, a traditional Chinese architectural element. Its circular opening, or oculus, appears to be rising out of the ground, just as a rising moon on the horizon seems to lift out of the landscape. This reference to the perpetual cycle of the moon, rising and falling, symbolizes the continuous cycle of birth, growth and decay. The gate's shape frames the scene behind it, but interrupts the view outwards, too, generating both concealment and surprise.

[4] WATER AND ROCKS
A body of water, no matter how small, represents the spiritual heart of any Chinese or Japanese garden. Here, at the end of the path, a 'pool-within-a-pool' is set before the oculus of the moon gate. The two pools mimic the moon gate's configuration, a circle in a rectangle, and the water feature is painted the same red colour. In a slightly Hollywood-like touch, Chiron has installed a device that generates an artificial mist; this swirls around the bases of the rocks beyond, making the scene seem even more intriguing.

EAST MEETS WEST

Another example of Chiron's blending of East and West is this garden, also in the Loire. The landscape gardener has cocooned the garden within red concrete walls, drawing inspiration from the enclosed gardens of China and Japan. The strict geometry of the straight box hedge that borders the edges of the garden is reminiscent of a formal French garden, as are the balls of sculpted box. Chiron's main concern is to show the plants he uses in an unfamiliar light. He regards sculptures and hard landscaping essentially as showcases for his planting.

Front Yard Retreat

DESIGNER IVE HAUGELAND

COMPLETED 2010

LOCATION DANVILLE, CALIFORNIA, USA

FRONT GARDENS tend to be difficult and underused spaces. Many house owners are not tempted to linger in them, or make anything of them, because they are so readily overlooked by adjacent streets or paths. This can be a waste, especially if the space is large, orientated towards the afternoon sun, or has good views. Often, all that is needed is to introduce a sense of seclusion.

For the owners of this corner property in Danville, a sleepy surburban town on the outskirts of Oakland in California, it was time for a change. The large front yard was dedicated to lawn and there was no connection between the driveway and the front door. The couple's children had grown into teenagers, so the outside space no longer needed to function as a play area. The owners wanted to spend less time mowing, watering and maintaining the lawn, and they suspected that they should also increase the appeal of their property from the curb – one they knew was largely missing.

Landscape architect Ive Haugeland, of Shades of Green Landscape Architecture, was commissioned to rework the largely featureless garden into something contemporary. First of all, she reduced the area of lawn to conserve water and reduce the time spent in lawn maintenance. In its place, she introduced drought-tolerant plants and surfaces of permeable, decomposed granite.

To establish a better connection between the street and the front door, Haugeland installed a new, generous flight of concrete steps. These were laid out in two offset sections, with lighting installed into the risers to make the access clear and welcoming at night. The designer also laid a path to connect the garage and drive to the front door, facilitating the comings and goings of the family. But perhaps the most significant feature was a new semi-private seating area, built to the side of the staircase. This is now a favourite gathering place for the family's teenagers and their friends.

DESIGN INGREDIENTS

· Flow

· Movement

· Screening

· Mystery

· Proportion

[1] SECLUDED PATIO A pair of free-standing semi-circular walls, 3 ft 3 in. (1 m) high, mark the boundary of a round terrace on its street side, embracing those within and preventing them from being observed from below. The walls were made in situ from poured concrete, the plywood moulds leaving them with an attractive imprint. The walled terrace is especially striking when lit at night. The opening between the walls gives those on the terrace the opportunity to look down onto the street and check any activity.

[2] PLANTING EFFECTS

The plant most used in the garden, gathered en masse as here, is *Pennisetum alopecuroides* 'Little Bunny', a dwarf fountain grass. It makes a big impact on the space with its soft, creamy, brush-like flowerheads, which appear in late summer. Also placed in front of the grey concrete walls is *Anigozanthos* 'Yellow Gem' (yellow kangaroo paw), which presents a splash of bright colour against the neutral backdrop. The flowering stems of both plants sway in response to the wind and catch the light pleasingly.

[3] INDIRECT PASSAGEWAY Connecting the driveway, the new patio and the main entrance to the house, a series of large, rectangular, concrete pavers zigzags its way through the garden. They give dynamism to a routine journey. Wide enough to walk along comfortably, the pavers are strips of concrete poured in situ; here, each moulding gives the impression of being six pavers laid on end; a texture provides a nonslip surface. As well as tying parts of the property together, the path brings to the design a sense of informality and playfulness.

[4] INTERRUPTED CLIMB The steps to the front door are split into two offset flights, set between two free-standing concrete walls that are of similar appearance to those around the patio. The walls anchor the steps, and also partly screen the front door from the street, making that area seem more private. Ascent and descent are naturally slowed by the break. This, together with the steps' generous proportions, makes the approach less steep and daunting. The entrance way now has authority as well as the desired curb appeal.

[5] MATURE TREES Haugeland decided to include most of the existing mature trees in her design because they comprised an instant established framework around the house. One plane tree was chosen to become the centrepiece of the round terrace, with its canopy providing ample shade in hot weather. The presence of the large tree adds to the sense of privacy enjoyed by users of the terrace, this time from the house side – which is perhaps a welcome feature for the teenagers and their parents alike. The tree also casts a welcome dappled shade.

Provençal Oasis

DESIGNER DOMINIQUE LAFOURCADE

COMPLETED 2008

LOCATION ST-REMY-DE-PROVENCE, FRANCE

PEACEFUL FOUNTAIN

Close to the house, in the centre of the dining terrace, a circular concrete water feature is enlivened by a single, central jet (see right). In visual terms, the pool forms the first step of the journey down the garden. Visual play emerges in how the circular form of the water feature, in the horizontal surface plane, interacts with the circle of the oculus, in the vertical plane, directly beyond. The peaceful murmur of the water masks conversation from any outsiders without causing difficulty in conversing at normal levels.

[3] CHEQUERBOARD PLANTING

In an informal twist on the concept of the parterre, concrete pavers moulded to resemble timber decking form a chequerboard with the squares of low-growing plants set between them. Aromatics such as thyme jostle with *Armeria maritima* (sea thrift), *Sagina subulata* (heath pearlwort), sedums and *Erigeron karvinskianus* (Mexican fleabane). Tufts of *Ophiopogon planiscapus* 'Nigrescens' (mondo grass) add texture and colour, while in spring the colour is provided by bulbs such as narcissus and crocus.

[4] STAGGERED HEDGE

To the side of the pool, behind the fountains, three different shrubs make up a staggered hedge. The staggering is a clever device for lightening and softening the effect of a tall and heavy boundary hedge. At the back is *Cupressus arizonica* (Arizona cypress); in the middle, *Elaeagnus* x *ebbingei* (oleaster); and at the front, *Taxus baccata* (common yew). The contrasting blue of the cypress, the silvery green of the oleaster and the dark green of the yew emphasize the staggered structure and pull the feature together.

Rustic Backyard

DESIGNER OEHME VAN SWEDEN

COMPLETED 1977

LOCATION WASHINGTON, DC, USA

THE IDEA OF USING backyard or outdoor space as an extension of a house's living area was unheard of in the United States in the 1970s. But people were beginning to stay at home more, and wanting to make the most of their available space. Pioneers of the prairie-inspired 'New American Garden' were garden designer James van Sweden and landscape architect Wolfgang Oehme.

Early in its career, the Oehme van Sweden partnership was approached by clients to redesign the garden of their historic Georgian brick house in Georgetown, Washington. The pair were presented with a patch of bare concrete with a garage at the far end. Garden design hitherto had been mostly limited to important or very large, well-heeled rural properties, and this space was small, 48 x 35 ft (15 x 11 m). Americans were not making use of their outdoor urban spaces as they do now, but by expanding the living space into the exterior, the partners heralded a new form of outdoor living.

The garden lent itself naturally to being an extension of the kitchen, with double French doors opening from the room into the outdoor space. This framework was enhanced by the Oehme van Sweden planting scheme, which was designed to have a soft natural look for year-round interest, lush and green in summer yet keeping some structure in winter.

Layers, screens and interesting focal points create mystery, especially in small gardens, and deepen the visitor's experience of the space. The sound of running water attracts attention and creates an auditory event for the visitor to experience while moving through the garden. Textures further enhance the sensation of moving around.

The owners were thrilled with their new environment and started to use their garden as a living room as soon it was warm enough to do so. In the extreme summer temperatures, the garden was doubly welcome as a cool, shady retreat.

DESIGN INGREDIENTS

· Mystery

· Texture

· Enclosure

· Sensual expression

· Architectural elements

[1] TEXTURE UNDERFOOT The route through the garden is marked by changes at ground level. The terrace immediately outside the French doors of the house is rough fieldstone framed by a border pattern of bluestone flags. The fieldstone leads into a path of more rustic and randomly laid stones, and this in turn arrives at a neatly laid bluestone terrace. The flags and stones are infilled with striking bluestone pebbles. The changes in the texture of the path materials define the separate garden areas and the functions allotted to them.

[2] PLANTING Although the whole garden seems swathed in plants, the main planted area lies between the pool and the terrace. Prairie favourites, including sulphur-yellow coreopsis, purple *Liatris spicata*, *Hydrangea quercifolia* (oakleaf hydrangea), hellebores and *Perovskia atriplicifolia* (Russian sage), form swathes below the structured frame of an evergreen magnolia tree. Oehme van Sweden were pioneers in prairie planting and railed against the ubiquitous use of English lawn with its accompanying regimented shrubs.

[3] **LILY POND** The owners wished to include water in the garden design but did not want the bother of maintaining a swimming pool. Oehme van Sweden added a square lily pond, placing it obliquely to the boundaries. Goldfish were introduced into the pond, and a simple jet throws a small arc of water into the air, creating a pleasing sound. A pond, stocked with fish and interesting water plants, slows down the visitor's movement around the garden and provides a place where it is pleasant to linger for contemplation.

[4] **ARBOUR** By the house, the transition from indoors to outdoors is framed by an arbour of narrow beams supported by four elegant wrought iron brackets, which tally well with the architecture of the house. In winter the arbour casts stripes of shadow across the terrace, while in summer it luxuriates under a blanket of rampant *Clematis* 'Jackmanii', which bears large purple flowers. Later in the year these are supplemented by the sweet-smelling, frothy white flowers of *Clematis terniflora* (sweet autumn clematis).

[5] **SCULPTURE** The low, capped wall surrounding the pond provides the perfect seat for a concrete sculpture, by Mary Brownstein, of a woman with her canine companion at her feet. Brownstein produces bronze sculptures for home display and concrete ones for the garden, some figurative, some abstract. Sculptures such as this are used increasingly in gardens because they have a powerful calming effect. Reproductions of ancient Buddhist statues and contemplative Buddha heads are also popular for their spiritual air.

Uplifting Path

DESIGNER DAN PEARSON

COMPLETED 2008

LOCATION LONDON, UK

IT IS WELL KNOWN that visiting a garden with a peaceful atmosphere, with the smell of the earth, beautiful flowers and the sounds of birds, can have a calming, soothing effect on people facing a crisis. Combine this with a venue dedicated to helping with that specific crisis, where the issue can be talked through and advice sought, and the result is an environment that offers hope and support.

The charity known as Maggie's, founded by the late Maggie Keswick Jencks, sets up and maintains uplifting cancer caring centres where anyone affected by cancer can drop in for emotional and practical support. At the time of writing there are seventeen of these centres in the United Kingdom, online, and around the world, with more planned. The first was opened in Edinburgh in 1996, and Maggie's West London (pictured), the first in England, opened to much acclaim twelve years later in Hammersmith. The award-winning building was designed by architect Richard Rogers, while garden designer Dan Pearson laid out a series of gardens around and inside the building.

The location, between a major road and a busy hospital, presented a challenge to both architect and designer. In response, the paprika-coloured building and its gardens were set behind a matching, 'embracing' perimeter wall, which plays a defensive role. In the sliver of land between the wall and the pavement, Pearson planted a row of *Betula albosinensis* var. *septentrionalis* (northern Chinese red birch). Attractive with their coppery-pink bark, the trees filter the din and traffic pollution while resonating with the orange-coloured wall.

The path into the centre passes beneath a substantial stand of mature *Platanus* x *hispanica* (London plane). The trees suggested a range of woodland favourites, including scented *Sarcococca confusa* (sweet box), hellebores, ferns, *Galium odoratum* (sweet woodruff) and spring bulbs. In recognition of the fact that every day counts for potentially terminally ill patients, the garden has much of interest all year round, with plantings organized to mark events significant to the centre.

An adept synergy exists between the building and garden. Peaceful internal courtyard gardens are arranged to take advantage of views out onto the garden outside, while the exterior planting fosters an upbeat and comfortable atmosphere.

413

DESIGN INGREDIENTS

· Enclosure

· Tranquil atmosphere

· Lush planting

· Functional elements

[1] WOODLAND WALK A gravel path winds its way through the trees towards the centre building, transporting visitors through what Pearson calls a 'decompression zone'. The designer is acutely aware of the benefits of gardens as feel-good environments, and the unpretentious simplicity of his scheme contains nothing that will jar or overwhelm. In time, a grove of white *Magnolia* x *loebneri* 'Merrill' will increase the experience of concealment and surprise. Views of the orange walls are softened by the planting.

[2] SMOOTH STONES A series of seven sensual, boulder-shaped sculptures by artist Hannah Bennett are distributed through the exterior space, some in the woodland borders, some grouped on the paved courtyard outside the building, where they double as impromptu seating. Their smooth, rounded, mushroom-cap shapes contrast with the strong horizontals and verticals of the building. Their light grey hue stands out from the dark green planting but harmonizes with the many white flowers. Their presence in the beds inevitably becomes a talking point.

[3] PLANTING The planting in the exterior courtyard has a woodland theme, with white being the dominant flower colour, set against restful green. Here the white is provided by *Anemone* x *hybrida* 'Honorine Jobert', a Japanese anemone with pure white, single flowers on wiry stems; it lasts for weeks, flowering from August until well into October. Herbs such as rosemary and lavender are also grown in the garden, some for medicinal purposes, while lemon verbena in the courtyard invites a trailing hand for a waft of its powerful fragrance.

[4] INTERNAL COURTYARDS

Visitors have a choice of three different courtyards to use for their discussions. The central internal garden space (see right) has the advantage of a wide picture window that gives on to the external courtyard. An *Albizia julibrissin*, which is known in China as the 'Tree of Happiness' for its calming herbal properties, shades a large table and benches. Planters contain scented *Trachelospermum jasminoides* and *Euphorbia mellifera,* and visitors can pick lemon verbena or peppermint leaves to make tea.

HORATIO'S GARDEN

Student Horatio Chapple was a volunteer at the Duke of Cornwall Spinal Treatment Centre in Salisbury, England. He and his father planned an uplifting garden for the patients, with a variety of different spaces to enjoy, appropriate to their needs. Tragically, Horatio was killed on a school trip at the age of seventeen, but a subsequent collection raised enough to make the garden a reality (see left). Designed by RHS Chelsea Flower Show medal-winner Cleve West, the garden cleverly refers to the spine in its low, limestone walls, which double as seating.

Meditation Space

DESIGNER MARJA VAN ASPEREN
COMPLETED 2008
LOCATION GELDERLAND, NETHERLANDS

THE PURPOSE OF MEDITATION is to focus the mind and achieve an inner equilibrium that offers release from the stresses and negative emotions of everyday life. Meditation is best accomplished in a place without distractions, in an atmosphere of quiet and calm. Left to oneself in a peaceful garden, it is easy to become lost in thought, reaching a calmer place mentally.

The south-west of Gelderland, the largest Dutch province, confirms common preconceptions of Holland: traditional windmills, winding dykes disappearing into endless horizons and old fortified towns. The area's name, Rivierenland, translates as 'Land of Rivers', a reference to its many waterways.

Asperen is a small and characterful village that lies halfway between Rotterdam and Arnhem in the centre of Rivierenland. A local resident knew that her garden was crying out for attention, so she called in local garden designer Marja van Asperen to help her transform the space.

The owner wanted to create a sleek, low-maintenance garden that would suit the character of her house. She envisioned the place as presenting an attractive view from the kitchen inside the house. No less important, the garden was to have a calm and welcoming atmosphere, conducive to meditation but also relaxing for the friends that she would entertain from time to time. The existing garden, bordered by an ugly wall on one side, was a mess, and the owner wanted to raise the mood.

Van Asperen took her lead from the large head of a Buddha that the client stipulated should be included in the design. The head became the garden's focal point and instantly established the meditative spirit of the place. The designer has drawn on its Eastern presence and a cool palette of green, purple and white to transform the wilderness into a calm environment that has plenty of seating and space for meals and social gatherings.

DESIGN INGREDIENTS

· Unity

· Symmetry

· Focal point

· Muted colour palette

· Screening

[1] BUDDHA'S HEAD Buddhists and non-Buddhists alike are receptive to the peaceful energy that this likeness of the sage's head, eyes closed in meditation, imparts to the space. The bust has an influence that is very grounding, and everything else in the garden seems to respond to it. The bust is big, almost 32 in. (80 cm) tall, and rests on a plinth, surrounded by a bed of *Helleborus foetidus* (stinking hellebore). The head's size is important: any smaller and it would not register in this particular space; any larger, and it would overwhelm it. The pleached pear trees above extend to cross its face with shadows, at the same time drawing it into the space.

[2] LIVING UMBRELLAS Four *Platanus* x *hispanica* (London plane) trees have been pruned to lift their crowns to an equal height, while their branches are being trained to conform to a square bamboo frame. The technique involved is a form of pleaching; the frame is removed eventually to leave a self-supporting, shallow canopy of interwoven branches that shades the table below while screening it from overlooking houses. Shady arbours of this kind have been created for centuries in hot countries – French towns, for example, often boast a central square shaded by a large canopy of heavily pollarded plane trees.

[3] COOL PLANTING Van
Asperen's planting plan contains
Hydrangea arborescens 'Annabelle'
for its flower colour and its bulky
foliage, and has white roses (*Rosa*
'Iceberg') sprawling through the beds
and taking up positions to the rear as
standard specimens. White-flowered
Salvia nemorosa works through the
lower levels, joined by the purple
highlights of lavender and catmint.
The client requested a restrained
colour palette, and Van Asperen's
calming, restful colours meld into the
mellow, grey painted wall behind.

[4] FORMAL FRAMING In a
garden where the atmosphere is
relaxed and the planting loose, the
introduction of clipped box hedges
immediately focuses the story.
The peeling plane trunks appear to
be raised by plinths of box, while low,
open-ended box hedges confer a
degree of formality and underline the
symmetry of the beds and pergola.
The plants are widely spaced in
well-weeded beds. Good maintenance
is essential in a meditation garden, if
only because few gardeners can resist
the temptation to start weeding.

[5] SIMPLE SURFACES The
garden's forecourt and the wide path
that leads to the dining area are
surfaced with old terracotta bricks
that tally with the house walls. Most
of the bricks are laid in the same
direction, but a line of half-bricks laid
in the opposite direction signals the
start of the connecting path and
extends to define the beds on either
side; another line forms the border
with the sympathetically coloured
gravel of the dining area. The change
of surface material from brick to
gravel delineates the different
functions of the two areas.

American Zen

DESIGNER KOICHI KAWANA

COMPLETED 1986

LOCATION BAINBRIDGE ISLAND,
WASHINGTON, USA

NO SCHOOL OF GARDEN design is more successful at creating an atmosphere of calm and contemplation than that of *karesansui,* or the Japanese rock garden (see also p. 86). The rock garden is deliberately minimal and free of superfluous elements that might distract the onlooker or disturb their absorption in the space. In Japan, such gardens were usually created in the restricted confines of monastery grounds, for the use of the monks. In the West, the rock garden was adopted more for its aesthetic qualities; its purpose was the same, but now it could be placed in a natural landscape, one flowing into the other.

Once a summer home with gardens belonging to a wealthy Seattle family, the 150-acre (60-ha) Bloedel Reserve is reached from Seattle by a ferry ride across Puget Sound, then a short drive across Bainbridge Island. Prentice and Virginia Bloedel lived and worked on the Reserve from 1951 to 1986, their dream being to 'provide refreshment and tranquillity in the presence of natural beauty, and enrich people's lives through a premier public garden of natural and designed Pacific Northwest landscapes'. They endowed their exceptional garden and nature reserve to the Arbor Fund in 1985, and this body continues to run it as a quasi-public garden.

DESIGN INGREDIENTS

· Formal layout

· Lavish planting

· Visual enticement

· Unity

· Enclosure

[1] ROOM DIVIDERS As solid and massive in their effect as fortifications, yew hedges 8 ft (2.4 m) tall provide enclosure and introduce structure to this formal space. The visitor has no choice but to halt and explore how to pass through or around the hedge. The view is blocked and the visitor is left wondering what is beyond, which adds drama to the experience. In garden design, even low hedges force a reaction by interrupting the line of vision. The viewer has to make an effort to see beyond, and that can be more rewarding than an easy glance.

[2] ABUNDANT BORDERS
The garden is closely packed with what Schoellkopf calls 'a generous abundance' of tall trees, shrubs and perennials, and these increase the visitor's sense of enclosure within rooms. Here, a bank of tall green- and red-foliaged plants acts as a backdrop for waterside planting that includes white-, yellow- and purple-flowered iris, alchemilla and catmint. Despite their lavish numbers, the plants are carefully placed where they will perform best, either alone or in contrasting groups that work well in concert with their neighbours.

Ind

[3] FORMALLY ENCLOSED INFORMALITY
Beautifully trimmed, low box hedges in a geometric
design provide a formal structure that here is
overlaid with informal planting. The strong lines
have been taken as giving licence to loosen up on
the soft landscaping. Schoellkopf sees the rectilinear
geometry as an elegant and very civilized
arrangement, but he allows plants to overflow it and
intermingle. The look is a little wild, and progress
along paths is interrupted by plants such as ferns
and hostas spilling out of the beds. The escapees
break up the monotony of the straight paths.

[4] VARIEGATED ELEMENTS Among the
plants to be found on the paths are the delicately
variegated *Hosta undulata* var. *albomarginata*.
Schoellkopf maintains that leaves are as important
as flowers in a garden, and, while he admits that
variegation is not to everyone's taste, he believes
that variegated foliage provides an extra source of
colour. It is especially useful in darker corners,
where white or silver variegation has a lightening
effect. Another example in the garden, *Actinidia
kolomikta* (kolomikta vine) is instantly recognizable
for its leaves splashed with pink and white.

BECKONING VISTAS

The garden is configured to provide intriguing
vistas and cross-vistas at every turn. Carefully
considered walkways and portals enable the
visitor to glimpse new spaces, even while
enjoying the ones they are in. There is a sense
of a surprise waiting round every corner – it
might be an interesting ornament, or nothing
less than a complete change of scenery. The
apertures boost the spontaneous experience of
the garden, making visitors more aware of, and
attentive to, the details of their surroundings.

De